One-Dimensional Man

ONE-DIMENSIONAL MAN

Studies in the Ideology of
Advanced Industrial Society

Herbert Marcuse

With a new Introduction
by Douglas Kellner

BEACON PRESS · BOSTON

Beacon Press
25 Beacon Street
Boston, Massachusetts 02108-2892

Beacon Press books
are published under the auspices of
the Unitarian Universalist Association of Congregations.

08 07 06 05 04   16 15 14 13 12

Library of Congress Cataloging-in-Publication Data

Marcuse, Herbert, 1898–
    One-dimensional man : studies in the ideology of advanced
    industrial society / Herbert Marcuse ; with a new introduction by
    Douglas Kellner.
        p.   cm.
    Includes bibliographical references and index.
    ISBN 0-8070-1417-6
    1. Civilization, Modern—20th century.   I. Title.
HM101.M268   1991
301—dc20   91-18246
                                                   CIP

For Inge

Contents

Acknowledgments   ix

Introduction to the Second Edition
by Douglas Kellner   xi

Introduction to the First Edition
The Paralysis of Criticism: Society Without Opposition   xli

One-Dimensional Society

1. *The New Forms of Control*   1
2. *The Closing of the Political Universe*   19
3. *The Conquest of the Unhappy Consciousness: Repressive Desublimation*   56
4. *The Closing of the Universe of Discourse*   84

One-Dimensional Thought

5. *Negative Thinking: The Defeated Logic of Protest*   123
6. *From Negative to Positive Thinking: Technological Rationality and the Logic of Domination*   144
7. *The Triumph of Positive Thinking: One-Dimensional Philosophy*   170

The Chance of the Alternatives

8. *The Historical Commitment of Philosophy*   203
9. *The Catastrophe of Liberation*   225
10. *Conclusion*   247

Index   259

Acknowledgments

My wife is at least partly responsible for the opinions expressed in this book. I am infinitely grateful to her.

My friend Barrington Moore, Jr., has helped me greatly by his critical comments; in discussions over a number of years, he has forced me to clarify my ideas.

Robert S. Cohen, Arno J. Mayer, Hans Meyerhoff, and David Ober read the manuscript at various stages and offered valuable suggestions.

The American Council of Learned Societies, the Louis M. Rabinowitz Foundation, the Rockefeller Foundation, and the Social Science Research Council have extended to me grants which greatly facilitated the completion of these studies.

Introduction to the Second Edition

Douglas Kellner

Herbert Marcuse's *One-Dimensional Man* was one of the most important books of the 1960s.[1] First published in 1964, it was immediately recognized as a significant critical diagnosis of the present age and was soon taken up by the emergent New Left as a damning indictment of contemporary Western societies, capitalist and communist. Conceived and written in the 1950s and early 1960s, the book reflects the stifling conformity of the era and provides a powerful critique of new modes of domination and social control. Yet it also expresses the hopes of a radical philosopher that human freedom and happiness could be greatly expanded beyond the one-dimensional thought and behavior prevalent in the established society. Holding onto the vision of liberation articulated in his earlier book *Eros and Civilization*,[2] Marcuse, in his critique of existing forms of domination and oppression, urges that what is be constantly compared with what could be: a freer and happier mode of human existence.

On one hand, *One-Dimensional Man* is an important work of critical social theory that continues to be relevant today as the forces of domination that Marcuse dissected have become even stronger and more prevalent in the years since he wrote the book. In a prospectus describing his work, Marcuse writes: "This book deals with certain basic tendencies in contemporary industrial society which seem to indicate a new phase of civilization. These tendencies

1. For a fuller discussion of the themes, contributions, and influence of *One-Dimensional Man*, see Chapters 7–10 of my book *Herbert Marcuse and the Crisis of Marxism* (London and Berkeley: MacMillan Press and University of California Press, 1984).
2. Herbert Marcuse, *Eros and Civilization* (Boston: Beacon Press, 1955).

have engendered a mode of thought and behavior which undermines the very foundations of the traditional culture. The chief characteristic of this new mode of thought and behavior is the repression of all values, aspirations, and ideas which cannot be defined in terms of the operations and attitudes validated by the prevailing forms of rationality. The consequence is the weakening and even the disappearance of all genuinely radical critique, the integration of all opposition in the established system."[3]

The book contains a theory of "advanced industrial society" that describes how changes in production, consumption, culture, and thought have produced an advanced state of conformity in which the production of needs and aspirations by the prevailing societal apparatus integrates individuals into the established societies. Marcuse describes what has become known as the "technological society," in which technology restructures labor and leisure, influencing life from the organization of labor to modes of thought. He also describes the mechanisms through which consumer capitalism integrates individuals into its world of thought and behavior. Rather than seeing these developments as beneficial to the individual, Marcuse sees them as a threat to human freedom and individuality in a totally administered society.

Justifying these claims requires Marcuse to develop a critical, philosophical perspective from which he can criticize existing forms of thought, behavior, and social organization. Thus, *One-Dimensional Man* is also Marcuse's major philosophical work, articulating his Hegelian-Marxian concept of philosophy and critique of dominant philosophical and intellectual currents: positivism, analytic philosophy, technological rationality, and a variety of

---

3. Herbert Marcuse, prospectus for *One-Dimensional Man*, Beacon Press archives, no date.

modes of conformist thinking. In this text, he both expli-
cates his conception of dialectical philosophy and produces
analyses of society and culture which exemplify his dialectical categories and method. Consequently, *One-Dimensional Man* presents a model both of Marcuse's critical social
theory and of his critical philosophy inspired by his philosophical studies and his work with the Frankfurt School.[4]

The Frankfurt School and *One-Dimensional Man*

During the 1920s and early 1930s Marcuse studied with
Martin Heidegger in Freiburg, Germany and intensely appropriated the works of Hegel, Marx, phenomenology, existentialism, German idealism, and the classics of the
Western philosophical tradition. While he later broke with
Heidegger after the rise of National Socialism in Germany
and Heidegger's affiliation with the Nazi party, he was influenced by Heidegger's critique of Western philosophy
and his attempts to develop a new philosophy. He followed
Heidegger and existentialism in seeking to deal with the
concrete problems of the existing individual and was im-
pressed with the phenomenological method of Husserl and
Heidegger which attempted to break with abstract philosophical theorizing and to conceptualize "the things themselves" as they appeared to consciousness.

In his early works, Marcuse himself attempted to syn-
thesize Heidegger's phenomenological existentialism with
Marxism, and in *One-Dimensional Man* one recognizes
Husserlian and Heideggerian motifs in Marcuse's critiques
of scientific civilization and modes of thought. In particular,

---

4. On the Frankfurt School, see Martin Jay, *The Dialectical Imagination* (Boston: Little, Brown and Company, 1973) and Douglas Kellner, *Critical Theory, Marxism, and Modernity* (Cambridge and Baltimore: Polity Press and Johns Hopkins
University Press, 1989).

Marcuse develops a conception of a technological world, similar in some respects to that developed by Heidegger, and, like Husserl and Heidegger, sees technological rationality colonizing everyday life, robbing individuals of freedom and individuality by imposing technological imperatives, rules, and structures upon their thought and behavior.

Marcuse thought that dialectical philosophy could promote critical thinking. *One-Dimensional Man* is perhaps Marcuse's most sustained attempt to present and develop the categories of the dialectical philosophy developed by Hegel and Marx. For Marcuse, dialectical thinking involved the ability to abstract one's perception and thought from existing forms in order to form more general concepts. This conception helps explain the difficulty of *One-Dimensional Man* and the demands that it imposes upon its reader. For Marcuse abstracts from the complexity and multiplicity of the existing society its fundamental tendencies and constituents, as well as those categories which constitute for him the forms of critical thinking. This demands that the reader also abstract from existing ways of looking at society and modes of thinking and attempt to perceive and think in a new way.

Uncritical thinking derives its beliefs, norms, and values from existing thought and social practices, while critical thought seeks alternative modes of thought and behavior from which it creates a standpoint of critique. Such a critical standpoint requires developing what Marcuse calls "negative thinking," which "negates" existing forms of thought and reality from the perspective of higher possibilities. This practice presupposes the ability to make a distinction between existence and essence, fact and potentiality, and appearance and reality. Mere existence would be negated in favor of realizing higher potentialities while norms discovered by reason would be used to criticize and overcome lower forms of thought and social organization. Thus grasping potentialities for freedom and happiness would make possible the negation of conditions that inhibited individuals' full development and realization. In other words, perceiving the possibility of self-determination and constructing one's own needs and values could enable individuals to break with the existing world of thought and behavior. Philosophy was thus to supply the norms for social criticism and the ideal of liberation which would guide social change and individual self-transformation.

It is probably Marcuse's involvement with the Critical Theory of the Frankfurt School that most decisively influenced the genesis and production of *One-Dimensional Man*. After the emergence of Heidegger's public support of National Socialism, and just on the eve of the triumph of the Nazi party, Marcuse had a job interview with the Frankfurt Institute for Social Research, received a position with them, and joined them in exile after Hitler's ascendancy to power. First in Geneva, Switzerland, and then in New York, where the Institute affiliated with Columbia University, Marcuse enthusiastically joined in the Institute's collective attempt to develop a critical theory of society. Along with the Institute's director, Max Horkheimer, Marcuse was one of their philosophy specialists. He began his work with the Institute by producing a critique of fascist ideology; having turned away from his former teacher, he now appraised Heidegger's work as part of the new tendency toward totalitarian thought that was dominant in Germany and which threatened the rest of the world as well.

During the 1930s, Marcuse worked intensively, attempting to explicate and develop philosophical concepts that would be most useful for critical social theory. This project involved the interrogation of the concepts of essence, happiness, freedom, and, especially, critical reason, which he believed was the central category of philosophical thought and critique. In each case, he took standard philosophical categories and provided them with a materialist base, showing how concepts of essence, for instance, are directly relevant to concrete human life.[5] Understanding the essential features of the human being, on this view, illuminates the potentialities that can be realized by individuals and the social conditions that inhibit or foster their development.

This concern with critical reason and Hegelian and Marxian modes of dialectical thinking is evident in *Reason and Revolution* (1941), Marcuse's first major work in English,[6] in which he traces the rise of modern social theory through Hegel, Marx, and positivism. Marcuse's Hegel is a critical dialectical thinker whom he tries to absolve of responsibility for the totalitarian states with which Hegel was often associated as a spiritual progenitor. Marcuse claims that Hegel instituted a method of rational critique that utilized the "power of negative thinking" to criticize irrational forms of social life. The close connection between Hegel and Marx and the ways that Marx developed and concretized Hegel's dialectical method are the focal points of Marcuse's interpretation, which remains to this day one of the most insightful studies of the relation between Hegel and Marx and the origins of modern social theory.

The contrast between one-dimensional and dialectical thinking is made already in his 1930s essays. For Marcuse, one-dimensional thought and action derive their standards and criteria from the existing society, eschewing transcendent standards and norms. Critical and dialectical thinking, by contrast, postulates norms of criticism, based on rational potentials for human happiness and freedom, which are used to negate existing states of affairs that oppress indi-

---

5. See the essays in Herbert Marcuse, *Negations* (Boston: Beacon Press, 1968).
6. Herbert Marcuse, *Reason and Revolution*, 2d ed. (Boston: Beacon Press, 1960).

viduals and restrict human freedom and well-being. Dialectical thought thus posits the existence of another realm of ideas, images, and imagination that serves as a potential guide for a social transformation that would realize the unrealized potentialities for a better life. Marcuse believes that great philosophy and art are the locus of these potentialities and critical norms, and he decodes the best products of Western culture in this light.

Throughout the first decade of their period of exile, there was constant discussion within the Institute for Social Research of the need for a systematic treatise on dialectics which would lay out the categories, modes of thought, and method of dialectical and critical theory.[7] Max Horkheimer was especially interested in this project and consulted with Marcuse, Theodor Adorno, Karl Korsch, and others concerning how such an ambitious project might be developed. In the United States, Horkheimer and his associates found themselves in an environment in which scientific and pragmatic modes of thinking were dominant and dialectics was seen as a sort of obscurantist thinking. Concerned to establish the importance of dialectical thinking, Horkheimer and his associates discussed how the great book on dialectics might be conceived and written.

Marcuse was extremely eager to work on this project with Horkheimer, who felt himself to be too involved in his work as director of the Institute to be able to devote sufficient time and energy to the project. During the 1940s, however, Horkheimer, Marcuse, and Adorno moved to California where they had an opportunity to devote themselves full time to philosophical studies. Soon after, following the outbreak of World War Two, Marcuse went to Washington to work for the Office of Strategic Services and then the State Department as his contribution to the fight

---

7. See Rolf Wiggershaus, *Die Frankfurter Schule* (Munich: Hanser, 1986), esp. pp. 338ff.

against fascism. Thus Adorno ended up as Horkheimer's collaborator on the project on dialectics, which became their book *Dialectic of Enlightenment*.[8]

The Genesis and Development of One-Dimensional Man

In retrospect, *One-Dimensional Man* articulates precisely the Hegelian-Marxian philosophical project that Marcuse began developing in the 1930s in his work with the Frankfurt School. In particular, in the sections on "One-Dimensional Thought" and "The Chance of the Alternatives" Marcuse develops the modes of critical thinking and ideology critique distinctive of the Frankfurt School most fully. His analyses here exemplify Hegelian/Marxian dialectical philosophy both in his relentless critique of existing modes of what he considers uncritical thought and in his working out of the categories of critical and dialectical thinking.

Chapters 1 through 4 of *One-Dimensional Man*, by contrast, connect with the Frankfurt School's project of developing a Critical Theory of contemporary society, which they began producing in the 1930s.[9] The Frankfurt School critical social theorists were among the first to analyze the new configurations of the state and economy in contemporary capitalist societies, to criticize the key roles of mass culture and communications, to analyze new modes of technology and forms of social control, to discuss new modes of socialization and the decline of the individual in mass society, and—vis-à-vis classical Marxism—to analyze and

8. Max Horkheimer and Theodor W. Adorno, *Dialectic of Enlightenment* (New York: Seabury, 1972; original 1947).
9. On the critical social theory of the Frankfurt School, see Kellner, *Critical Theory, Marxism, and Modernity* and the essays collected in Stephen Bronner and Douglas Kellner, eds., *Critical Theory and Society. A Reader* (New York and London: Routledge, 1989).

confront the consequences of the integration of the working classes and the stabilization of capitalism for the project of radical social change. Marcuse's *One-Dimensional Man* is perhaps the fullest and most concrete development of these themes within the tradition of Frankfurt School Critical Theory.

One can trace the genesis of the major themes of Marcuse's magnus opus in his works from the early 1930s until its publication in 1964. In essays from the early 1940s, Marcuse is already describing how tendencies toward technological rationality were producing a system of totalitarian social control and domination. In a 1941 article, "Some Social Implications of Modern Technology," Marcuse sketches the historical decline of individualism from the time of the bourgeois revolutions to the rise of modern technological society.[10] Individual rationality, he claims, was won in the struggle against regnant superstitions, irrationality, and domination, and posed the individual in a critical stance against society. Critical reason was thus a creative principle which was the source of both the individual's liberation and society's advancement. The development of modern industry and technological rationality, however, undermined the basis of individual rationality. As capitalism and technology developed, advanced industrial society demanded increasing accommodation to the economic and social apparatus and submission to increasing domination and administration. Hence, a "mechanics of conformity" spread throughout the society. The efficiency and power of administration overwhelmed the in-

10. Herbert Marcuse, "Some Social Implications of Modern Technology," collected in Andrew Arato and Eike Gebhardt, *The Essential Frankfurt School Reader* (New York: Continuum, 1985), pp. 138–62. Marcuse indicates in letters from the 1940s that he was working on a large manuscript criticizing contemporary forms of thought such as positivism, behaviorism, and other forms of one-dimensional thought; see the discussion in Wiggershaus, *Die Frankfurter Schule*, and the collected letters from the period in the Marcuse Archive. Unfortunately, the manuscript has not yet turned up and may be lost.

dividual, who gradually lost the earlier traits of critical rationality (i.e., autonomy, dissent, the power of negation), thus producing a "one-dimensional society" and "one-dimensional man."

At the same time, however, Marcuse was working with Franz Neumann on a project entitled "Theory of Social Change"[11] which they described as

A historical and theoretical approach to the development of a positive theory of social change for contemporary society.

The major historical changes of social systems, and the theories associated with them will be discussed. Particular attention will be paid to such transitions as those from feudalism to capitalism, from laissez-faire to organized industrial society, from capitalism to socialism and communism.

A handwritten note, in Marcuse's writing, on the themes of the project indicates that he and Neumann intended to analyze conflicting tendencies toward social change and social cohesion; forces of freedom and necessity in social change; subjective and objective factors that produce social change; patterns of social change, such as evolution and revolution; and the nature of social change, whether progressive, regressive, or cyclical. They ultimately intended to develop a "theory of social change for our society." A seventeen-page typed manuscript in the Marcuse Archive, entitled "A History of the Doctrine of Social Change," presents an overview of the project. Marcuse and Neumann open by writing:

Since sociology as an independent science was not established before the 19th century, the theory of society up to that time was an integral part of philosophy or of those sciences

---

11. Herbert Marcuse and Franz Neumann, "Theory of Social Change," unpublished text in Marcuse Archive, no date. The Marcuse Archive was opened in Frankfurt, Germany in October of 1990; it contains a wealth of unpublished manuscripts, lectures, and letters which will be published in forthcoming volumes.

(such as the economic or juristic), the conceptual structure of which was to a large extent based upon specific philosophical doctrines. This intrinsic connection between philosophy and the theory of society (a connection which will be explained in the text) formulates the pattern of all particular theories of social change occurring in the ancient world, in the middle ages, and on the commencement of modern times. One decisive result is the emphasis on the fact that social change cannot be interpreted within a particular social science, but must be understood within the social and natural totality of human life. This conception uses, to a large extent, psychological factors in the theories of social change. However, the derivation of social and political concepts from the "psyche" of man is not a psychological method in the modern sense but rather involves the negation of psychology as a special science. For the Greeks, psychological concepts were essentially ethical, social and political ones, to be integrated into the ultimate science of philosophy.[12]

This passage clearly reveals the typically Marcusean tendency, shared by the Frankfurt School, to integrate philosophy, social theory, and politics. While standard academic practice tended to separate these disciplines, Marcuse and his colleagues perceived their interrelation. Thus Marcuse and Neumann read ancient philosophy as containing a theory of social change that was basically determined by a search for the conditions that would produce the highest fulfillment of the individual. They read Plato, therefore, as elaborating "that form of social order which can best guarantee the development of human potentialities under the prevailing conditions." For Plato, this involves conceptualizing the ideal forms of life and the reconstruction of society according to them: "The radical change of the traditional city state into the platonic state of estates implies a reconstruction of the economy in such a manner

12. Herbert Marcuse and Franz Neumann, "A History of the Doctrine of Social Change," unpublished text in Marcuse Archive, no date.

that the economic no longer determines the faculties and powers of man, but is rather determined by them."

Marcuse and Neumann propose a systematic examination of ancient, medieval, and modern theories of social change with a view toward developing a contemporary theory of society and social change. They note that modern sociology "has severed the intrinsic connection between the theory of society and philosophy which is still operative in Marxism and has treated the problem of social change as a particular sociological question." They propose, by contrast, integrating philosophy, sociology, and political theory in a theory of social change for the present age.

A larger, forty-seven-page manuscript, titled "A Theory of Social Change," presents a more comprehensive analysis of some of the specific theories of social change that Marcuse and Neumann would analyze. This project is extremely interesting within the history of Critical Theory since it shows that in the 1940s there were two tendencies within Critical Theory: (1) the philosophical-cultural analysis of the trends of Western civilization being developed by Horkheimer and Adorno in *Dialectic of Enlightenment*, and (2) the more practical-political development of Critical Theory as a theory of social change proposed by Marcuse and Neumann. For Marcuse and Neumann, Critical Theory would be developed as a theory of social change that would connect philosophy, social theory, and radical politics— precisely the project of 1930s Critical Theory that Horkheimer and Adorno were abandoning in the early 1940s in their turn toward philosophical and cultural criticism divorced from social theory and radical politics. Marcuse and Neumann, by contrast, were focusing precisely on the issue that Horkheimer and Adorno had neglected: the theory of social change.[13]

13. In *The Origins of Negative Dialectics* (New York: The Free Press, 1977), Susan Buck-Morss argues that in the 1930s there were two models and tendencies

With their involvement in antifascist work for the U.S. government during the Second World War their work on the project was suspended, and there is no evidence that Marcuse and Neumann attempted to take it up again after the war. During his years of government service—from 1942 until the early 1950s—Marcuse continued to develop his Critical Theory and the themes that would become central to *One-Dimensional Man*. In a 1946 essay that contained thirty-three theses on the current world situation, Marcuse sketched what he saw as the social and political tendencies of the present moment.[14] The text was prepared for the journal *Zeitschrift für Sozialforschung*, which the Institute for Social Research hoped to relaunch. The plan was for Marcuse, Horkheimer, Neumann, Adorno, and others to write articles on contemporary philosophy, art, social theory, politics, and so on, but this project also failed to come to fruition, perhaps because of growing philosophical and political differences between the members of the Institute. The return of Adorno and Horkheimer to Germany to re-establish the Institute for Social Research in Frankfurt might also have undermined the project.

Marcuse's "Theses," like his later *One-Dimensional Man*, contain a Hegelian overview of the contemporary world situation that was deeply influenced by classical Marxism. In the theses, Marcuse anticipates many of the key positions of *One-Dimensional Man*, including the integration of the proletariat, the stabilization of capitalism, the bureaucratization of socialism, the demise of the rev-

---

of Critical Theory: the attempt by Marcuse, Horkheimer, and others to develop a Critical Theory of contemporary society and the attempts to develop a radical theory and cultural criticism developed by T. W. Adorno and Walter Benjamin. The discovery of the manuscripts by Marcuse and Neumann on theories of social change suggest that there were also two distinct tendencies within Critical Theory in the 1940s.

    14. Herbert Marcuse, unpublished manuscript with no title, dated 1946, in Marcuse Archive. For a discussion of the manuscript's history, see Wiggershaus, *Die Frankfurter Schule*, pp. 429ff.

olutionary left, and the absence of genuine forces of progressive social change.

In general, the characteristic themes of Marcuse's post-Second World War writings build on the Frankfurt School's analyses of the role of technology and technological rationality, administration and bureaucracy, the capitalist state, mass media and consumerism, and new modes of social control, which in their view produced both a decline in the revolutionary potential of the working class and a decline of individuality, freedom, and democracy, as well as the stabilization of capitalism. In a 1954 epilogue to the second edition of *Reason and Revolution,* Marcuse claims that: "The defeat of Fascism and National Socialism has not arrested the trend towards totalitarianism. Freedom is on the retreat—in the realm of thought as well as in that of society."[15] In Marcuse's view, the powers of reason and freedom are declining in "late industrial society": "With the increasing concentration and effectiveness of economic, political, and cultural controls, the opposition in all these fields has been pacified, co-ordinated, or liquidated." Indeed, reason has become an instrument of domination: "It helps to organize, administer, and anticipate the powers that be, and to liquidate the 'power of Negativity.' Reason has identified itself with the reality: what is actual is reasonable, although what is reasonable has not yet become actuality."

Not only Hegel's hope that reason would shape and control reality, but Marx's hope that reason would be embodied in a revolutionary class and rational socialist society, had come to naught. The proletariat was not the "absolute negation of capitalist society presupposed by Marx," and the contradictions of capitalism were not as explosive as Marx had forecast. Marcuse took over the term "organized

15. Herbert Marcuse, "Epilogue," *Reason and Revolution,* 2d ed. (New York: Humanities Press, 1954), pp. 433ff.

capitalism" developed by the Austro-Marxist Rudolf Hilferding to describe the administrative-bureaucratic apparatus which organizes, manages, and stabilizes capitalist society.[16] Economic planning in the state, automatization in the economy, the rationalization of culture in the mass media, and the increased bureaucratization of all modes of social, political, and economic life had created a "totally administered society" that was resulting in "the decline of the individual."

By the 1950s, Marcuse thus perceived that the unparalleled affluence of the consumer society and the apparatus of planning and management in advanced capitalism had produced new forms of social administration and a "society without opposition" that threatened individuality and that closed off possibilities of radical social change. In studies of the 1950s, he began sketching out a theory of a new type of technological society which would receive its fullest development in *One-Dimensional Man*. Marcuse's analysis is based on a conception of the historical rise of a technological world which overpowers and controls its subjects. In this technological world, Marcuse claims that metaphysics is superseded by technology, in that the previous metaphysical concept of subjectivity, which postulates an active subject confronting a controllable world of objects, is replaced by a one-dimensional technical world where "pure instrumentality" and "efficacy" of arranging means and ends within a pre-established universe is the "common principle of thought and action." The self-contained and self-perpetuating technological world allows change only within its own institutions and parameters. In this sense, it is "one-dimensional" and "has become a universal means of domination" which congeals into a "second nature, *schlechte Unmittelbarkeit* (bad immediacy) which is perhaps more

16. Rudolf Hilferding, *Finance Capital* (London: Routledge, 1981; originally published 1910).

hostile and more destructive than *primary* nature, the pre-technical nature."[17]

There are two ways to read Marcuse's theory of the one-dimensional technical world and society, which is the primary focus of *One-Dimensional Man*. One can interpret Marcuse's theory as a global, totalizing theory of a new type of society that transcends the contradictions of capitalist society in a new order that eliminates individuality, dissent, and opposition. Indeed, there is a recurrent tendency in reading Marcuse to use "one-dimensionality" as a totalizing concept to describe an era of historical development which supposedly absorbs all opposition into a totalitarian, monolithic system. However, Marcuse himself rarely, if ever, uses the term "one-dimensionality" (i.e., as a totalizing noun) but instead tends to speak of "one-dimensional" man, society, or thought, applying the term as an adjective describing deficient conditions which he criticizes and contrasts with an alternative state of affairs. In fact, Marcuse introduces "one-dimensional" in his earlier writing as an epistemological concept that makes a distinction between one-dimensional and dialectical thought; in *One-Dimensional Man* it is extended to describe social and anthropological phenomena. In light of Marcuse's criticism of "one-dimensional" states of affairs by posing alternatives that are to be fought for and realized, it is wrong to read him solely as a theorist of the totally administered society who completely rejects contradiction, conflict, revolt, and alternative thought and action. In *One-Dimensional Man* and later works, he rejects a monolithic interpretation of the text as an epic of total domination that in a quasi-Hegelian fashion subsumes everything into a one-

17. Herbert Marcuse, "From Ontology to Technology: Fundamental Tendencies of Industrial Society," in Stephen Bronner and Douglas Kellner, eds., *Critical Theory and Society. A Reader* (New York and London: Routledge, 1989), p. 122.

dimensional totality; it is preferable to read it as a dialectical text which contrasts one-dimensional with multidimensional thought and behavior.

Thus, I would propose interpreting "one-dimensional" as conforming to existing thought and behavior and lacking a critical dimension and a dimension of potentialities that transcend the existing society. In Marcuse's usage the adjective "one-dimensional" describes practices that conform to pre-existing structures, norms, and behavior, in contrast to multidimensional discourse, which focuses on possibilities that transcend the established state of affairs. This epistemological distinction presupposes antagonism between subject and object so that the subject is free to perceive possibilities in the world that do not yet exist but which can be realized. In the one-dimensional society, the subject is assimilated into the object and follows the dictates of external, objective norms and structures, thus losing the ability to discover more liberating possibilities and to engage in transformative practice to realize them. Marcuse's theory presupposes the existence of a human subject with freedom, creativity, and self-determination who stands in opposition to an object-world, perceived as substance, which contains possibilities to be realized and secondary qualities like values, aesthetic traits, and aspirations, which can be cultivated to enhance human life.

In Marcuse's analysis, "one-dimensional man" has lost, or is losing, individuality, freedom, and the ability to dissent and to control one's own destiny. The private space, the dimension of negation and individuality, in which one may become and remain a self, is being whittled away by a society which shapes aspirations, hopes, fears, and values, and even manipulates vital needs. In Marcuse's view, the price that one-dimensional man pays for satisfaction is to surrender freedom and individuality. One-dimensional man does not know its true needs because its needs are not its own—they are administered, superimposed, and heteronomous; it is not able to resist domination, nor to act autonomously, for it identifies with public behavior and imitates and submits to the powers that be. Lacking the power of authentic self-activity, one-dimensional man submits to increasingly total domination.

Marcuse is thus a radical individualist who is deeply disturbed by the decline of the traits of authentic individuality that he so highly values. One-dimensional society and one-dimensional man are the results of a long historical erosion of individuality which Marcuse criticized over several decades. *One-Dimensional Man* can thus be interpreted as an extended protest against the decline of individuality in advanced industrial society. The cognitive costs include the loss of an ability to perceive another dimension of possibilities that transcend the one-dimensional thought and society. Rooting his conception in Hegel's dialectical philosophy, Marcuse insists on the importançe of distinguishing between existence and essence, fact and potential, and appearance and reality. One-dimensional thought is not able to make these distinctions and thus submits to the power of the existing society, deriving its view of the world and mode of behavior from existing practices and modes of thought.

Marcuse is again reworking here the Hegelian-Marxian theme of reification and alienation, where the individual loses the power of comprehending and transforming subjectivity as it becomes dominated by alien powers and objects. For Marcuse, the distinguishing features of a human being are free and creative subjectivity. If in one's economic and social life one is administered by a technical labor apparatus and conforms to dominant social norms, one is losing one's potentialities of self-determination and individuality. Alienated from the powers of being-a-self, one-dimensional man thus becomes an object of administration and conformity.

The Critical Theory of One-Dimensional Society

One-Dimensional Man raises the specter of the closing-off, or "atrophying," of the very possibilities of radical social change and human emancipation. Marcuse depicts a situation in which there are no revolutionary classes or groups to militate for radical social change and in which individuals are integrated into the existing society, content with their lot and unable to perceive possibilities for a happier and freer life. There are tensions in the book, however, between the development of a more general theory of "advanced industrial society" and a more specific critique of contemporary capitalist societies, especially U.S. society, from which he derives most of his examples. Marcuse draws on the social analyses of C. Wright Mills, Daniel Bell, Vance Packard, and critical journalists like Fred Cook for examples of the trends that he sees in contemporary U.S. society. Yet he also draws on European theories, such as French theories of the technological society and the new working class, and he depicts trends in contemporary communist societies that he believes are similar to those in capitalist ones. Thus one can read the book as a general theory of contemporary advanced industrial, or technological, societies, or as a more specific analysis and critique of contemporary U.S. society during a period of affluence and muted social opposition.

Marcuse combines the perspectives of Marxian theory, the Critical Theory of the Frankfurt School, French social theory, and American social science to present a critical social theory of the present age. What is striking about the book is Marcuse's posture of total critique and resolute opposition to contemporary advanced industrial societies, capitalist and communist, in their totality. While he frequently criticizes communist societies, building on his earlier critiques of *Soviet Marxism* (1958),[18] he rejects the Cold War demonology which celebrates capitalist society in contrast to communism. Marcuse perceives destructive tendencies in advanced capitalism's most celebrated achievements and sees irrationality in its self-proclaimed rationality. He maintains that the society's prosperity and growth are based on waste and destruction, its progress fueled by exploitation and repression, while its freedom and democracy are based on manipulation. Marcuse slices through the ideological celebrations of capitalism and sharply criticizes the dehumanization and alienation in its opulence and affluence, the slavery in its labor system, the ideology and indoctrination in its culture, the fetishism in its consumerism, and the danger and insanity in its military-industrial complex. He concludes that despite its achievements, "this society is irrational as a whole. Its productivity is destructive of the free development of human needs and faculties . . . its growth dependent on the repression of the real possibilities for pacifying the struggle for existence— individual, national and international" (*One-Dimensional Man*, pp. ix–x).

For Marcuse, commodities and consumption play a far greater role in contemporary capitalist society than that envisaged by Marx and most orthodox Marxists. Marcuse was one of the first critical theorists to analyze the consumer society through analyzing how consumerism, advertising, mass culture, and ideology integrate individuals into and stabilize the capitalist system. In describing how needs are produced which integrate individuals into a whole universe of thought, behavior, and satisfactions, he distinguishes be-

18. Herbert Marcuse, *Soviet Marxism* (New York: Columbia University Press, 1985; original 1958).

tween true and false needs and describes how individuals can liberate themselves from the prevailing needs and satisfactions to live a freer and happier life. He claims that the system's widely touted individualism and freedom are forms from which individuals need to liberate themselves in order to be truly free. His argument is that the system's much lauded economic, political, and social freedoms, formerly a source of social progress, lose their progressive function and become subtle instruments of domination which serve to keep individuals in bondage to the system that they strengthen and perpetuate. For example, economic freedom to sell one's labor power in order to compete on the labor market submits the individual to the slavery of an irrational economic system; political freedom to vote for generally indistinguishable representatives of the same system is but a delusive ratification of a nondemocratic political system; intellectual freedom of expression is ineffectual when the media either co-opt and defuse, or distort and suppress, oppositional ideas, and when the image-makers shape public opinion so that it is hostile or immune to oppositional thought and action. Marcuse concludes that genuine freedom and well-being depend on liberation from the entire system of one-dimensional needs and satisfactions and require "new modes of realization . . . corresponding to the new capabilities of society" (*One-Dimensional Man*, p. 4).

Marcuse also analyzes changes in the labor process and new forms of integration of the working class into the existing capitalist society; developments within the capitalist state and the emergence of a one-dimensional politics; and the integration of thought, language, and culture. His critiques of contemporary modes of thought are especially provocative. He also critically analyzes new forms of technology and technological rationality which are producing a qualitatively different social structure, a totally administered society. Together, these analyses provide theoretical perspectives on the new forms of capitalist hegemony and stabilization which had emerged in the 1950s and early 1960s.

One-Dimensional Man continues to be relevant because of its grasp of the underlying structures and tendencies of contemporary socioeconomic and political development. The scientific and technological rationalities that Marcuse describes are even more powerful today with the emergence of computerization, the proliferation of media and information, and the development of new techniques and forms of social control. And yet the society is more irrational than previously. Marcuse's description of 1964 still rings true today: "The union of growing productivity and growing destruction; the brinkmanship of annihilation; the surrender of thought, hope, and fear to the decisions of the powers that be; the preservation of misery in the face of unprecedented wealth constitute the most impartial indictment. . . . [Society's] sweeping rationality, which propels efficiency and growth is itself irrational" (*One-Dimensional Man*, p. xiii).

Marcuse's critical theory of society brilliantly analyzes the tendencies toward social stability and integration achieved by contemporary capitalist societies, but downplays their crisis-tendencies and contradictions. Consequently, his theory of "one-dimensional society" cannot account either for the eruption of social revolt on a global scale in the 1960s, or the global crises of capitalism that have been occurring from the early 1970s to the present. In a sense, *One-Dimensional Man* articulates a stage of historical development that would soon be coming to a close and would give way to a new era marked by social turmoil and upheaval in the 1960s and a world crisis of capitalism in the 1970s. By failing to analyze in more detail countertendencies against one-dimensional society, he created a picture of a new type of social order able to absorb all opposition and to control thought and action indefinitely, thus permanently stabilizing the capitalist system. Yet methodologically, Marcuse indicates that he is analyzing trends of social development to which there are counter-trends (*One-Dimensional Man,* pp. xv–xviii). In the introduction he writes that his study "will vacillate throughout between two contradictory hypotheses: (1) that advanced industrial society is capable of containing qualitative change for the foreseeable future; (2) that forces and tendencies exist which may break this containment and explode the society" (p. xv). Near the end of the book he writes: "The unification of opposites in the medium of technological rationality must be, *in all its reality,* an illusory unification, which eliminates neither the contradiction between the growing productivity and its repressive use, nor the vital need for solving the contradiction" (p. 256).

Thus Marcuse recognizes that both social conflicts and tendencies toward change continue to exist and that radical social transformation may eventually be possible. Although the focus of his analysis is on the containment of social change, he describes the society in the passage just cited as a "forced unity" or "illusory unification" rather than as one which has eliminated all contradictions and conflicts. Thus, to interpret properly both *One-Dimensional Man* and Marcuse's project as a whole, *One-Dimensional Man* should be read in relation to *Eros and Civilization* as well as to the works that follow, such as *An Essay on Liberation* and *Counterrevolution and Revolt.* It is precisely the vision of "what could be" articulated in these texts that highlights the bleakness of "what is" in *One-Dimensional Man.* Marcuse continues to believe that contradictions exist between the higher possibilities of a free and pacified society and the existing social system. The problem presented in *One-Dimensional Man* is that one-dimensional thought cannot perceive this distinction, but Marcuse insists that it continues to exist, and, if perceived, could be a vehicle of individual and social transformation.

In his writings after *One-Dimensional Man,* Marcuse focuses more on social contradictions, struggles, and the disintegrating factors in existing societies, capitalist and communist. *One-Dimensional Man* should thus be read as a theory of the containment of social contradictions, forces of negation, and possibilities of liberation that exist but are suppressed. Even in *One-Dimensional Man* Marcuse continues to point to these forces and possibilities, and to recognize the liberating potential hidden in the oppressive social system, especially in technology, which could be used to eliminate alienated labor and to produce a better life for all. Marcuse always stresses liberation, and his thought is animated by a utopian vision that life could be as it is in art and dreams if only a revolution would take place that would eliminate its repressive features.

A lesson that might be drawn from his work is that critical and dialectical social theory should analyze containment and stabilization as well as contestation and struggle. In some eras, stabilization and containment may predominate, while in others upheaval and struggle may be dominant, or both trends could be posed against each other. Certainly, from the 1980s to the present, conservative trends have been dominant. Yet to present an adequate model for contemporary social theory and politics, forms of both domination and resistance should be analyzed. Consequently, rather than conceptualizing contemporary societies as closed monoliths of domination, they should be analyzed as systems of contradictions, tensions, and conflicts which oscillate from stasis to change, from oppression and domination to struggle and resistance, and from stability and containment to conflict and crisis.

Reception and Contemporary Relevance

In sharply criticizing contemporary capitalist societies, Marcuse went against the currents of conformist academic thinking and anticipated the multifaceted critiques of U.S. society that were to emerge in the 1960s. *One-Dimensional Man* had a curious reception and impact. It angered both orthodox Marxists, who could not accept such thorough-going revision of Marxism, and many others who were unable to assent to such radical critiques of contemporary capitalist society. The book was, however, well received by the New Left and a generation dissatisfied with the current social order and the orthodoxies of the dominant Marxist and academic theories. For the New Left, *One-Dimensional Man* articulated what young radicals felt was wrong with society, and the book's dialectic of liberation and domination provided a framework for radical politics which struggled against domination and for liberation. Moreover, *One-Dimensional Man* showed that the problems confronting the emerging radical movement were not simply the Vietnam war, racism or inequality, but the system itself, and that solving a wide range of social problems required fundamental social restructuring. In this way, *One-Dimensional Man* played an important role in the political education of a generation of radicals and to this day has inspired those involved in the development of critical philosophy and social theory.

While *One-Dimensional Man* became associated with the radicalism of the New Left in the 1960s, the text has a paradoxical relation with the new radicalism whose possibility its analyses seem to deny. At the conclusion of the book, Marcuse speculated that there was only a slight chance that the most exploited and persecuted outsiders, in alliance with an enlightened intelligentsia, might mark "the beginning of the end" and signify some hope for social change. He thought there was hope that the civil rights movement might produce ferment which would lead to a new era of struggle, and he held onto the concept of the "Great Refusal" of forms of oppresion and domination as his political ideal.

Almost on the eve of *One-Dimensional Man*'s publication, in fact, the New Left and antiwar movement began to grow in response to the accelerating U.S. military intervention in Vietnam. During this period, a generation of radicals turned to Marcuse's book, which seemed to have denied the possibility of fundamental political change. During the heroic period of the New Left in the 1960s, *One-Dimensional Man* helped to show a generation of political and cultural radicals what was wrong with the system they were struggling against, and thus played an important role in the student movement. Marcuse himself quickly rallied to the student activists' cause and was exhilarated when the Great Refusal was being acted out on a grand scale.

One-Dimensional Man also achieved a quite respectable, even laudatory, academic reception. It was reviewed in most major intellectual journals, many national magazines and newspapers, and many specialized academic journals in a wide variety of fields. The text was read as a classical study of contemporary trends of the current society in the same league with the works of C. Wright Mills, Daniel Bell, John Galbraith, and other critics of contemporary American society. The book also generated much controversy, however, especially when Marcuse was presented in the media as a "guru of the New Left." For a generation of young radicals took up Marcuse's texts as essential criticism of existing forms of thought and behavior, and Marcuse himself identified with the New Left and defended their politics and opposition.

During the late 1960s and early 1970s, Marcuse's work

was probably the most influential social theory of its day and was read and criticized by individuals from a variety of different perspectives. He modified some of his positions in his later writings in response to some of these criticisms, though he continued to be a radical critic of forms of domination and to champion what he perceived as forces of liberation. In particular, he went beyond his model of one-dimensional society in books like *An Essay on Liberation* (1969) and *Counterrevolution and Revolt* (1972) and celebrated all the most radical forms of oppositional thought and action. And then, in his last years, Marcuse turned positively to feminism and new social movements after the demise of the New Left in the early 1970s.

Near the end of his life, when I asked him what he thought of *One-Dimensional Man,* Marcuse replied that: "I stick to what I wrote in *One-Dimensional Man,*" insisting that his analysis of social trends had been confirmed by recent assaults on the changes that the struggles of the 1960s had been producing. Marcuse mentioned attacks on welfare programs, typified by Proposition 13 in California, which cut taxes for welfare spending; demands by government and business for cutbacks on social programs and a decrease in government regulation; the *Berufsverbot* in Germany and other repressions of radicals throughout the world; conservative attacks on abortion, feminism, and the Equal Rights Amendment; the increased strength of major transnational corporations; and conservative and neoconservative offenses in many areas of social and political life. He added, however, that the 1960s had unleashed new social forces, opening up new space for struggle that still existed and should be used by forces of opposition to militate for radical social change.

Marcuse died in 1979. Had he lived through the eras of Reagan and Bush no doubt he would have insisted that *One-Dimensional Man* is more relevant than ever after a decade of conservative hegemony, rampant capitalism, and a series of U.S. military interventions and covert operations in Grenada, Nicaragua, Panama, and many parts of the world, culminating in the Persian Gulf war. Marcuse was a sharp critic of militarism and a lover of life who hated death and killing. He feared that more sophisticated technologies would "instrumentalize" war and produce ever more brutal forms of destruction—a vision amply confirmed in the Vietnam and Persian Gulf wars.

Indeed, *One-Dimensional Man* provides a model analysis of the synthesis of business, the state, the media, and other cultural institutions under the hegemony of corporate capital which characterizes the U.S. economy and polity in the 1980s and early 1990s. While Marcuse does not adequately analyze the antagonisms that always exist between ruling groups and those in opposition to oppressive policies, he certainly provides illuminating perspectives on the sort of conservativism dominant in the past decade. In particular, Reagan and Reaganism exemplified one-dimensional "positive thinking" to an extreme degree. The way that the media and political establishment went along with "Reaganism" in the 1980s indicates trends toward one-dimensional thought and politics that have only intensified in the early 1990s.

Marcuse's *One-Dimensional Man* is especially relevant in regard to the resurgence of militarism during and after the Persian Gulf war. The syndrome of denial and projection and unleashing of aggressive energies was a familiar one for the Freudian Herbert Marcuse, who constantly argued that advanced industrial societies unleashed ever more lethal destructiveness which finds a mass base of approval in those who have been conditioned to approve of aggression. One-dimensional society operates by steering erotic and destructive instinctual energies into socially controlled modes of thought and behavior. Aggressive behavior thus provides a social bond, unifying those who gain in power and self-esteem through identifying with forms of aggression against shared objects of hate. This trend is all too visible in current American society, and Marcuse's analyses of aggression and militarism should be read anew during this era of resurgent aggression and one-dimensional conservativism.

Yet the legacy of the 1960s, of which Marcuse was a vital part, lives on, and the Great Refusal is still practiced by oppositional groups and individuals who refuse to conform to existing oppression and domination. Marcuse should be widely read and studied again to help nourish a renewal of critical thinking and radical politics. For social domination continues to be a block to human freedom and happiness, and liberation continues to be a hope for those who refuse to join the contemporary celebration of militarism, the forces of conservatism, and unrestrained capitalism. For, quoting Walter Benjamin at the end of *One-Dimensional Man*, "It is only for the sake of those without hope that hope is given to us."

Introduction to the First Edition

The Paralysis of Criticism: Society Without Opposition

Does not the threat of an atomic catastrophe which could wipe out the human race also serve to protect the very forces which perpetuate this danger? The efforts to prevent such a catastrophe overshadow the search for its potential causes in contemporary industrial society. These causes remain unidentified, unexposed, unattacked by the public because they recede before the all too obvious threat from without—to the West from the East, to the East from the West. Equally obvious is the need for being prepared, for living on the brink, for facing the challenge. We submit to the peaceful production of the means of destruction, to the perfection of waste, to being educated for a defense which deforms the defenders and that which they defend.

If we attempt to relate the causes of the danger to the way in which society is organized and organizes its members, we are immediately confronted with the fact that advanced industrial society becomes richer, bigger, and better as it perpetuates the danger. The defense structure makes life easier for a greater number of people and extends man's mastery of nature. Under these circumstances, our mass media have little difficulty in selling particular interests as those of all sensible men. The political needs of society become individual needs and aspirations, their satisfaction promotes business and the commonweal, and the whole appears to be the very embodiment of Reason.

And yet this society is irrational as a whole. Its productivity is destructive of the free development of human needs and faculties, its peace maintained by the constant threat of war, its growth dependent on the repression of the real possibilities for pacifying the struggle for existence—

individual, national, and international. This repression, so different from that which characterized the preceding, less developed stages of our society, operates today not from a position of natural and technical immaturity but rather from a position of strength. The capabilities (intellectual and material) of contemporary society are immeasurably greater than ever before—which means that the scope of society's domination over the individual is immeasurably greater than ever before. Our society distinguishes itself by conquering the centrifugal social forces with Technology rather than Terror, on the dual basis of an overwhelming efficiency and an increasing standard of living.

To investigate the roots of these developments and examine their historical alternatives is part of the aim of a critical theory of contemporary society, a theory which analyzes society in the light of its used and unused or abused capabilities for improving the human condition. But what are the standards for such a critique?

Certainly value judgments play a part. The established way of organizing society is measured against other possible ways, ways which are held to offer better chances for alleviating man's struggle for existence; a specific historical practice is measured against its own historical alternatives. From the beginning, any critical theory of society is thus confronted with the problem of historical objectivity, a problem which arises at the two points where the analysis implies value judgments:

1. the judgment that human life is worth living, or rather can be and ought to be made worth living. This judgment underlies all intellectual effort; it is the *a priori* of social theory, and its rejection (which is perfectly logical) rejects theory itself;

2. the judgment that, in a given society, specific possibilities exist for the amelioration of human life and specific

ways and means of realizing these possibilities. Critical analysis has to demonstrate the objective validity of these judgments, and the demonstration has to proceed on empirical grounds. The established society has available an ascertainable quantity and quality of intellectual and material resources. How can these resources be used for the optimal development and satisfaction of individual needs and faculties with a minimum of toil and misery? Social theory is historical theory, and history is the realm of chance in the realm of necessity. Therefore, among the various possible and actual modes of organizing and utilizing the available resources, which ones offer the greatest chance of an optimal development?

The attempt to answer these questions demands a series of initial abstractions. In order to identify and define the possibilities of an optimal development, the critical theory must abstract from the actual organization and utilization of society's resources, and from the results of this organization and utilization. Such abstraction which refuses to accept the given universe of facts as the final context of validation, such "transcending" analysis of the facts in the light of their arrested and denied possibilities, pertains to the very structure of social theory. It is opposed to all metaphysics by virtue of the rigorously historical character of the transcendence.[1] The "possibilities" must be within the reach of the respective society; they must be definable goals of practice. By the same token, the abstraction from the established institutions must be expressive of an actual tendency—that is, their transformation must be the real need of the underlying population. Social theory is concerned with the historical

1. The terms "transcend" and "transcendence" are used throughout in the empirical, critical sense: they designate tendencies in theory and practice which, in a given society, "overshoot" the established universe of discourse and action toward its historical alternatives (real possibilities).

alternatives which haunt the established society as subversive tendencies and forces. The values attached to the alternatives do become facts when they are translated into reality by historical practice. The theoretical concepts terminate with social change.

But here, advanced industrial society confronts the critique with a situation which seems to deprive it of its very basis. Technical progress, extended to a whole system of domination and coordination, creates forms of life (and of power) which appear to reconcile the forces opposing the system and to defeat or refute all protest in the name of the historical prospects of freedom from toil and domination. Contemporary society seems to be capable of containing social change—qualitative change which would establish essentially different institutions, a new direction of the productive process, new modes of human existence. This containment of social change is perhaps the most singular achievement of advanced industrial society; the general acceptance of the National Purpose, bipartisan policy, the decline of pluralism, the collusion of Business and Labor within the strong State testify to the integration of opposites which is the result as well as the prerequisite of this achievement.

A brief comparison between the formative stage of the theory of industrial society and its present situation may help to show how the basis of the critique has been altered. At its origins in the first half of the nineteenth century, when it elaborated the first concepts of the alternatives, the critique of industrial society attained concreteness in a historical mediation between theory and practice, values and facts, needs and goals. This historical mediation occurred in the consciousness and in the political action of the two great classes which faced each other in the society: the bourgeoisie and the proletariat. In the capitalist world, they are still the basic classes. However, the capitalist development has altered the structure and function of these two classes in such a way that they no longer appear to be agents of historical transformation. An overriding interest in the preservation and improvement of the institutional status quo unites the former antagonists in the most advanced areas of contemporary society. And to the degree to which technical progress assures the growth and cohesion of communist society, the very idea of qualitative change recedes before the realistic notions of a non-explosive evolution. In the absence of demonstrable agents and agencies of social change, the critique is thus thrown back to a high level of abstraction. There is no ground on which theory and practice, thought and action meet. Even the most empirical analysis of historical alternatives appears to be unrealistic speculation, and commitment to them a matter of personal (or group) preference.

And yet: does this absence refute the theory? In the face of apparently contradictory facts, the critical analysis continues to insist that the need for qualitative change is as pressing as ever before. Needed by whom? The answer continues to be the same: by the society as a whole, for every one of its members. The union of growing productivity and growing destruction; the brinkmanship of annihilation; the surrender of thought, hope, and fear to the decisions of the powers that be; the preservation of misery in the face of unprecedented wealth constitute the most impartial indictment —even if they are not the *raison d'être* of this society but only its by-product: its sweeping rationality, which propels efficiency and growth, is itself irrational.

The fact that the vast majority of the population accepts, and is made to accept, this society does not render it less irrational and less reprehensible. The distinction between true and false consciousness, real and immediate interest still is meaningful. But this distinction itself must be validated. Men must come to see it and to find their way from false to true consciousness, from their immediate to their real interest. They can do so only if they live in need of changing their way of life, of denying the positive, of refusing. It is precisely this need which the established society manages to repress to the degree to which it is capable of "delivering the goods" on an increasingly large scale, and using the scientific conquest of nature for the scientific conquest of man.

Confronted with the total character of the achievements of advanced industrial society, critical theory is left without the rationale for transcending this society. The vacuum empties the theoretical structure itself, because the categories of a critical social theory were developed during the period in which the need for refusal and subversion was embodied in the action of effective social forces. These categories were essentially negative and oppositional concepts, defining the actual contradictions in nineteenth century European society. The category "society" itself expressed the acute conflict between the social and political sphere—society as antagonistic to the state. Similarly, "individual," "class," "private," "family" denoted spheres and forces not yet integrated with the established conditions—spheres of tension and contradiction. With the growing integration of industrial society, these categories are losing their critical connotation, and tend to become descriptive, deceptive, or operational terms.

An attempt to recapture the critical intent of these categories, and to understand how the intent was cancelled by the social reality, appears from the outset to be regression from a theory joined with historical practice to abstract, speculative thought: from the critique of political economy to philosophy. This ideological character of the critique results from the fact that the analysis is forced to proceed from a position "outside" the positive as well as negative, the productive as well as destructive tendencies in society. Modern industrial society is the pervasive identity of these opposites —it is the whole that is in question. At the same time, the position of theory cannot be one of mere speculation. It must be a historical position in the sense that it must be grounded on the capabilities of the given society.

This ambiguous situation involves a still more fundamental ambiguity. *One-Dimensional Man* will vacillate throughout between two contradictory hypotheses: (1) that advanced industrial society is capable of containing qualitative change for the foreseeable future; (2) that forces and tendencies exist which may break this containment and explode the society. I do not think that a clear answer can be given. Both tendencies are there, side by side—and even the one in the other. The first tendency is dominant, and whatever preconditions for a reversal may exist are being used to prevent it. Perhaps an accident may alter the situation, but unless the recognition of what is being done and what is being prevented subverts the consciousness and the behavior of man, not even a catastrophe will bring about the change.

The analysis is focused on advanced industrial society, in which the technical apparatus of production and distribution (with an increasing sector of automation) functions, not as the sum-total of mere instruments which can be isolated from their social and political effects, but rather as a system which determines *a priori* the product of the apparatus as well as the operations of servicing and extending it. In this society, the productive apparatus tends to become totalitarian to the extent to which it determines not only the socially needed occupations, skills, and attitudes, but also individual needs and aspirations. It thus obliterates the opposition between the private and public existence, between individual and social needs. Technology serves to institute new, more effective, and more pleasant forms of social control and social cohesion. The totalitarian tendency of these controls seems to assert itself in still another sense

—by spreading to the less developed and even to the pre-industrial areas of the world, and by creating similarities in the development of capitalism and communism.

In the face of the totalitarian features of this society, the traditional notion of the "neutrality" of technology can no longer be maintained. Technology as such cannot be isolated from the use to which it is put; the technological society is a system of domination which operates already in the concept and construction of techniques.

The way in which a society organizes the life of its members involves an initial *choice* between historical alternatives which are determined by the inherited level of the material and intellectual culture. The choice itself results from the play of the dominant interests. It *anticipates* specific modes of transforming and utilizing man and nature and rejects other modes. It is one "project" of realization among others.[2] But once the project has become operative in the basic institutions and relations, it tends to become exclusive and to determine the development of the society as a whole. As a technological universe, advanced industrial society is a *political* universe, the latest stage in the realization of a specific historical *project*—namely, the experience, transformation, and organization of nature as the mere stuff of domination.

As the project unfolds, it shapes the entire universe of discourse and action, intellectual and material culture. In the medium of technology, culture, politics, and the economy merge into an omnipresent system which swallows up or repulses all alternatives. The productivity and growth potential of this system stabilize the society and contain technical progress within the framework of domination. Technological rationality has become political rationality.

2. The term "project" emphasizes the element of freedom and responsibility in historical determination: it links autonomy and contingency. In this sense, the term is used in the work of Jean-Paul Sartre. For a further discussion see chapter VIII below.

In the discussion of the familiar tendencies of advanced industrial civilization, I have rarely given specific references. The material is assembled and described in the vast sociological and psychological literature on technology and social change, scientific management, corporative enterprise, changes in the character of industrial labor and of the labor force, etc. There are many unideological analyses of the facts—such as Berle and Means, *The Modern Corporation and Private Property,* the reports of the 76th Congress' Temporary National Economic Committee on the *Concentration of Economic Power,* the publications of the AFL-CIO on *Automation and Major Technological Change,* but also those of *News and Letters* and *Correspondence* in Detroit. I should like to emphasize the vital importance of the work of C. Wright Mills, and of studies which are frequently frowned upon because of simplification, overstatement, or journalistic ease—Vance Packard's *The Hidden Persuaders, The Status Seekers,* and *The Waste Makers,* William H. Whyte's *The Organization Man,* Fred J. Cook's *The Warfare State* belong in this category. To be sure, the lack of theoretical analysis in these works leaves the roots of the described conditions covered and protected, but left to speak for themselves, the conditions speak loudly enough. Perhaps the most telling evidence can be obtained by simply looking at television or listening to the AM radio for one consecutive hour for a couple of days, not shutting off the commercials, and now and then switching the station.

My analysis is focused on tendencies in the most highly developed contemporary societies. There are large areas within and without these societies where the described tendencies do not prevail—I would say: not yet prevail. I am projecting these tendencies and I offer some hypotheses, nothing more.

One-Dimensional Man

1: The New Forms of Control

A comfortable, smooth, reasonable, democratic unfreedom prevails in advanced industrial civilization, a token of technical progress. Indeed, what could be more rational than the suppression of individuality in the mechanization of socially necessary but painful performances; the concentration of individual enterprises in more effective, more productive corporations; the regulation of free competition among unequally equipped economic subjects; the curtailment of prerogatives and national sovereignties which impede the international organization of resources. That this technological order also involves a political and intellectual coordination may be a regrettable and yet promising development.

The rights and liberties which were such vital factors in the origins and earlier stages of industrial society yield to a higher stage of this society: they are losing their traditional rationale and content. Freedom of thought, speech, and conscience were—just as free enterprise, which they served to promote and protect—essentially *critical* ideas, designed to replace an obsolescent material and intellectual culture by a more productive and rational one. Once institutionalized, these rights and liberties shared the fate of the society of which they had become an integral part. The achievement cancels the premises.

To the degree to which freedom from want, the concrete substance of all freedom, is becoming a real possibility, the liberties which pertain to a state of lower productivity are losing their former content. Independence of thought, autonomy, and the right to political opposition are being deprived of their basic critical function in a society which seems increasingly capable of satisfying the needs of the individuals through the way in which it is organized. Such a society may justly demand acceptance of its principles and institutions, and reduce the opposition to the discussion and promotion of alternative policies *within* the status quo. In this respect, it seems to make little difference whether the increasing satisfaction of needs is accomplished by an authoritarian or a non-authoritarian system. Under the conditions of a rising standard of living, non-conformity with the system itself appears to be socially useless, and the more so when it entails tangible economic and political disadvantages and threatens the smooth operation of the whole. Indeed, at least in so far as the necessities of life are involved, there seems to be no reason why the production and distribution of goods and services should proceed through the competitive concurrence of individual liberties.

Freedom of enterprise was from the beginning not altogether a blessing. As the liberty to work or to starve, it spelled toil, insecurity, and fear for the vast majority of the population. If the individual were no longer compelled to prove himself on the market, as a free economic subject, the disappearance of this kind of freedom would be one of the greatest achievements of civilization. The technological processes of mechanization and standardization might release individual energy into a yet uncharted realm of freedom beyond necessity. The very structure of human existence would be altered; the individual would be liberated from the work world's imposing upon him alien needs and alien possibilities. The individual would be free to exert autonomy over a life that would be his own. If the productive apparatus could be organized and directed toward the satisfaction of the vital needs, its control might well be centralized; such control would not prevent individual autonomy, but render it possible.

This is a goal within the capabilities of advanced industrial civilization, the "end" of technological rationality. In actual fact, however, the contrary trend operates: the apparatus imposes its economic and political requirements for defense and expansion on labor time and free time, on the material and intellectual culture. By virtue of the way it has organized its technological base, contemporary industrial society tends to be totalitarian. For "totalitarian" is not only a terroristic political coordination of society, but also a nonterroristic economic-technical coordination which operates through the manipulation of needs by vested interests. It thus precludes the emergence of an effective opposition against the whole. Not only a specific form of government or party rule makes for totalitarianism, but also a specific system of production and distribution which may well be compatible with a "pluralism" of parties, newspapers, "countervailing powers," etc.[1]

Today political power asserts itself through its power over the machine process and over the technical organization of the apparatus. The government of advanced and advancing industrial societies can maintain and secure itself only when it succeeds in mobilizing, organizing, and exploiting the technical, scientific, and mechanical productivity available to industrial civilization. And this productivity mobilizes society as a whole, above and beyond any particular individual or group interests. The brute fact that the machine's physical (only physical?) power surpasses that of the individual, and of any particular group of individuals, makes the machine the most effective political instrument in any society whose basic organization is that of the machine process. But the political trend may be reversed; essentially the power of the machine is only the stored-up and projected power of man. To the extent to which the work world is conceived of as a machine and mechanized accordingly, it becomes the *potential* basis of a new freedom for man.

Contemporary industrial civilization demonstrates that it has reached the stage at which "the free society" can no

1. See p. 50.

longer be adequately defined in the traditional terms of economic, political, and intellectual liberties, not because these liberties have become insignificant, but because they are too significant to be confined within the traditional forms. New modes of realization are needed, corresponding to the new capabilities of society.

Such new modes can be indicated only in negative terms because they would amount to the negation of the prevailing modes. Thus economic freedom would mean freedom *from* the economy—from being controlled by economic forces and relationships; freedom from the daily struggle for existence, from earning a living. Political freedom would mean liberation of the individuals *from* politics over which they have no effective control. Similarly, intellectual freedom would mean the restoration of individual thought now absorbed by mass communication and indoctrination, abolition of "public opinion" together with its makers. The unrealistic sound of these propositions is indicative, not of their utopian character, but of the strength of the forces which prevent their realization. The most effective and enduring form of warfare against liberation is the implanting of material and intellectual needs that perpetuate obsolete forms of the struggle for existence.

The intensity, the satisfaction and even the character of human needs, beyond the biological level, have always been preconditioned. Whether or not the possibility of doing or leaving, enjoying or destroying, possessing or rejecting something is seized as a *need* depends on whether or not it can be seen as desirable and necessary for the prevailing societal institutions and interests. In this sense, human needs are historical needs and, to the extent to which the society demands the repressive development of the individual, his needs themselves and their claim for satisfaction are subject to overriding critical standards.

We may distinguish both true and false needs. "False"

are those which are superimposed upon the individual by particular social interests in his repression: the needs which perpetuate toil, aggressiveness, misery, and injustice. Their satisfaction might be most gratifying to the individual, but this happiness is not a condition which has to be maintained and protected if it serves to arrest the development of the ability (his own and others) to recognize the disease of the whole and grasp the chances of curing the disease. The result then is euphoria in unhappiness. Most of the prevailing needs to relax, to have fun, to behave and consume in accordance with the advertisements, to love and hate what others love and hate, belong to this category of false needs.

Such needs have a societal content and function which are determined by external powers over which the individual has no control; the development and satisfaction of these needs is heteronomous. No matter how much such needs may have become the individual's own, reproduced and fortified by the conditions of his existence; no matter how much he identifies himself with them and finds himself in their satisfaction, they continue to be what they were from the beginning—products of a society whose dominant interest demands repression.

The prevalence of repressive needs is an accomplished fact, accepted in ignorance and defeat, but a fact that must be undone in the interest of the happy individual as well as all those whose misery is the price of his satisfaction. The only needs that have an unqualified claim for satisfaction are the vital ones—nourishment, clothing, lodging at the attainable level of culture. The satisfaction of these needs is the prerequisite for the realization of *all* needs, of the unsublimated as well as the sublimated ones.

For any consciousness and conscience, for any experience which does not accept the prevailing societal interest as the supreme law of thought and behavior, the established universe of needs and satisfactions is a fact to be questioned

—questioned in terms of truth and falsehood. These terms are historical throughout, and their objectivity is historical. The judgment of needs and their satisfaction, under the given conditions, involves standards of *priority*—standards which refer to the optimal development of the individual, of all individuals, under the optimal utilization of the material and intellectual resources available to man. The resources are calculable. "Truth" and "falsehood" of needs designate objective conditions to the extent to which the universal satisfaction of vital needs and, beyond it, the progressive alleviation of toil and poverty, are universally valid standards. But as historical standards, they do not only vary according to area and stage of development, they also can be defined only in (greater or lesser) *contradiction* to the prevailing ones. What tribunal can possibly claim the authority of decision?

In the last analysis, the question of what are true and false needs must be answered by the individuals themselves, but only in the last analysis; that is, if and when they are free to give their own answer. As long as they are kept incapable of being autonomous, as long as they are indoctrinated and manipulated (down to their very instincts), their answer to this question cannot be taken as their own. By the same token, however, no tribunal can justly arrogate to itself the right to decide which needs should be developed and satisfied. Any such tribunal is reprehensible, although our revulsion does not do away with the question: how can the people who have been the object of effective and productive domination by themselves create the conditions of freedom? [2]

The more rational, productive, technical, and total the repressive administration of society becomes, the more unimaginable the means and ways by which the administered

2. See p. 40.

individuals might break their servitude and seize their own liberation. To be sure, to impose Reason upon an entire society is a paradoxical and scandalous idea—although one might dispute the righteousness of a society which ridicules this idea while making its own population into objects of total administration. All liberation depends on the consciousness of servitude, and the emergence of this consciousness is always hampered by the predominance of needs and satisfactions which, to a great extent, have become the individual's own. The process always replaces one system of preconditioning by another; the optimal goal is the replacement of false needs by true ones, the abandonment of repressive satisfaction.

The distinguishing feature of advanced industrial society is its effective suffocation of those needs which demand liberation—liberation also from that which is tolerable and rewarding and comfortable—while it sustains and absolves the destructive power and repressive function of the affluent society. Here, the social controls exact the overwhelming need for the production and consumption of waste; the need for stupefying work where it is no longer a real necessity; the need for modes of relaxation which soothe and prolong this stupefication; the need for maintaining such deceptive liberties as free competition at administered prices, a free press which censors itself, free choice between brands and gadgets.

Under the rule of a repressive whole, liberty can be made into a powerful instrument of domination. The range of choice open to the individual is not the decisive factor in determining the degree of human freedom, but *what* can be chosen and what *is* chosen by the individual. The criterion for free choice can never be an absolute one, but neither is it entirely relative. Free election of masters does not abolish the masters or the slaves. Free choice among a wide variety of goods and services does not signify freedom if these goods and services sustain social controls over a life of toil and fear—that is, if they sustain alienation. And the spontaneous reproduction of superimposed needs by the individual does not establish autonomy; it only testifies to the efficacy of the controls.

Our insistence on the depth and efficacy of these controls is open to the objection that we overrate greatly the indoctrinating power of the "media," and that by themselves the people would feel and satisfy the needs which are now imposed upon them. The objection misses the point. The preconditioning does not start with the mass production of radio and television and with the centralization of their control. The people enter this stage as preconditioned receptacles of long standing; the decisive difference is in the flattening out of the contrast (or conflict) between the given and the possible, between the satisfied and the unsatisfied needs. Here, the so-called equalization of class distinctions reveals its ideological function. If the worker and his boss enjoy the same television program and visit the same resort places, if the typist is as attractively made up as the daughter of her employer, if the Negro owns a Cadillac, if they all read the same newspaper, then this assimilation indicates not the disappearance of classes, but the extent to which the needs and satisfactions that serve the preservation of the Establishment are shared by the underlying population. Indeed, in the most highly developed areas of contemporary society, the transplantation of social into individual needs is so effective that the difference between them seems to be purely theoretical. Can one really distinguish between the mass media as instruments of information and entertainment, and as agents of manipulation and indoctrination? Between the automobile as nuisance and as convenience? Between the horrors and the comforts of functional architecture? Between the work for national defense and the work for corporate gain? Between the private pleasure and the commercial and political utility involved in increasing the birth rate? We are again confronted with one of the most vexing aspects of advanced industrial civilization: the rational character of its irrationality. Its productivity and efficiency, its capacity to increase and spread comforts, to turn waste into need, and destruction into construction, the extent to which this civilization transforms the object world into an extension of man's mind and body makes the very notion of alienation questionable. The people recognize themselves in their commodities; they find their soul in their automobile, hi-fi set, split-level home, kitchen equipment. The very mechanism which ties the individual to his society has changed, and social control is anchored in the new needs which it has produced.

The prevailing forms of social control are technological in a new sense. To be sure, the technical structure and efficacy of the productive and destructive apparatus has been a major instrumentality for subjecting the population to the established social division of labor throughout the modern period. Moreover, such integration has always been accompanied by more obvious forms of compulsion: loss of livelihood, the administration of justice, the police, the armed forces. It still is. But in the contemporary period, the technological controls appear to be the very embodiment of Reason for the benefit of all social groups and interests— to such an extent that all contradiction seems irrational and all counteraction impossible.

No wonder then that, in the most advanced areas of this civilization, the social controls have been introjected to the point where even individual protest is affected at its roots. The intellectual and emotional refusal "to go along" appears neurotic and impotent. This is the socio-psychological aspect of the political event that marks the contemporary period: the passing of the historical forces which, at the preceding stage of industrial society, seemed to represent the possibility of new forms of existence.

But the term "introjection" perhaps no longer describes the way in which the individual by himself reproduces and perpetuates the external controls exercised by his society. Introjection suggests a variety of relatively spontaneous processes by which a Self (Ego) transposes the "outer" into the "inner." Thus introjection implies the existence of an inner dimension distinguished from and even antagonistic to the external exigencies—an individual consciousness and an individual unconscious *apart from* public opinion and behavior.[3] The idea of "inner freedom" here has its reality: it designates the private space in which man may become and remain "himself."

Today this private space has been invaded and whittled down by technological reality. Mass production and mass distribution claim the *entire* individual, and industrial psychology has long since ceased to be confined to the factory. The manifold processes of introjection seem to be ossified in almost mechanical reactions. The result is, not adjustment but *mimesis:* an immediate identification of the individual with *his* society and, through it, with the society as a whole.

This immediate, automatic identification (which may have been characteristic of primitive forms of association) reappears in high industrial civilization; its new "immediacy," however, is the product of a sophisticated, scientific management and organization. In this process, the "inner" dimension of the mind in which opposition to the status quo can take root is whittled down. The loss of this dimension, in

3. The change in the function of the family here plays a decisive role: its "socializing" functions are increasingly taken over by outside groups and media. See my *Eros and Civilization* (Boston: Beacon Press, 1955), p. 96 ff.

which the power of negative thinking—the critical power of Reason—is at home, is the ideological counterpart to the very material process in which advanced industrial society silences and reconciles the opposition. The impact of progress turns Reason into submission to the facts of life, and to the dynamic capability of producing more and bigger facts of the same sort of life. The efficiency of the system blunts the individuals' recognition that it contains no facts which do not communicate the repressive power of the whole. If the individuals find themselves in the things which shape their life, they do so, not by giving, but by accepting the law of things—not the law of physics but the law of their society.

I have just suggested that the concept of alienation seems to become questionable when the individuals identify themselves with the existence which is imposed upon them and have in it their own development and satisfaction. This identification is not illusion but reality. However, the reality constitutes a more progressive stage of alienation. The latter has become entirely objective; the subject which is alienated is swallowed up by its alienated existence. There is only one dimension, and it is everywhere and in all forms. The achievements of progress defy ideological indictment as well as justification; before their tribunal, the "false consciousness" of their rationality becomes the true consciousness.

This absorption of ideology into reality does not, however, signify the "end of ideology." On the contrary, in a specific sense advanced industrial culture is *more* ideological than its predecessor, inasmuch as today the ideology is in the process of production itself.[4] In a provocative form, this proposition reveals the political aspects of the prevailing technological rationality. The productive apparatus and the

4. Theodor W. Adorno, *Prismen. Kulturkritik und Gesellschaft.* (Frankfurt: Suhrkamp, 1955), p. 24 f.

goods and services which it produces "sell" or impose the social system as a whole. The means of mass transportation and communication, the commodities of lodging, food, and clothing, the irresistible output of the entertainment and information industry carry with them prescribed attitudes and habits, certain intellectual and emotional reactions which bind the consumers more or less pleasantly to the producers and, through the latter, to the whole. The products indoctrinate and manipulate; they promote a false consciousness which is immune against its falsehood. And as these beneficial products become available to more individuals in more social classes, the indoctrination they carry ceases to be publicity; it becomes a way of life. It is a good way of life—much better than before—and as a good way of life, it militates against qualitative change. Thus emerges a pattern of *one-dimensional thought and behavior* in which ideas, aspirations, and objectives that, by their content, transcend the established universe of discourse and action are either repelled or reduced to terms of this universe. They are redefined by the rationality of the given system and of its quantitative extension.

The trend may be related to a development in scientific method: operationalism in the physical, behaviorism in the social sciences. The common feature is a total empiricism in the treatment of concepts; their meaning is restricted to the representation of particular operations and behavior. The operational point of view is well illustrated by P. W. Bridgman's analysis of the concept of length:[5]

5. P. W. Bridgman, *The Logic of Modern Physics* (New York: Macmillan, 1928), p. 5. The operational doctrine has since been refined and qualified. Bridgman himself has extended the concept of "operation" to include the "paper-and-pencil" operations of the theorist (in Philipp J. Frank, *The Validation of Scientific Theories* [Boston: Beacon Press, 1954], Chap. II). The main impetus remains the same: it is "desirable" that the paper-and-pencil operations "be capable of eventual contact, although perhaps indirectly, with instrumental operations."

We evidently know what we mean by length if we can tell what the length of any and every object is, and for the physicist nothing more is required. To find the length of an object, we have to perform certain physical operations. The concept of length is therefore fixed when the operations by which length is measured are fixed: that is, the concept of length involves as much and nothing more than the set of operations by which length is determined. In general, we mean by any concept nothing more than a set of operations; *the concept is synonymous with the corresponding set of operations.*

Bridgman has seen the wide implications of this mode of thought for the society at large:[6]

To adopt the operational point of view involves much more than a mere restriction of the sense in which we understand 'concept,' but means a far-reaching change in all our habits of thought, in that we shall no longer permit ourselves to use as tools in our thinking concepts of which we cannot give an adequate account in terms of operations.

Bridgman's prediction has come true. The new mode of thought is today the predominant tendency in philosophy, psychology, sociology, and other fields. Many of the most seriously troublesome concepts are being "eliminated" by showing that no adequate account of them in terms of operations or behavior can be given. The radical empiricist onslaught (I shall subsequently, in chapters VII and VIII, examine its claim to be empiricist) thus provides the methodological justification for the debunking of the mind by the intellectuals—a positivism which, in its denial of the transcending elements of Reason, forms the academic counterpart of the socially required behavior.

Outside the academic establishment, the "far-reaching change in all our habits of thought" is more serious. It serves to coordinate ideas and goals with those exacted by the

6. P. W. Bridgman, *The Logic of Modern Physics,* loc. cit., p. 31.

prevailing system, to enclose them in the system, and to repel those which are irreconcilable with the system. The reign of such a one-dimensional reality does not mean that materialism rules, and that the spiritual, metaphysical, and bohemian occupations are petering out. On the contrary, there is a great deal of "Worship together this week," "Why not try God," Zen, existentialism, and beat ways of life, etc. But such modes of protest and transcendence are no longer contradictory to the status quo and no longer negative. They are rather the ceremonial part of practical behaviorism, its harmless negation, and are quickly digested by the status quo as part of its healthy diet.

One-dimensional thought is systematically promoted by the makers of politics and their purveyors of mass information. Their universe of discourse is populated by self-validating hypotheses which, incessantly and monopolistically repeated, become hypnotic definitions or dictations. For example, "free" are the institutions which operate (and are operated on) in the countries of the Free World; other transcending modes of freedom are by definition either anarchism, communism, or propaganda. "Socialistic" are all encroachments on private enterprises not undertaken by private enterprise itself (or by government contracts), such as universal and comprehensive health insurance, or the protection of nature from all too sweeping commercialization, or the establishment of public services which may hurt private profit. This totalitarian logic of accomplished facts has its Eastern counterpart. There, freedom is the way of life instituted by a communist regime, and all other transcending modes of freedom are either capitalistic, or revisionist, or leftist sectarianism. In both camps, non-operational ideas are non-behavioral and subversive. The movement of thought is stopped at barriers which appear as the limits of Reason itself.

Such limitation of thought is certainly not new. Ascending modern rationalism, in its speculative as well as empirical form, shows a striking contrast between extreme critical radicalism in scientific and philosophic method on the one hand, and an uncritical quietism in the attitude toward established and functioning social institutions. Thus Descartes' *ego cogitans* was to leave the "great public bodies" untouched, and Hobbes held that "the present ought always to be preferred, maintained, and accounted best." Kant agreed with Locke in justifying revolution *if and when* it has succeeded in organizing the whole and in preventing subversion.

However, these accommodating concepts of Reason were always contradicted by the evident misery and injustice of the "great public bodies" and the effective, more or less conscious rebellion against them. Societal conditions existed which provoked and permitted real dissociation from the established state of affairs; a private as well as political dimension was present in which dissociation could develop into effective opposition, testing its strength and the validity of its objectives.

With the gradual closing of this dimension by the society, the self-limitation of thought assumes a larger significance. The interrelation between scientific-philosophical and societal processes, between theoretical and practical Reason, asserts itself "behind the back" of the scientists and philosophers. The society bars a whole type of oppositional operations and behavior; consequently, the concepts pertaining to them are rendered illusory or meaningless. Historical transcendence appears as metaphysical transcendence, not acceptable to science and scientific thought. The operational and behavioral point of view, practiced as a "habit of thought" at large, becomes the view of the established universe of discourse and action, needs and aspirations. The "cunning of Reason" works, as it so often did, in the interest of the powers that be. The insistence on operational and behavioral concepts turns against the efforts to free thought and behavior *from* the given reality and *for* the suppressed alternatives. Theoretical and practical Reason, academic and social behaviorism meet on common ground: that of an advanced society which makes scientific and technical progress into an instrument of domination.

"Progress" is not a neutral term; it moves toward specific ends, and these ends are defined by the possibilities of ameliorating the human condition. Advanced industrial society is approaching the stage where continued progress would demand the radical subversion of the prevailing direction and organization of progress. This stage would be reached when material production (including the necessary services) becomes automated to the extent that all vital needs can be satisfied while necessary labor time is reduced to marginal time. From this point on, technical progress would transcend the realm of necessity, where it served as the instrument of domination and exploitation which thereby limited its rationality; technology would become subject to the free play of faculties in the struggle for the pacification of nature and of society.

Such a state is envisioned in Marx's notion of the "abolition of labor." The term "pacification of existence" seems better suited to designate the historical alternative of a world which—through an international conflict which transforms and suspends the contradictions within the established societies—advances on the brink of a global war. "Pacification of existence" means the development of man's struggle with man and with nature, under conditions where the competing needs, desires, and aspirations are no longer organized by vested interests in domination and scarcity— an organization which perpetuates the destructive forms of this struggle.

Today's fight against this historical alternative finds a firm mass basis in the underlying population, and finds its ideology in the rigid orientation of thought and behavior to the given universe of facts. Validated by the accomplishments of science and technology, justified by its growing productivity, the status quo defies all transcendence. Faced with the possibility of pacification on the grounds of its technical and intellectual achievements, the mature industrial society closes itself against this alternative. Operationalism, in theory and practice, becomes the theory and practice of *containment*. Underneath its obvious dynamics, this society is a thoroughly static system of life: self-propelling in its oppressive productivity and in its beneficial coordination. Containment of technical progress goes hand in hand with its growth in the established direction. In spite of the political fetters imposed by the status quo, the more technology appears capable of creating the conditions for pacification, the more are the minds and bodies of man organized against this alternative.

The most advanced areas of industrial society exhibit throughout these two features: a trend toward consummation of technological rationality, and intensive efforts to contain this trend within the established institutions. Here is the internal contradiction of this civilization: the irrational element in its rationality. It is the token of its achievements. The industrial society which makes technology and science its own is organized for the ever-more-effective domination of man and nature, for the ever-more-effective utilization of its resources. It becomes irrational when the success of these efforts opens new dimensions of human realization. Organization for peace is different from organization for war; the institutions which served the struggle for existence cannot serve the pacification of existence. Life as an end is qualitatively different from life as a means.

Such a qualitatively new mode of existence can never be envisaged as the mere by-product of economic and political changes, as the more or less spontaneous effect of the new institutions which constitute the necessary prerequisite. Qualitative change also involves a change in the *technical* basis on which this society rests—one which sustains the economic and political institutions through which the "second nature" of man as an aggressive object of administration is stabilized. The techniques of industrialization are political techniques; as such, they prejudge the possibilities of Reason and Freedom.

To be sure, labor must precede the reduction of labor, and industrialization must precede the development of human needs and satisfactions. But as all freedom depends on the conquest of alien necessity, the realization of freedom depends on the *techniques* of this conquest. The highest productivity of labor can be used for the perpetuation of labor, and the most efficient industrialization can serve the restriction and manipulation of needs.

When this point is reached, domination—in the guise of affluence and liberty—extends to all spheres of private and public existence, integrates all authentic opposition, absorbs all alternatives. Technological rationality reveals its political character as it becomes the great vehicle of better domination, creating a truly totalitarian universe in which society and nature, mind and body are kept in a state of permanent mobilization for the defense of this universe.

2: The Closing of the Political Universe

The society of total mobilization, which takes shape in the most advanced areas of industrial civilization, combines in productive union the features of the Welfare State and the Warfare State. Compared with its predecessors, it is indeed a "new society." Traditional trouble spots are being cleaned out or isolated, disrupting elements taken in hand. The main trends are familiar: concentration of the national economy on the needs of the big corporations, with the government as a stimulating, supporting, and sometimes even controlling force; hitching of this economy to a world-wide system of military alliances, monetary arrangements, technical assistance and development schemes; gradual assimilation of blue-collar and white-collar population, of leadership types in business and labor, of leisure activities and aspirations in different social classes; fostering of a pre-established harmony between scholarship and the national purpose; invasion of the private household by the togetherness of public opinion; opening of the bedroom to the media of mass communication.

In the political sphere, this trend manifests itself in a marked unification or convergence of opposites. Bipartisanship in foreign policy overrides competitive group interests under the threat of international communism, and spreads to domestic policy, where the programs of the big parties become ever more undistinguishable, even in the degree of hypocrisy and in the odor of the clichés. This unification of opposites bears upon the very possibilities of social change where it embraces those strata on whose back the system progresses—that is, the very classes whose existence once embodied the opposition to the system as a whole.

In the United States, one notices the collusion and alliance between business and organized labor; in *Labor Looks at Labor: A Conversation,* published by the Center for the Study of Democratic Institutions in 1963, we are told that:

"What has happened is that the union has become almost indistinguishable in *its own eyes* from the corporation. We see the phenomenon today of unions and corporations *jointly* lobbying. The union is not going to be able to convince missile workers that the company they work for is a fink outfit when both the union and the corporation are out lobbying for bigger missile contracts and trying to get other defense industries into the area, or when they jointly appear before Congress and jointly ask that missiles instead of bombers should be built or bombs instead of missiles, depending on what contract they happen to hold."

The British Labor Party, whose leaders compete with their Conservative counterparts in advancing national interests, is hard put to save even a modest program of partial nationalization. In West Germany, which has outlawed the Communist Party, the Social Democratic Party, having officially rejected its Marxist programs, is convincingly proving its respectability. This is the situation in the leading industrial countries of the West. In the East, the gradual reduction of direct political controls testifies to increasing reliance on the effectiveness of technological controls as instruments of domination. As for the strong Communist parties in France and Italy, they bear witness to the general trend of circumstances by adhering to a minimum program which shelves the revolutionary seizure of power and complies with the rules of the parliamentary game.

However, while it is incorrect to consider the French and Italian parties "foreign" in the sense of being sustained by a foreign power, there is an unintended kernel of truth in this propaganda: they are foreign inasmuch as they are witnesses of a past (or future?) history in the present reality. If they have agreed to work within the framework of the established system, it is not merely on tactical grounds and as short-range strategy, but because their social base has been weakened and their objectives altered by the transformation of the capitalist system (as have the objectives of the Soviet Union which has endorsed this change in policy). These national Communist parties play the historical role of legal opposition parties "condemned" to be non-radical. They testify to the depth and scope of capitalist integration, and to the conditions which make the qualitative difference of conflicting interests appear as quantitative differences within the established society.

No analysis in depth seems to be necessary in order to find the reasons for these developments. As to the West: the former conflicts within society are modified and arbitrated under the double (and interrelated) impact of technical progress and international communism. Class struggles are attenuated and "imperialist contradictions" suspended before the threat from without. Mobilized against this threat, capitalist society shows an internal union and cohesion unknown at previous stages of industrial civilization. It is a cohesion on very material grounds; mobilization against the enemy works as a mighty stimulus of production and employment, thus sustaining the high standard of living.

On these grounds, there arises a universe of administration in which depressions are controlled and conflicts stabilized by the beneficial effects of growing productivity and threatening nuclear war. Is this stabilization "temporary" in the sense that it does not affect the *roots* of the conflicts which Marx found in the capitalist mode of production (contradiction between private ownership of the means of production and social productivity), or is it a transformation of the antagonistic structure itself, which resolves the contradictions by making them tolerable? And, if the second alternative is true, how does it change the relationship between capitalism and socialism which made the latter appear the historical negation of the former?

Containment of Social Change

The classical Marxian theory envisages the transition from capitalism to socialism as a political revolution: the proletariat destroys the *political* apparatus of capitalism but retains the *technological* apparatus, subjecting it to socialization. There is continuity in the revolution: technological rationality, freed from irrational restrictions and destructions, sustains and consummates itself in the new society. It is interesting to read a Soviet Marxist statement on this continuity, which is of such vital importance for the notion of socialism as the determinate negation of capitalism:[1]

"(1) Though the development of technology is subject to the economic laws of each social formation, it does not, like other economic factors, end with the cessation of the laws of the formation. When in the process of revolution the old relations of production are broken up, technology remains and, subordinated to the economic laws of the new economic formation, continues to develop further, with added speed. (2) Contrary to the development of the economic basis in antagonistic societies, technology does not develop through leaps but by a gradual accumulation of elements of a new quality, while the elements of the old quality disappear. (3) [irrelevant in this context]."

In advanced capitalism, technical rationality is embodied, in spite of its irrational use, in the productive apparatus. This applies not only to mechanized plants, tools, and exploitation of resources, but also to the mode of labor as adaptation to and handling of the machine process, as arranged by "scientific management." Neither nationalization nor socialization alter *by themselves* this physical embodiment of technological rationality; on the contrary, the *latter* remains

1. A. Zworikine, "The History of Technology as a Science and as a Branch of Learning; a Soviet view," *Technology and Culture*. (Detroit: Wayne State University Press, Winter 1961), p. 2.

a precondition for the socialist development of all productive forces.

To be sure, Marx held that organization and direction of the productive apparatus by the "immediate producers" would introduce a *qualitative* change in the technical continuity: namely, production toward the satisfaction of freely developing individual needs. However, to the degree to which the established technical apparatus engulfs the public and private existence in all spheres of society—that is, becomes the medium of control and cohesion in a political universe which incorporates the laboring classes—to that degree would the qualitative change involve a change in the *technological structure itself.* And such change would *presuppose* that the laboring classes are alienated from this universe in their very existence, that their consciousness is that of the total impossibility to continue to exist in this universe, so that the need for qualitative change is a matter of life and death. Thus, the negation exists *prior* to the change itself, the notion that the liberating historical forces develop *within* the established society is a cornerstone of Marxian theory.[2]

Now it is precisely this new consciousness, this "space within," the space for the transcending historical practice, which is being barred by a society in which subjects as well as objects constitute instrumentalities in a whole that has its *raison d'être* in the accomplishments of its overpowering productivity. Its supreme promise is an ever-more-comfortable life for an ever-growing number of people who, in a strict sense, cannot imagine a qualitatively different universe of discourse and action, for the capacity to contain and manipulate subversive imagination and effort is an integral part of the given society. Those whose life is the hell of the Affluent Society are kept in line by a brutality which revives medieval and early modern practices. For the other, less

2. See p. 41.

underprivileged people, society takes care of the need for liberation by satisfying the needs which make servitude palatable and perhaps even unnoticeable, and it accomplishes this fact in the process of production itself. Under its impact, the laboring classes in the advanced areas of industrial civilization are undergoing a decisive transformation, which has become the subject of a vast sociological research. I shall enumerate the main factors of this transformation:

(1) Mechanization is increasingly reducing the quantity and intensity of physical energy expended in labor. This evolution is of great bearing on the Marxian concept of the worker (proletarian). To Marx, the proletarian is primarily the manual laborer who expends and exhausts his physical energy in the work process, even if he works with machines. The purchase and use of this physical energy, under subhuman conditions, for the private appropriation of surplus-value entailed the revolting inhuman aspects of exploitation; the Marxian notion denounces the physical pain and misery of labor. This is the material, tangible element in wage slavery and alienation—the physiological and biological dimension of classical capitalism.

"Pendant les siècles passés, une cause importante d'aliénation résidait dans le fait que l'être humain prêtait son individualité biologique à l'organisation technique: il était porteur d'outils; les ensembles techniques ne pouvaient se constituer qu'en incorporant l'homme comme porteur d'outils. Le caractère déformant de la profession était à la fois psychique et somatique." [3]

3. "During the past centuries, one important reason for alienation was that the human being lent his biological individuality to the technical apparatus: he was the bearer of tools; technical units could not be established without incorporating man as bearer of tools into them. The nature of this occupation was such that it was both psychologically and physiologically deforming in its effect." Gilbert Simondon, *Du Mode d'existence des objets techniques* (Paris: Aubier, 1958), p. 103, note.

Now the ever-more-complete mechanization of labor in advanced capitalism, while sustaining exploitation, modifies the attitude and the status of the exploited. Within the technological ensemble, mechanized work in which automatic and semi-automatic reactions fill the larger part (if not the whole) of labor time remains, as a life-long occupation, exhausting, stupefying, inhuman slavery—even more exhausting because of increased speed-up, control of the machine operators (rather than of the product), and isolation of the workers from each other.[4] To be sure, this form of drudgery is expressive of *arrested, partial* automation, of the coexistence of automated, semi-automated, and non-automated sections within the same plant, but even under these conditions, "for muscular fatigue technology has substituted tension and/or mental effort."[5] For the more advanced automated plants, the transformation of physical energy into technical and mental skills is emphasized:

". . . skills of the head rather than of the hand, of the logician rather than the craftsman; of nerve rather than muscle; of the pilot rather than the manual worker; of the maintenance man rather than the operator."[6]

This kind of masterly enslavement is not essentially different from that of the typist, the bank teller, the high-pressure salesman or saleswoman, and the television announcer. Standardization and the routine assimilate productive and non-productive jobs. The proletarian of the previous stages of capitalism was indeed the beast of burden, by the labor of his body procuring the necessities and luxuries of life while living in filth and poverty. Thus he was the living

4. See Charles Denby, "Workers Battle Automation" (*News and Letters*, Detroit, 1960).
5. Charles R. Walker, *Toward the Automatic Factory* (New Haven: Yale University Press, 1957), p. XIX.
6. *Ibid.*, p. 195.

denial of his society.[7] In contrast, the organized worker in the advanced areas of the technological society lives this denial less conspicuously and, like the other human objects of the social division of labor, he is being incorporated into the technological community of the administered population. Moreover, in the most successful areas of automation, some sort of technological community seems to integrate the human atoms at work. The machine seems to instill some drugging rhythm in the operators:

"It is generally agreed that interdependent motions performed by a group of persons which follow a rhythmic pattern yield satisfaction—quite apart from what is being accomplished by the motions";[8]

and the sociologist-observer believes this to be a reason for the gradual development of a "general climate" more "favorable both to production and to certain important kinds of human satisfaction." He speaks of the "growth of a strong in-group feeling in each crew" and quotes one worker as stating: "All in all we are in the swing of things . . ."[9] The phrase admirably expresses the change in mechanized enslavement: things swing rather than oppress, and they swing the human instrument—not only its body but also its mind and even its soul. A remark by Sartre elucidates the depth of the process:

"Aux premiers temps des machines semi-automatiques, des enquêtes ont montré que les ouvrières spécialisées se laissaient aller, en travaillant, à une rêverie d'ordre sexuel, elles se rappellaient la chambre, le lit, la nuit, tout ce qui ne concerne que

7. One must insist on the inner connection between the Marxian concepts of exploitation and impoverishment in spite of later redefinitions, in which impoverishment either becomes a cultural aspect, or relative to such an extent that it applies also to the suburban home with automobile, television, etc. "Impoverishment" connotes the *absolute need and necessity* of subverting *intolerable* conditions of existence, and such absolute need appears in the beginnings of all revolution against the basic social institutions.
8. Charles R. Walker, *loc. cit.*, p. 104.
9. *Ibid.*, p. 104 f.

la personne dans la solitude du couple fermé sur soi. Mais c'est la machine en elle qui rêvait de caresses. . . ." [10]

The machine process in the technological universe breaks the innermost privacy of freedom and joins sexuality and labor in one unconscious, rhythmic automatism—a process which parallels the assimilation of jobs.

(2) The assimilating trend shows forth in the occupational stratification. In the key industrial establishments, the "blue-collar" work force declines in relation to the "white-collar" element; the number of non-production workers increases.[11] This quantitative change refers back to a change in the character of the basic instruments of production.[12] At the advanced stage of mechanization, as part of the technological reality, the machine is not

"une unité absolue, mais seulement une réalité technique individualisée, ouverte selon deux voies: celle de la relation aux éléments, et celle des relations interindividuelles dans l'ensemble technique." [13]

To the extent to which the machine becomes itself a system of mechanical tools and relations and thus extends far beyond the individual work process, it asserts its larger domin-

10. "Shortly after semi-automatic machines were introduced, investigations showed that female skilled workers would allow themselves to lapse while working into a sexual kind of daydream; they would recall the bedroom, the bed, the night and all that concerns only the person within the solitude of the couple alone with itself. But it was the machine in her which was dreaming of caresses . . ." Jean-Paul Sartre, *Critique de la raison dialectique*, tome I (Paris: Gallimard, 1960), p. 290.

11. *Automation and Major Technological Change:* Impact on Union Size, Structure, and Function. (Industrial Union Dept. AFL.-CIO, Washington, 1958) p. 5 ff. Solomon Barkin, *The Decline of the Labor Movement* (Santa Barbara, Center for the Study of Democratic Institutions, 1961), p. 10 ff.

12. See p. 23.

13. "an absolute unity, but only an individualized technical reality open in two directions, that of the relation to the elements and that of the relation among the individuals in the technical whole." Gilbert Simondon, *loc. cit.*, p. 146.

ion by reducing the "professional autonomy" of the laborer and integrating him with other professions which suffer and direct the technical ensemble. To be sure, the former "professional" autonomy of the laborer was rather his professional enslavement. But this *specific* mode of enslavement was at the same time the source of his specific, professional power of negation—the power to stop a process which threatened him with annihilation as a human being. Now the laborer is losing the professional autonomy which made him a member of a class set off from the other occupational groups because it embodied the refutation of the established society.

The technological change which tends to do away with the machine as *individual* instrument of production, as "absolute unit," seems to cancel the Marxian notion of the "organic composition of capital" and with it the theory of the creation of surplus value. According to Marx, the machine never creates value but merely transfers its own value to the product, while surplus value remains the result of the exploitation of living labor. The machine is embodiment of human labor power, and through it, past labor (dead labor) preserves itself and determines living labor. Now automation seems to alter qualitatively the relation between dead and living labor; it tends toward the point where productivity is determined "by the machines, and not by the individual output." [14] Moreover, the very measurement of individual output becomes impossible:

"Automation in its largest sense means, in effect, the *end* of measurement of work. . . . With automation, you can't measure output of a single man; you now have to measure simply equipment utilization. If that is generalized as a kind of concept . . . there is no longer, for example, any reason at all to pay a man by the piece or pay him by the hour," that is to say, there is no more reason to keep up the "dual pay system" of salaries and wages." [15]

14. Serge Mallet, in *Arguments*, no. 12-13, Paris 1958, p. 18.
15. *Automation and Major Technological Change*, loc. cit., p. 8.

Daniel Bell, the author of this report, goes further; he links this technological change to the historical system of industrialization itself: the meaning of

industrialization did not arise with the introduction of factories, it "arose out of the *measurement of work*. It's when work can be measured, when you can hitch a man to the job, when you can put a harness on him, and measure his output in terms of a single piece and pay him by the piece or by the hour, that you have got modern industrialization." [16]

What is at stake in these technological changes is far more than a pay system, the relation of the worker to other classes, and the organization of work. What is at stake is the compatibility of technical progress with the very institutions in which industrialization developed.

(3) These changes in the character of work and the instruments of production change the attitude and the consciousness of the laborer, which become manifest in the widely discussed "social and cultural integration" of the laboring class with capitalist society. Is this a change in consciousness only? The affirmative answer, frequently given by Marxists, seems strangely inconsistent. Is such a fundamental change in consciousness understandable without assuming a corresponding change in the "societal existence"? Granted even a high degree of ideological independence, the links which tie this change to the transformation of the productive process militate against such an interpretation. Assimilation in needs and aspirations, in the standard of living, in leisure activities, in politics derives from an integration *in the plant* itself, in the material process of production. It is certainly questionable whether one can speak of "voluntary integration" (Serge Mallet) in any other than an ironical sense. In the present situation, the negative features of auto-

16. *Ibid.*

mation are predominant: speed-up, technological unemployment, strengthening of the position of management, increasing impotence and resignation on the part of the workers. The chances of promotion decline as management prefers engineers and college graduates.[17] However, there are other trends. The same technological organization which makes for a mechanical community at work also generates a larger interdependence which[18] integrates the worker with the plant. One notes an "eagerness" on the part of the workers "to share in the solution of production problems," a "desire to join actively in applying their own brains to technical and production problems which clearly fitted in with the technology."[19] In some of the technically most advanced establishments, the workers even show a vested interest in the establishment—a frequently observed effect of "workers' participation" in capitalist enterprise. A provocative description, referring to the highly Americanized Caltex refineries at Ambès, France, may serve to characterize this trend. The workers of the plant are conscious of the links which attach them to the enterprise:

Liens professionnels, liens sociaux, liens matériels: le métier appris dans la raffinerie, l'habitude des rapports de production qui s'y sont établis, les multiples avantages sociaux qui, en cas de mort subite, de maladie grave, d'incapacité de travail, de vieillesse enfin, lui sont assurés par sa seule appartenance à la firme, prolongeant au-delà de la période productive de leur vie la sûreté des lendemains. Ainsi, la notion de ce contrat vivant et indestructible avec la 'Caltex' les amène à se préoccuper, avec une attention et une lucidité inattendue, de la gestion financière de l'entreprise. Les délégués aux Comités d'entreprise épluchent la comptabilité

17. Charles R. Walker, *loc. cit.*, p. 97 ff. See also Ely Chinoy, *Automobile Workers and the American Dream*, (Garden City: Doubleday, 1955) passim.
18. Floyd C. Mann and L. Richard Hoffman, *Automation and the Worker. A Study of Social Change in Power Plants* (New York, Henry Holt: 1960), p. 189.
19. Charles R. Walker, *loc. cit.*, p. 213 f.

de la société avec le soin jaloux qu'y accorderaient des action-
naires consciencieux. La direction de la Caltex peut certes se
frotter les mains lorsque les syndicats acceptent de surseoir à
leurs revendications de salaires en présence des besoins d'inves-
tissements nouveaux. Mais elle commence à manifester les plus
'légitimes' inquiétudes lorsque, prenant au mot les bilans truqués
de la filiale française, ils s'inquiètent des marchés 'désavantageux'
passés par celles-ci et poussent l'audace jusqu'à contester les prix
de revient et suggérer des propositions économiques! [20]

(4) The new technological work-world thus enforces a
weakening of the negative position of the working class: the
latter no longer appears to be the living contradiction to
the established society. This trend is strengthened by the
effect of the technological organization of production on the

---

20. "Professional, social, material links: the skill they acquired in the
refinery, the fact that they got used to certain production relationships
which were established there; the manifold social benefits on which they
can count in case of sudden death, serious illness, incapacity to work,
finally old age, merely because they belong to the firm, extending their
security beyond the productive period of their lives. Thus the notion of a
living and indestructible contract with Caltex makes them think with
unexpected attention and lucidity about the financial management of the
firm. The delegates to the "Comités d'entreprise" examine and discuss the
accounts of the company with the same jealous care that conscientious
shareholders would devote to it. The board of directors of Caltex can certainly rub their hands with joy when the unions agree to put off their
salary demands because of the need for new investments. But they begin
to show signs of 'legitimate' anxiety when the delgates take seriously the
faked balance sheets of the French branches and worry about disadvanta-
geous deals concluded by these branches, daring to go as far as to contest
the production costs and suggesting money-saving measures." Serge Mallet,
Le Salaire de la technique, in: *La Nef*, no. 25, Paris 1959, p. 40. For the
integrating trend in the United States here is an amazing statement by a
union leader of the United Automobile Workers: "Many times . . . we
would meet in a union hall and talk about the grievances that workers had
brought in and what we are going to do about them. By the time I had
arranged a meeting with management the next day, the problem had been
corrected and the union didn't get credit for redressing the grievance. It's
become a battle of loyalties. . . . All the things we fought for the corporation
is now giving the workers. What we have to find are other things the worker
wants which the employer is not willing to give him. . . . We're searching.
We're searching." *Labor Looks At Labor. A Conversation,* (Santa Barbara:
Center for the Study of Democratic Institutions, 1963) p. 16 f.

other side of the fence: on management and direction. Domination is transfigured into administration.[21] The capitalist bosses and owners are losing their identity as responsible agents; they are assuming the function of bureaucrats in a corporate machine. Within the vast hierarchy of executive and managerial boards extending far beyond the individual establishment into the scientific laboratory and research institute, the national government and national purpose, the tangible source of exploitation disappears behind the façade of objective rationality. Hatred and frustration are deprived of their specific target, and the technological veil conceals the reproduction of inequality and enslavement.[22] With technical progress as its instrument, unfreedom—in the sense of man's subjection to his productive apparatus—is perpetuated and intensified in the form of many liberties and comforts. The novel feature is the overwhelming rationality in this irrational enterprise, and the depth of the preconditioning which shapes the instinctual drives and aspirations of the individuals and obscures the difference between false and true consciousness. For in reality, neither the utilization of administrative rather than physical controls (hunger, personal dependence, force), nor the change in the character of heavy work, nor the assimilation of occupational classes, nor the equalization in the sphere of consumption compensate for the fact that the decisions over life and death, over personal and national security are made at places over which the individuals have no control. The slaves of developed industrial civilization are sublimated slaves, but they are slaves, for slavery is determined

21. Is it still necessary to denounce the ideology of the "managerial revolution?" Capitalist production proceeds through the investment of private capital for the private extraction and appropriation of surplus value, and capital is a social instrument for the domination of man by man. The essential features of this process are in no way altered by the spread of stock-holdings, the separation of ownership from management, etc.
22. See p. 9.

"pas par l'obéissance, ni par la rudesse des labeurs, mais par le statu d'instrument et la réduction de l'homme à l'état de chose." [23] This is the pure form of servitude: to exist as an instrument, as a thing. And this mode of existence is not abrogated if the thing is animated and chooses its material and intellectual food, if it does not feel its being-a-thing, if it is a pretty, clean, mobile thing. Conversely, as reification tends to become totalitarian by virtue of its technological form, the organizers and administrators themselves become increasingly dependent on the machinery which they organize and administer. And this mutual dependence is no longer the dialectical relationship between Master and Servant, which has been broken in the struggle for mutual recognition, but rather a vicious circle which encloses both the Master and the Servant. Do the technicians rule, or is their rule that of the others, who rely on the technicians as their planners and executors?

". . . the pressures of today's highly technological arms race have taken the initiative and the power to make the crucial decisions out of the hands of responsible government officials and placed it in the hands of technicians, planners and scientists employed by vast industrial empires and charged with responsibility for their employers' interests. It is their job to dream up new weapons systems and persuade the military that the future of their military profession, as well as the country, depends upon buying what they have dreamed up." [24]

As the productive establishments rely on the military for self-preservation and growth, so the military relies on the corporations "not only for their weapons, but also for knowledge of what kind of weapons they need, how much they

23. "neither by obedience nor by hardness of labor but by the status of being a mere instrument, and the reduction of man to the state of a thing." François Perroux, *La Coexistence pacifique*, (Paris, Presses Universitaires, 1958), vol. III, p. 600.

24. Stewart Meacham, *Labor and the Cold War* (American Friends Service Committee, Philadelphia 1959), p. 9.

will cost, and how long it will take to get them." [25] A vicious circle seems indeed the proper image of a society which is self-expanding and self-perpetuating in its own preestablished direction—driven by the growing needs which it generates and, at the same time, contains.

Prospects of Containment

Is there any prospect that this chain of growing productivity and repression may be broken? An answer would require an attempt to project contemporary developments into the future, assuming a relatively normal evolution, that is, neglecting the very real possibility of a nuclear war. On this assumption, the Enemy would remain "permanent"—that is, communism would continue to coexist with capitalism. At the same time, the latter would continue to be capable of maintaining and even increasing the standard of living for an increasing part of the population—in spite of and through intensified production of the means of destruction, and methodical waste of resources and faculties. This capability has asserted itself in spite of and through two World Wars and immeasurable physical and intellectual regression brought about by the fascist systems.

The material base for this capability would continue to be available in

(a) the growing productivity of labor (technical progress);

(b) the rise in the birth rate of the underlying population;

(c) the permanent defense economy;

(d) the economic-political integration of the capitalist countries, and the building up of their relations with the underdeveloped areas.

25. *Ibid.*

But the continued conflict between the productive capabilities of society and their destructive and oppressive utilization would necessitate intensified efforts to impose the requirements of the apparatus on the population—to get rid of excess capacity, to create the need for buying the goods that must be profitably sold, and the desire to work for their production and promotion. The system thus tends toward both total administration and total dependence on administration by ruling public and private managements, strengthening the preestablished harmony between the interest of the big public and private corporations and that of their customers and servants. Neither partial nationalization nor extended participation of labor in management and profit would by themselves alter this system of domination—as long as labor itself remains a prop and affirmative force.

There are centrifugal tendencies, from within and from without. One of them is inherent in technical progress itself, namely, *automation.* I suggested that expanding automation is more than quantitative growth of mechanization—that it is a change in the character of the basic productive forces.[26] It seems that automation to the limits of technical possibility is incompatible with a society based on the private exploitation of human labor power in the process of production. Almost a century before automation became a reality, Marx envisaged its explosive prospects:

As large-scale industry advances, the creation of real wealth depends less on the labor time and the quantity of labor expended than on the power of the instrumentalities (*Agentien*) set in motion during the labor time. These instrumentalities, and their powerful effectiveness, are in no proportion to the immediate labor time which their production requires; their effectiveness rather depends on the attained level of science and technological progress; in other words, on the application of this science to

26. See p. 27.

production. . . . Human labor then no longer appears as enclosed in the process of production—man rather relates himself to the process of production as supervisor and regulator (*Wächter und Regulator*). . . . He stands outside of the process of production instead of being the principal agent in the process of production. . . . In this transformation, the great pillar of production and wealth is no longer the immediate labor performed by man himself, nor his labor time, but the appropriation of his own universal productivity (*Produktivkraft*), i.e., his knowledge and his mastery of nature through his societal existence—in one word: the development of the societal individual (*des gesellschaftlichen Individuums*). The *theft of another man's labor time, on which the* [*social*] *wealth still rests today,* then appears as a miserable basis compared with the new basis which large-scale industry itself has created. As soon as human labor, in its immediate form, has ceased to be the great source of wealth, labor time will cease, and must of necessity cease to be the measure of wealth, and the exchange value must of necessity cease to be the measure of use value. The *surplus labor of the mass* [of the population] has thus ceased to be the condition for the development of social wealth (*des allgemeinen Reichtums*), and the idleness of the few has ceased to be the condition for the development of the universal intellectual faculties of man. The mode of production which rests on the exchange value thus collapses . . .[27]

Automation indeed appears to be the great catalyst of advanced industrial society. It is an explosive or non-explosive catalyst in the material base of qualitative change, the technical instrument of the turn from quantity to quality. For the social process of automation expresses the transformation, or rather transubstantiation of labor power, in which the latter, separated from the individual, becomes an independent producing object and thus a subject itself.

Automation, once it became *the* process of material production, would revolutionize the whole society. The reifica-

27. Karl Marx, *Grundrisse der Kritik der politischen Oekonomie* (Berlin, Dietz Verlag, 1953), p. 592 f. See also p. 596. My translation.

tion of human labor power, driven to perfection, would shatter the reified form by cutting the chain that ties the individual to the machinery—the mechanism through which his own labor enslaves him. Complete automation in the realm of necessity would open the dimension of free time as the one in which man's private *and* societal existence would constitute itself. This would be the historical transcendence toward a new civilization.

At the present stage of advanced capitalism, organized labor rightly opposes automation without compensating employment. It insists on the extensive utilization of human labor power in material production, and thus opposes technical progress. However, in doing so, it also opposes the more efficient utilization of capital; it hampers intensified efforts to raise the productivity of labor. In other words, continued arrest of automation may weaken the competitive national and international position of capital, cause a long-range depression, and consequently reactivate the conflict of class interests.

This possibility becomes more realistic as the contest between capitalism and communism shifts from the military to the social and economic field. By the power of total administration, automation in the Soviet system can proceed more rapidly once a certain technical level has been attained. This threat to its competitive international position would compel the Western world to accelerate rationalization of the productive process. Such rationalization encounters stiff resistance on the part of labor, but resistance which is not accompanied by political radicalization. In the United States at least, the leadership of labor in its aims and means does not go beyond the framework common to the national and group interest, with the latter submitting or subjected to the former. These centrifugal forces are still manageable within this framework.

Here, too, the declining proportion of human labor

power in the productive process means a decline in political power of the opposition. In view of the increasing weight of the white-collar element in this process, political radicalization would have to be accompanied by the emergence of an independent political consciousness and action among the white-collar groups—a rather unlikely development in advanced industrial society. The stepped-up drive to organize the growing white-collar element in the industrial unions,[28] if successful at all, may result in a growth of trade union consciousness of these groups, but hardly in their political radicalization.

"Politically, the presence of more white-collar workers in labor unions will give liberal and labor spokesmen a chance more truthfully to identify 'the interests of labor' with those of the community as a whole. The mass base of labor as a pressure group will be further extended, and labor spokesmen will inevitably be involved in more far-reaching bargains over the national political economy." [29]

Under these circumstances, the prospects for a streamlined containment of the centrifugal tendencies depend primarily on the ability of the vested interests to adjust themselves and their economy to the requirements of the Welfare State. Vastly increased government spending and direction, planning on a national and international scope, an enlarged foreign aid program, comprehensive social security, public works on a grand scale, perhaps even partial nationalization belong to these requirements.[30] I believe that the dominant interests will gradually and hesitantly accept these requirements and entrust their prerogatives to a more effective power.

28. *Automation and Major Technological Change,* loc. cit., p. 11 f.
29. C. Wright Mills, *White Collar* (New York: Oxford University Press, 1956), p. 319 f.
30. In the less advanced capitalist countries, where strong segments of the militant labor movement are still alive (France, Italy), their force is pitted against that of accelerated technological and political rationalization

Turning now to the prospects for the containment of social change in the other system of industrial civilization, in Soviet society,[31] the discussion is from the outset confronted with a double incomparability: (a) chronologically, Soviet society is at an earlier stage of industrialization, with large sectors still at the pre-technological stage, and (b) structurally, its economic and its political institutions are essentially different (total nationalization, and dictatorship).

The interconnection between the two aspects aggravates the difficulties of the analysis. The historical backwardness not only enables but compels Soviet industrialization to proceed without planned waste and obsolescence, without the restrictions on productivity imposed by the interests of private profit, and with planned satisfaction of still unfulfilled vital needs after, and perhaps even simultaneously with, the priorities of military and political needs.

Is this greater rationality of industrialization only the token and advantage of historical backwardness, likely to disappear once the advanced level is reached? Is it the same historical backwardness which, on the other hand, enforces —under the conditions of the competitive coexistence with advanced capitalism—the total development and control of all resources by a dictatorial regime? And, after having attained the goal of "catching up and overtaking," would Soviet society then be able to liberalize the totalitarian controls to the point where a qualitative change could take place?

The argument from historical backwardness—according to which liberation must, under the prevailing conditions of material and intellectual immaturity, necessarily be the work of force and administration—is not only the core of Soviet

---

in authoritarian form. The exigencies of the international contest are likely to strengthen the latter and to make for adoption of and alliance with the predominant tendencies in the most advanced industrial areas.

31. For the following see my *Soviet Marxism*, (New York: Columbia University Press, 1958).

Marxism, but also that of the theoreticians of "educational dictatorship" from Plato to Rousseau. It is easily ridiculed but hard to refute because it has the merit to acknowledge, without much hypocrisy, the conditions (material and intellectual) which serve to prevent genuine and intelligent self-determination.

Moreover, the argument debunks the repressive ideology of freedom, according to which human liberty can blossom forth in a life of toil, poverty, and stupidity. Indeed, society must first create the material prerequisites of freedom for all its members before it can be a free society; it must first *create* the wealth before being able to *distribute* it according to the freely developing needs of the individual; it must first enable its slaves to learn and see and think before they know what is going on and what they themselves can do to change it. And, to the degree to which the slaves have been preconditioned to exist as slaves and be content in that role, their liberation necessarily appears to come from without and from above. They must be "forced to be free," to "see objects as they are, and sometimes as they ought to appear," they must be shown the "good road" they are in search of.[32]

But with all its truth, the argument cannot answer the time-honored question: who educates the educators, and where is the proof that they are in possession of "the good?" The question is not invalidated by arguing that it is equally applicable to certain democratic forms of government where the fateful decisions on what is good for the nation are made by elected representatives (or rather endorsed by elected representatives)—elected under conditions of effective and freely accepted indoctrination. Still, the only possible excuse (it is weak enough!) for "educational dictatorship" is that the terrible risk which it involves may not be more terrible

32. Rousseau, *The Social Contract*, Book I, Chap. VII; Book II, ch. VI.—See p. 6.

than the risk which the great liberal as well as the authoritarian societies are taking now, nor may the costs be much higher.

However, the dialectical logic insists, against the language of brute facts and ideology, that the slaves must be *free for* their liberation before they can become free, and that the end must be operative in the means to attain it. Marx's proposition that the liberation of the working class must be the action of the working class itself states this *a priori*. Socialism must become reality with the first act of the revolution because it must already be in the consciousness and action of those who carried the revolution.

True, there is a "first phase" of socialist construction during which the new society is "still stamped with the birth marks of the old society from whose womb it emerges," [33] but the qualitative change from the old to the new society occurred when this phase began. According to Marx, the "second phase" is literally constituted in the first phase. The qualitatively new mode of life generated by the new mode of production appears *in* the socialist revolution, which is the end and *at* the end of the capitalist system. Socialist construction begins with the first phase of the revolution.

By the same token, the transition from "to each according to his work" to "to each according to his needs" is determined by the first phase—not only by the creation of the technological and material base, but also (and this is decisive!) by the *mode* in which it is created. Control of the productive process by the "immediate producers" is supposed to initiate the development which distinguishes the history of free men from the prehistory of man. This is a society in which the former objects of productivity first

33. Marx, "Critique of the Gotha Programme," in Marx and Engels, *Selected Works* (Moscow: Foreign Languages Publ. House, 1958), vol. II, p. 23.

become the human individuals who plan and use the instruments of their labor for the realization of their own humane needs and faculties. For the first time in history, men would act freely and collectively under and against the necessity which limits their freedom and their humanity. Therefore all repression imposed by necessity would be truly self-imposed necessity. In contrast to this conception, the actual development in present-day communist society postpones (or is compelled to postpone, by the international situation) the qualitative change to the second phase, and the transition from capitalism to socialism appears, in spite of the revolution, still as quantitative change. The enslavement of man by the instruments of his labor continues in a highly rationalized and vastly efficient and promising form.

The situation of hostile coexistence may explain the terroristic features of Stalinist industrialization, but it also set in motion the forces which tend to perpetuate technical progress as the instrument of domination; the means prejudice the end. Again assuming that no nuclear warfare or other catastrophe cuts off its development, technical progress would make for continued increase in the standard of living and for continued liberalization of controls. The nationalized economy could exploit the productivity of labor and capital without structural resistance[34] while considerably reducing working hours and augmenting the comforts of life. And it could accomplish all this without abandoning the hold of total administration over the people. There is no reason to assume that technical progress plus nationalization will make for "automatic" liberation and release of the negating forces. On the contrary, the contradiction between the growing productive forces and their enslaving organization—openly admitted as a feature of Soviet socialist development even

34. On the difference between built-in and manageable resistance see my *Soviet Marxism,* loc. cit., p. 109 ff.

by Stalin[35]—is likely to flatten out rather than to aggravate. The more the rulers are capable of delivering the goods of consumption, the more firmly will the underlying population be tied to the various ruling bureaucracies.

But while these prospects for the containment of qualitative change in the Soviet system seem to be parallel to those in advanced capitalist society, the socialist base of production introduces a decisive difference. In the Soviet system, the organization of the productive process certainly separates the "immediate producers" (the laborers) from control over the means of production and thus makes for class distinctions at the very base of the system. This separation was established by political decision and power after the brief "heroic period" of the Bolshevik Revolution, and has been perpetuated ever since. And yet it is not the motor of the productive process itself; it is not built into this process as is the division between capital and labor, derived from private ownership of the means of production. Consequently, the ruling strata are themselves separable from the productive process—that is, they are replaceable without exploding the basic institutions of society.

This is the half-truth in the Soviet-Marxist thesis that the prevailing contradictions between the "lagging production relations and the character of the productive forces" can be resolved without explosion, and that "conformity" between the two factors can occur through "gradual change." [36] The other half of the truth is that quantitative change would still have to turn into qualitative change, into the disappearance of the State, the Party, the Plan, etc. as independent powers superimposed on the individuals. Inasmuch as this change would leave the material base of society (the nationalized productive process) intact, it would be

35. *"Economic Problems of Socialism in the U.S.S.R."* (1952), in: Leo Gruliow ed. *Current Soviet Policies,* (New York: F. A. Praeger, 1953), p. 5, 11, 14.
36. *Ibid.,* p. 14 f.

confined to a *political* revolution. If it could lead to self-determination at the very base of human existence, namely in the dimension of necessary labor, it would be the most radical and most complete revolution in history. Distribution of the necessities of life regardless of work performance, reduction of working time to a minimum, universal all-sided education toward exchangeability of functions—these are the preconditions but not the contents of self-determination. While the creation of these preconditions may still be the result of superimposed administration, their establishment would mean the end of this administration. To be sure, a mature and free industrial society would continue to depend on a division of labor which involves inequality of functions. Such inequality is necessitated by genuine social needs, technical requirements, and the physical and mental differences among the individuals. However, the executive and supervisory functions would no longer carry the privilege of ruling the life of others in some particular interest. The transition to such a state is a revolutionary rather than evolutionary process, even on the foundation of a fully nationalized and planned economy.

Can one assume that the communist system, in its established forms, would develop (or rather be *forced* to develop by virtue of the international contest) the conditions which would make for such a transition? There are strong arguments against this assumption. One emphasizes the powerful resistance which the entrenched bureaucracy would offer—a resistance which finds its *raison d'être* precisely on the same grounds that impel the drive for creating the preconditions for liberation, namely, the life-and-death competition with the capitalist world.

One can dispense with the notion of an innate "power-drive" in human nature. This is a highly dubious psychological concept and grossly inadequate for the analysis of societal developments. The question is not whether the communist bureaucracies would "give up" their privileged position once the level of a possible qualitative change has been reached, but whether they will be able to prevent the attainment of this level. In order to do so, they would have to arrest material and intellectual growth at a point where domination still is rational and profitable, where the underlying population can still be tied to the job and to the interest of the state or other established institutions. Again, the decisive factor here seems to be the global situation of coexistence, which has long since become a factor in the *internal* situation of the two opposed societies. The need for the all-out utilization of technical progress, and for survival by virtue of a superior standard of living may prove stronger than the resistance of the vested bureaucracies.

I should like to add a few remarks on the often-heard opinion that the new development of the backward countries might not only alter the prospects of the advanced industrial countries, but also constitute a "third force" that may grow into a relatively independent power. In terms of the preceding discussion: is there any evidence that the former colonial or semi-colonial areas might adopt a way of industrialization essentially different from capitalism and present-day communism? Is there anything in the indigenous culture and tradition of these areas which might indicate such an alternative? I shall confine my remarks to models of backwardness already in the process of industrialization—that is, to countries where industrialization coexists with an unbroken pre- and anti-industrial culture (India, Egypt).

These countries enter upon the process of industrialization with a population untrained in the values of self-propelling productivity, efficiency, and technological rationality. In other words, with a vast majority of population which has not yet been transformed into a labor force separated from the means of production. Do these conditions favor a new confluence of industrialization and liberation—an essentially different mode of industrialization which would build the productive apparatus not only in accord with the vital needs of the underlying population, but also with the aim of pacifying the struggle for existence?

Industrialization in these backward areas does not take place in a vacuum. It occurs in a historical situation in which the social capital required for primary accumulation must be obtained largely from without, from the capitalist or communist bloc—or from both. Moreover, there is a widespread presumption that remaining independent would require *rapid* industrialization and attainment of a level of productivity which would assure at least relative autonomy in competition with the two giants.

In these circumstances, the transformation of underdeveloped into industrial societies must as quickly as possible discard the pre-technological forms. This is especially so in countries where even the most vital needs of the population are far from being satisfied, where the terrible standard of living calls first of all for quantities *en masse*, for mechanized and standardized mass production and distribution. And in these same countries, the dead weight of pre-technological and even pre-"bourgeois" customs and conditions offers a strong resistance to such a superimposed development. The machine process (as social process) requires obedience to a system of anonymous powers—total secularization and the destruction of values and institutions whose de-sanctification has hardly begun. Can one reasonably assume that, under the impact of the two great systems of total technological administration, the dissolution of this resistance will proceed in liberal and democratic forms? That the underdeveloped countries can make the historical leap from the pre-technological to the *post*-technological society, in which the mastered technological apparatus may provide the basis for a genuine democracy? On the contrary, it rather seems that the superimposed development of these countries will bring about a period of total administration more violent and more rigid than that traversed by the advanced societies which can build on the achievements of the liberalistic era. To sum up: the backward areas are likely to succumb either to one of the various forms of neo-colonialism, or to a more or less terroristic system of primary accumulation.

However, another alternative seems possible.[37] If industrialization and the introduction of technology in the backward countries encounter strong resistance from the indigenous and traditional modes of life and labor—a resistance which is not abandoned even at the very tangible prospect of a better and easier life—could this pre-technological tradition itself become the source of progress and industrialization?

Such indigenous progress would demand a planned policy which, instead of superimposing technology on the traditional modes of life and labor, would extend and improve them on their own grounds, eliminating the oppressive and exploitative forces (material and religious) which made them incapable of assuring the development of a human existence. Social revolution, agrarian reform, and reduction of over-population would be prerequisites, but not industrialization after the pattern of the advanced societies. Indigenous progress seems indeed possible in areas where the natural resources, if freed from suppressive encroachment, are still sufficient not only for subsistence but also for a human life. And where they are not, could they not be made sufficient by the gradual and piecemeal aid of technology—within the framework of the traditional forms? If this is the case, then conditions would prevail which

37. For the following see the magnificent books by René Dumont, especially *Terres vivantes* (Paris: Plon, 1961).

do not exist in the old and advanced industrial societies (and never existed there)—namely, the "immediate producers" themselves would have the chance to create, by their own labor and leisure, their own progress and determine its rate and direction. Self-determination would proceed from the base, and work for the necessities could transcend itself toward work for gratification.

But even under these abstract assumptions, the brute limits of self-determination must be acknowledged. The initial revolution which, by abolishing mental and material exploitation, is to establish the prerequisites for the new development, is hardly conceivable as spontaneous action. Moreover, indigenous progress would presuppose a change in the policy of the two great industrial power blocs which today shape the world—abandonment of neo-colonialism in all its forms. At present, there is no indication of such a change.

The Welfare and Warfare State

By way of summary: the prospects of containment of change, offered by the politics of technological rationality, depend on the prospects of the Welfare State. Such a state seems capable of raising the standard of *administered* living, a capability inherent in all advanced industrial societies where the streamlined technical apparatus—set up as a separate power over and above the individuals—depends for its functioning on the intensified development and expansion of productivity. Under such conditions, decline of freedom and opposition is not a matter of moral or intellectual deterioration or corruption. It is rather an objective societal process insofar as the production and distribution of an increasing quantity of goods and services make compliance a rational technological attitude.

However, with all its rationality, the Welfare State is a state of unfreedom because its total administration is systematic restriction of (a) "technically" available free time;[38] (b) the quantity and quality of goods and services "technically" available for vital individual needs; (c) the intelligence (conscious and unconscious) capable of comprehending and realizing the possibilities of self-determination.

Late industrial society has increased rather than reduced the need for parasitical and alienated functions (for the society as a whole, if not for the individual). Advertising, public relations, indoctrination, planned obsolescence are no longer unproductive overhead costs but rather elements of basic production costs. In order to be effective, such production of socially necessary waste requires continuous rationalization—the relentless utilization of advanced techniques and science. Consequently, a rising standard of living is the almost unavoidable by-product of the politically manipulated industrial society, once a certain level of backwardness has been overcome. The growing productivity of labor creates an increasing surplus-product which, whether privately or centrally appropriated and distributed, allows an increased consumption—notwithstanding the increased diversion of productivity. As long as this constellation prevails, it reduces the use-value of freedom; there is no reason to insist on self-determination if the administered life is the comfortable and even the "good" life. This is the rational and material ground for the unification of opposites, for one-dimensional political behavior. On this ground, the transcending political forces *within* society are arrested, and qualitative change appears possible only as a change from *without.*

38. "Free" time, not "leisure" time. The latter thrives in advanced industrial society, but it is unfree to the extent to which it is administered by business and politics.

Rejection of the Welfare State on behalf of abstract ideas of freedom is hardly convincing. The loss of the economic and political liberties which were the real achievement of the preceding two centuries may seem slight damage in a state capable of making the administered life secure and comfortable.[39] If the individuals are satisfied to the point of happiness with the goods and services handed down to them by the administration, why should they insist on different institutions for a different production of different goods and services? And if the individuals are pre-conditioned so that the satisfying goods also include thoughts, feelings, aspirations, why should they wish to think, feel, and imagine for themselves? True, the material and mental commodities offered may be bad, wasteful, rubbish—but *Geist* and knowledge are no telling arguments against satisfaction of needs.

The critique of the Welfare State in terms of liberalism and conservatism (with or without the prefix "neo-") rests, for its validity, on the existence of the very conditions which the Welfare State has surpassed—namely, a lower degree of social wealth and technology. The sinister aspects of this critique show forth in the fight against comprehensive social legislation and adequate government expenditures for services other than those of military defense.

Denunciation of the oppressive capabilities of the Welfare State thus serves to protect the oppressive capabilities of the society *prior* to the Welfare State. At the most advanced stage of capitalism, this society is a system of subdued pluralism, in which the competing institutions concur in solidifying the power of the whole over the individual. Still, for the administered individual, pluralistic administration is far better than total administration. One institution might protect him against the other; one organization might mitigate the impact of the other; possibilities of escape and

39. See p. 2.

redress can be calculated. The rule of law, no matter how restricted, is still infinitely safer than rule above or without law.

However, in view of prevailing tendencies, the question must be raised whether this form of pluralism does not accelerate the destruction of pluralism. Advanced industrial society is indeed a system of countervailing powers. But these forces cancel each other out in a higher unification— in the common interest to defend and extend the established position, to combat the historical alternatives, to contain qualitative change. The countervailing powers do not include those which counter the whole.[40] They tend to make the whole immune against negation from within as well as without; the foreign policy of containment appears as an extension of the domestic policy of containment.

The reality of pluralism becomes ideological, deceptive. It seems to extend rather than reduce manipulation and co-ordination, to promote rather than counteract the fateful integration. Free institutions compete with authoritarian ones in making the Enemy a deadly force *within* the system. And this deadly force stimulates growth and initiative, not by virtue of the magnitude and economic impact of the defense "sector," but by virtue of the fact that the society as a whole becomes a defense society. For the Enemy is permanent. He is not in the emergency situation but in the normal state of affairs. He threatens in peace as much as in war (and perhaps more than in war); he is thus being built into the system as a cohesive power.

Neither the growing productivity nor the high standard of living depend on the threat from without, but their use for the containment of social change and perpetuation of

40. For a critical and realistic appraisal of Galbraith's ideological concept see Earl Latham, "The Body Politic of the Corporation," in: E. S. Mason, *The Corporation in Modern Society* (Cambridge: Harvard University Press, 1959), p. 223, 235 f.

servitude does. The Enemy is the common denominator of all doing and undoing. And the Enemy is not identical with actual communism or actual capitalism—he is, in both cases, the real spectre of liberation.

Once again: the insanity of the whole absolves the particular insanities and turns the crimes against humanity into a rational enterprise. When the people, aptly stimulated by the public and private authorities, prepare for lives of total mobilization, they are sensible not only because of the present Enemy, but also because of the investment and employment possibilities in industry and entertainment. Even the most insane calculations are rational: the annihilation of five million people is preferable to that of ten million, twenty million, and so on. It is hopeless to argue that a civilization which justifies its defense by such a calculus proclaims its own end.

Under these circumstances, even the existing liberties and escapes fall in place within the organized whole. At this stage of the regimented market, is competition alleviating or intensifying the race for bigger and faster turnover and obsolescence? Are the political parties competing for pacification or for a stronger and more costly armament industry? Is the production of "affluence" promoting or delaying the satisfaction of still unfulfilled vital needs? If the first alternatives are true, the contemporary form of pluralism would strengthen the potential for the containment of qualitative change, and thus prevent rather than impel the "catastrophe" of self-determination. Democracy would appear to be the most efficient system of domination.

The image of the Welfare State sketched in the preceding paragraphs is that of a historical freak between organized capitalism and socialism, servitude and freedom, totalitarianism and happiness. Its possibility is sufficiently indicated by prevalent tendencies of technical progress, and

sufficiently threatened by explosive forces. The most powerful, of course, is the danger that preparation for total nuclear
war may turn into its realization: the deterrent also serves
to deter efforts to eliminate the *need* for the deterrent. Other
factors are at play which may preclude the pleasant juncture
of totalitarianism and happiness, manipulation and democracy, heteronomy and autonomy—in short, the perpetuation
of the preestablished harmony between organized and spontaneous behavior, preconditioned and free thought, expedi-
ency and conviction.

Even the most highly organized capitalism retains the
social need for private appropriation and distribution of
profit as the regulator of the economy. That is, it continues
to link the realization of the general interest to that of particular vested interests. In doing so, it continues to face the
conflict between the growing potential of pacifying the
struggle for existence, and the need for intensifying this
struggle; between the progressive "abolition of labor" and
the need for preserving labor as the source of profit. The
conflict perpetuates the inhuman existence of those who
form the human base of the social pyramid—the outsiders
and the poor, the unemployed and unemployable, the persecuted colored races, the inmates of prisons and mental
institutions.

In contemporary communist societies, the enemy without, backwardness, and the legacy of terror perpetuate the
oppressive features of "catching up with and surpassing"
the achievements of capitalism. The priority of the means
over the end is thereby aggravated—a priority which could
be broken only if pacification is achieved—and capitalism
and communism continue to compete without military force,
on a global scale and through global institutions. This pacification would mean the emergence of a genuine world economy—the demise of the nation state, the national interest,
national business together with their international alliances.

And this is precisely the possibility against which the present world is mobilized:

L'ignorance et l'inconscience sont telles que les nationalismes demeurent florissants. Ni l'armement ni l'industrie du XXe siècle ne permettent aux *patries* d'assurer leur sécurité et leur vie sinon en ensembles organisés de poids mondial, dans l'ordre militaire et économique. Mais à l'Ouest non plus qu'à l'Est, les croyances collectives n'assimilent les changements réels. Les Grands forment leurs empires, ou en réparent les architectures sans accepter les changements de régime économique et politique qui donneraient efficacité et sens à l'une et à l'autre coalitions.

and:

Dupes de la nation et dupes de la classe, les masses souffrantes sont partout engagées dans les duretés de conflits où leurs seuls ennemis sont des maîtres qui emploient sciemment les mystifications de l'industrie et du pouvoir.

La collusion de l'industrie moderne et du pouvoir territorialisé est un vice dont la réalité est plus profonde que les institutions et les structures capitalistes et communistes et qu'aucune dialectique nécessaire ne doit nécessairement extirper.[41]

41. "Ignorance and unconsciousness are such that nationalism continues to flourish. Neither twentieth century armaments nor industry allow "fatherlands" to insure their security and their existence except through organisations which carry weight on a world wide scale in military and economic matters. But in the East as well as in the West, collective beliefs don't adapt themselves to real changes. The great powers shape their empires or repair the architecture thereof without accepting changes in the economic and political regime which would give effectiveness and meaning to one or the other of the coalitions."

(and:)

"Duped by the nation and duped by the class, the suffering masses are everywhere involved in the harshness of conflict in which their only enemies are masters who knowingly use the mystifications of industry and power.

The collusion of modern industry and territorial power is a vice which is more profoundly real than capitalist and communist institutions and structures and which no necessary dialectic necessarily eradicates." François Perroux, loc. cit., vol. III, p. 631-632; 633.

The fateful interdependence of the only two "sovereign" social systems in the contemporary world is expressive of the fact that the conflict between progress and politics, between man and his masters has become total. When capitalism meets the challenge of communism, it meets its own capabilities: spectacular development of all productive forces after the subordination of the private interests in profitability which arrest such development. When communism meets the challenge of capitalism, it too meets its own capabilities: spectacular comforts, liberties, and alleviation of the burden of life. Both systems have these capabilities distorted beyond recognition and, in both cases, the reason is in the last analysis the same—the struggle against a form of life which would dissolve the basis for domination.

3: The Conquest
of the Unhappy Consciousness:
Repressive Desublimation

Having discussed the political integration of advanced industrial society, an achievement rendered possible by growing technological productivity and the expanding conquest of man and nature, we will now turn to a corresponding integration in the realm of culture. In this chapter, certain key notions and images of literature and their fate will illustrate how the progress of technological rationality is liquidating the oppositional and transcending elements in the "higher culture." They succumb in fact to the process of *desublimation* which prevails in the advanced regions of contemporary society.

The achievements and the failures of this society invalidate its higher culture. The celebration of the autonomous personality, of humanism, of tragic and romantic love appears to be the ideal of a backward stage of the development. What is happening now is not the deterioration of higher culture into mass culture but the refutation of this culture by the reality. The reality surpasses its culture. Man today can do *more* than the culture heros and half-gods; he has solved many insoluble problems. But he has also betrayed the hope and destroyed the truth which were preserved in the sublimations of higher culture. To be sure, the higher culture was always in contradiction with social reality, and only a privileged minority enjoyed its blessings and represented its ideals. The two antagonistic spheres of society have always coexisted; the higher culture has always been accommodating, while the reality was rarely disturbed by its ideals and its truth.

Today's novel feature is the flattening out of the antagonism between culture and social reality through the obliteration of the oppositional, alien, and transcendent elements in the higher culture by virtue of which it constituted *another dimension* of reality. This liquidation of *two-dimensional* culture takes place not through the denial and rejection of the "cultural values," but through their wholesale incorporation into the established order, through their reproduction and display on a massive scale.

In fact, they serve as instruments of social cohesion. The greatness of a free literature and art, the ideals of humanism, the sorrows and joys of the individual, the fulfillment of the personality are important items in the competitive struggle between East and West. They speak heavily against the present forms of communism, and they are daily administered and sold. The fact that they contradict the society which sells them does not count. Just as people know or feel that advertisements and political platforms must not be necessarily true or right, and yet hear and read them and even let themselves be guided by them, so they accept the traditional values and make them part of their mental equipment. If mass communications blend together harmoniously, and often unnoticeably, art, politics, religion, and philosophy with commercials, they bring these realms of culture to their common denominator—the commodity form. The music of the soul is also the music of salesmanship. Exchange value, not truth value counts. On it centers the rationality of the status quo, and all alien rationality is bent to it.

As the great words of freedom and fulfillment are pronounced by campaigning leaders and politicians, on the screens and radios and stages, they turn into meaningless sounds which obtain meaning only in the context of propaganda, business, discipline, and relaxation. This assimilation of the ideal with reality testifies to the extent to which the ideal has been surpassed. It is brought down from the sublimated realm of the soul or the spirit or the inner man, and translated into operational terms and problems. Here are the progressive elements of mass culture. The perversion is indicative of the fact that advanced industrial society is confronted with the possibility of a materialization of ideals. The capabilities of this society are progressively reducing the sublimated realm in which the condition of man was represented, idealized, and indicted. Higher culture becomes part of the material culture. In this transformation, it loses the greater part of its truth.

The higher culture of the West—whose moral, aesthetic, and intellectual values industrial society still professes —was a pre-technological culture in a functional as well as chronological sense. Its validity was derived from the experience of a world which no longer exists and which cannot be recaptured because it is in a strict sense invalidated by technological society. Moreover, it remained to a large degree a feudal culture, even when the bourgeois period gave it some of its most lasting formulations. It was feudal not only because of its confinement to privileged minorities, not only because of its inherent romantic element (which will be discussed presently), but also because its authentic works expressed a conscious, methodical alienation from the entire sphere of business and industry, and from its calculable and profitable order.

While this bourgeois order found its rich—and even affirmative—representation in art and literature (as in the Dutch painters of the seventeenth century, in Goethe's *Wilhelm Meister,* in the English novel of the nineteenth century, in Thomas Mann), it remained an order which was overshadowed, broken, refuted by another dimension which was irreconcilably antagonistic to the order of business, indicting it and denying it. And in the literature, this other dimension is represented *not* by the religious, spiritual, moral heroes (who often sustain the established order) but rather by such disruptive characters as the artist, the prostitute, the adulteress, the great criminal and outcast, the warrior, the rebel-poet, the devil, the fool—those who don't earn a living, at least not in an orderly and normal way.

To be sure, these characters have not disappeared from the literature of advanced industrial society, but they survive essentially transformed. The vamp, the national hero, the beatnik, the neurotic housewife, the gangster, the star, the charismatic tycoon perform a function very different from and even contrary to that of their cultural predecessors. They are no longer images of another way of life but rather freaks or types of the same life, serving as an affirmation rather than negation of the established order.

Surely, the world of their predecessors was a backward, pre-technological world, a world with the good conscience of inequality and toil, in which labor was still a fated misfortune; but a world in which man and nature were not yet organized as things and instrumentalities. With its code of forms and manners, with the style and vocabulary of its literature and philosophy, this past culture expressed the rhythm and content of a universe in which valleys and forests, villages and inns, nobles and villains, salons and courts were a part of the experienced reality. In the verse and prose of this pre-technological culture is the rhythm of those who wander or ride in carriages, who have the time and the pleasure to think, contemplate, feel and narrate.

It is an outdated and surpassed culture, and only dreams and childlike regressions can recapture it. But this culture is, in some of its decisive elements, also a *post*-technological one. Its most advanced images and positions seem to survive their absorption into administered comforts and stimuli; they continue to haunt the consciousness with the possibility of their rebirth in the consummation of technical progress. They are the expression of that free and conscious alienation from the established forms of life with which literature and the arts opposed these forms even where they adorned them.

In contrast to the Marxian concept, which denotes man's relation to himself and to his work in capitalist society, the *artistic alienation* is the conscious transcendence of the alienated existence—a "higher level" or mediated alienation. The conflict with the world of progress, the negation of the order of business, the anti-bourgeois elements in bourgeois literature and art are neither due to the aesthetic lowliness of this order nor to romantic reaction—nostalgic consecration of a disappearing stage of civilization. "Romantic" is a term of condescending defamation which is easily applied to disparaging avant-garde positions, just as the term "decadent" far more often denounces the genuinely progressive traits of a dying culture than the real factors of decay. The traditional images of artistic alienation are indeed romantic in as much as they are in aesthetic incompatibility with the developing society. This incompatibility is the token of their truth. What they recall and preserve in memory pertains to the future: images of a gratification that would dissolve the society which suppresses it. The great surrealist art and literature of the 'Twenties and 'Thirties has still recaptured them in their subversive and liberating function. Random examples from the basic literary vocabulary may indicate the range and the kinship of these images, and the dimension which they reveal: Soul and Spirit and Heart; *la recherche de l'absolu, Les Fleurs du mal, la femme-enfant;* the Kingdom by the Sea; *Le Bateau ivre* and the Long-legged Bait; *Ferne* and *Heimat;* but also demon rum, demon machine, and demon money; Don Juan and Romeo; the Master Builder and When We Dead Awake.

Their mere enumeration shows that they belong to a lost dimension. They are invalidated not because of their literary obsolescence. Some of these images pertain to contemporary literature and survive in its most advanced creations. What has been invalidated is their subversive force, their destructive content—their truth. In this transformation, they find their home in everyday living. The alien and alienating oeuvres of intellectual culture become familiar goods and services. Is their massive reproduction and consumption only a change in quantity, namely, growing appreciation and understanding, democratization of culture?

The truth of literature and art has always been granted (if it was granted at all) as one of a "higher" order, which should not and indeed did not disturb the order of business. What has changed in the contemporary period is the difference between the two orders and their truths. The absorbent power of society depletes the artistic dimension by assimilating its antagonistic contents. In the realm of culture, the new totalitarianism manifests itself precisely in a harmonizing pluralism, where the most contradictory works and truths peacefully coexist in indifference.

Prior to the advent of this cultural reconciliation, literature and art were essentially alienation, sustaining and protecting the contradiction—the unhappy consciousness of the divided world, the defeated possibilities, the hopes unfulfilled, and the promises betrayed. They were a rational, cognitive force, revealing a dimension of man and nature which was repressed and repelled in reality. Their truth was in the illusion evoked, in the insistence on creating a world in which the terror of life was called up and suspended—mastered by recognition. This is the miracle of the *chef-d'oeuvre;* it is the tragedy, sustained to the last, and the end of tragedy—its impossible solution. To live one's love and hatred, to live that which one *is* means defeat, resignation, and death. The crimes of society, the hell that man has made for man become unconquerable cosmic forces.

The tension between the actual and the possible is transfigured into an insoluble conflict, in which reconciliation is by grace of the oeuvre as *form:* beauty as the "promesse de bonheur." In the form of the oeuvre, the actual circumstances are placed in another dimension where the given reality shows itself as that which it is. Thus it tells the truth about itself; its language ceases to be that of deˆeption, ignorance, and submission. Fiction calls the facts by their name and their reign collapses; fiction subverts everyday experience and shows it to be mutilated and false. But art has this magic power only as the power of negation. It can speak its own language only as long as the images are alive which refuse and refute the established order.

Flaubert's *Madame Bovary* is distinguished from equally sad love stories of contemporary literature by the fact that the humble vocabulary of her real-life counterpart still contained the heroine's images, or she read stories still containing such images. Her anxiety was fatal because there was no psychoanalyst, and there was no psychoanalyst because, in her world, he would not have been capable of curing her. She would have rejected him as part of the order of Yonville which destroyed her. Her story was "tragic" because the society in which it occurred was a backward one, with a sexual morality not yet liberalized, and a psychology not yet institutionalized. The society that was still to come has "solved" her problem by suppressing it. Certainly it would be nonsense to say that her tragedy or that of Romeo and Juliet is solved in modern democracy, but it would also be nonsense to deny the historical essence of the tragedy. The developing technological reality undermines not only the traditional forms but the very basis of the artistic alienation—that is, it tends to invalidate not only certain "styles" but also the very substance of art.

To be sure, alienation is not the sole characteristic of art. An analysis, and even a statement of the problem is outside the scope of this work, but some suggestions may be offered for clarification. Throughout whole periods of civilization, art appears to be entirely integrated into its society. Egyptian, Greek, and Gothic art are familiar examples; Bach and Mozart are usually also cited as testifying to the "positive" side of art. The place of the work of art in a pre-technological and two-dimensional culture is very different from that in a one-dimensional civilization, but alienation characterizes affirmative as well as negative art.

The decisive distinction is not the psychological one between art created in joy and art created in sorrow, between sanity and neurosis, but that between the artistic and the societal reality. The rupture with the latter, the magic or rational transgression, is an essential quality of even the most affirmative art; it is alienated also from the very public to which it is addressed. No matter how close and familiar the temple or cathedral were to the people who lived around them, they remained in terrifying or elevating contrast to the daily life of the slave, the peasant, and the artisan—and perhaps even to that of their masters.

Whether ritualized or not, art contains the rationality of negation. In its advanced positions, it is the Great Refusal —the protest against that which is. The modes in which man and things are made to appear, to sing and sound and speak, are modes of refuting, breaking, and recreating their factual existence. But these modes of negation pay tribute to the antagonistic society to which they are linked. Separated from the sphere of labor where society reproduces itself and its misery, the world of art which they create remains, with all its truth, a privilege and an illusion.

In this form it continues, in spite of all democratization and popularization, through the nineteenth and into the twentieth century. The "high culture" in which this alienation is celebrated has its own rites and its own style. The salon, the concert, opera, theater are designed to create and invoke another dimension of reality. Their attendance requires festive-like preparation; they cut off and transcend everyday experience.

Now this essential gap between the arts and the order of the day, kept open in the artistic alienation, is progressively closed by the advancing technological society. And with its closing, the Great Refusal is in turn refused; the "other dimension" is absorbed into the prevailing state of affairs. The works of alienation are themselves incorporated into this society and circulate as part and parcel of the equipment which adorns and psychoanalyzes the prevailing state of affairs. Thus they become commercials—they sell, comfort, or excite.

The neo-conservative critics of leftist critics of mass culture ridicule the protest against Bach as background music in the kitchen, against Plato and Hegel, Shelley and Baudelaire, Marx and Freud in the drugstore. Instead, they insist on recognition of the fact that the classics have left the mausoleum and come to life again, that people are just so much more educated. True, but coming to life as classics, they come to life as other than themselves; they are deprived of their antagonistic force, of the estrangement which was the very dimension of their truth. The intent and function of these works have thus fundamentally changed. If they once stood in contradiction to the status quo, this contradiction is now flattened out.

But such assimilation is historically premature; it establishes cultural equality while preserving domination. Society is eliminating the prerogatives and privileges of feudal-aristocratic culture together with its content. The fact that the transcending truths of the fine arts, the aesthetics of life and thought, were accessible only to the few wealthy and educated was the fault of a repressive society. But this fault is not corrected by paperbacks, general education, long-playing records, and the abolition of formal dress in the theater and concert hall.[1] The cultural privileges expressed the injustice of freedom, the contradiction between ideology and reality, the separation of intellectual from material productivity; but they also provided a protected realm in which the tabooed truths could survive in abstract integrity—remote from the society which suppressed them.

Now this remoteness has been removed—and with it the transgression and the indictment. The text and the tone are still there, but the distance is conquered which made them *Luft von anderen Planeten.*[2] The artistic alienation has become as functional as the architecture of the new theaters and concert halls in which it is performed. And here too, the rational and the evil are inseparable. Unquestionably the new architecture is better, i.e., more beautiful and more practical than the monstrosities of the Victorian era. But it is also more "integrated"—the cultural center is becoming a fitting part of the shopping center, or municipal center, or government center. Domination has its own aesthetics, and democratic domination has its democratic aesthetics. It is good that almost everyone can now have the fine arts at his fingertips, by just turning a knob on his set, or by just stepping into his drugstore. In this diffusion, however, they become cogs in a culture-machine which remakes their content.

Artistic alienation succumbs, together with other modes of negation, to the process of technological rationality. The change reveals its depth and the degree of its irreversibility if it is seen as a result of technical progress. The present stage redefines the possibilities of man and nature in accordance with the new means available for their realization and, in their light, the pre-technological images are losing their power.

1. No misunderstanding: as far as they go, paperbacks, general education, and long-playing records are truly a blessing.
2. Stefan George, in Arnold Schönberg's Quartet in F Sharp Minor. See Th. W. Adorno, *Philosophie der neuen Musik.* (J. C. B. Mohr, Tübingen, 1949), p. 19 ff.

Their truth value depended to a large degree on an un-comprehended and unconquered dimension of man and na-ture, on the narrow limits placed on organization and ma-nipulation, on the "insoluble core" which resisted integration. In the fully developed industrial society, this insoluble core is progressively whittled down by technological rationality. Obviously, the physical transformation of the world entails the mental transformation of its symbols, images, and ideas. Obviously, when cities and highways and National Parks replace the villages, valleys, and forests; when motorboats race over the lakes and planes cut through the skies—then these areas lose their character as a qualitatively different reality, as areas of contradiction.

And since contradiction is the work of the Logos—ra-tional confrontation of "that which is not" with "that which is"—it must have a medium of communication. The struggle for this medium, or rather the struggle against its absorption into the predominant one-dimensionality, shows forth in the avant-garde efforts to create an estrangement which would make the artistic truth again communicable.

Bertolt Brecht has sketched the theoretical foundations for these efforts. The total character of the established so-ciety confronts the playwright with the question of whether it is still possible to "represent the contemporary world in the theater"—that is, represent it in such a manner that the spectator recognizes the truth which the play is to convey. Brecht answers that the contemporary world can be thus represented only if it is represented as subject to change[3]—as the state of negativity which is to be negated. This is doctrine which has to be learned, comprehended, and acted upon; but the theater is and ought to be entertainment, pleasure. However, entertainment and learning are not op-

3. Bertolt Brecht, *Schriften zum Theater* (Berlin and Frankfurt, Suhr-kamp, 1957), p. 7, 9.

posites; entertainment may be the most effective mode of learning. To teach what the contemporary world really is behind the ideological and material veil, and how it can be changed, the theater must break the spectator's identification with the events on the stage. Not empathy and feeling, but distance and reflection are required. The "estrangement-effect" (*Verfremdungseffekt*) is to produce this dissociation in which the world can be recognized as what it is. "The things of everyday life are lifted out of the realm of the self-evident. . . ."[4] "That which is 'natural' must assume the features of the extraordinary. Only in this manner can the laws of cause and effect reveal themselves."[5]

The "estrangement-effect" is not superimposed on literature. It is rather literature's own answer to the threat of total behaviorism—the attempt to rescue the rationality of the negative. In this attempt, the great "conservative" of literature joins forces with the radical activist. Paul Valéry insists on the inescapable commitment of the poetic language to the negation. The verses of this language "ne parlent jamais que de choses absentes."[6] They speak of that which, though absent, haunts the established universe of discourse and behavior as its most tabooed possibility—neither heaven nor hell, neither good nor evil but simply "le bonheur." Thus the poetic language speaks of that which is of this world, which is visible, tangible, audible in man and nature—and of that which is not seen, not touched, not heard.

Creating and moving in a medium which presents the absent, the poetic language is a language of cognition—but a cognition which subverts the positive. In its cognitive function, poetry performs the great task of *thought*:

4. *Ibid.*, p. 76.
5. *Ibid.*, p. 63.
6. Paul Valéry, "Poésie et Pensée Abstraite," in *Oeuvres* (édition de la Pléiade, Paris, Gallimard, 1957), vol. I, p. 1324.

le travail qui fait vivre en nous ce qui n'existe pas.[7]

Naming the "things that are absent" is breaking the spell of the things that are; moreover, it is the ingression of a different order of things into the established one—"le commencement d'un monde."[8]

For the expression of this other order, which is transcendence within the one world, the poetic language depends on the transcendent elements in ordinary language.[9] However, the total mobilization of all media for the defense of the established reality has coordinated the means of expression to the point where communication of transcending contents becomes technically impossible. The spectre that has haunted the artistic consciousness since Mallarmé—the impossibility of speaking a non-reified language, of communicating the negative—has ceased to be a spectre. It has materialized.

The truly avant-garde works of literature communicate the break with communication. With Rimbaud, and then with dadaism and surrealism, literature rejects the very structure of discourse which, throughout the history of culture, has linked artistic and ordinary language. The propositional system[10] (with the sentence as its unit of meaning) was the medium in which the two dimensions of reality could meet, communicate and be communicated. The most sublime poetry and the lowest prose shared this medium of expression. Then, modern poetry "détruisait les rapports du langage et ramenait le discours à des stations de *mots*."[11]

The word refuses the unifying, sensible rule of the

---

7. "the effort which makes live in us that which does not exist." *Ibid.*, p. 1333.

8. *Ibid.*, p. 1327 (with reference to the language of music).

9. See chapter VII below.

10. See chapter V below.

11. "destroyed the relationships of the language and brought discourse back to the stage of *words*." Roland Barthes, *Le Degré zéro de l'écriture*. Paris, Editions du Sevil, 1953, p. 72 (my emphasis).

sentence. It explodes the pre-established structure of meaning and, becoming an "absolute object" itself, designates an intolerable, self-defeating universe—a discontinuum. This subversion of the linguistic structure implies a subversion of the experience of nature:

La Nature y devient un discontinu d'objets solitaires et terribles, parce qu'ils n'ont que des liaisons virtuelles; personne ne choisit pour eux un sens privilégié ou un emploi ou un service, personne ne les réduit à la signification d'un comportement mental ou d'une intention, c'est-à-dire finalement d'une tendresse . . . Ces mots-objets sans liaison, parés de toute la violence de leur éclatement . . . ces mots poétiques excluent les hommes; il n'y a pas d'humanisme poétique de la modernité: ce discours debout est un discours plein de terreur, c'est-à-dire qu'il met l'homme en liaison non pas avec les autres hommes, mais avec les images les plus inhumaines de la Nature; le ciel, l'enfer, le sacré, l'enfance, la folie, la matière pure, etc.[12]

The traditional stuff of art (images, harmonies, colors) reappears only as "quotes," residues of past meaning in a context of refusal. Thus, the surrealist paintings

sind der Inbegriff dessen, was die Sachlichkeit mit einem Tabu zudeckt, weil es sie an ihr eigenes dinghaftes Wesen gemahnt und daran, dass sie nicht damit fertig wird, dass ihre Rationalität irrational bleibt. Der Surrealismus sammelt ein, was die Sachlichkeit den Menschen versagt; die Entstellungen bezeugen, was das Verbot dem Begehrten antat. Durch sie errettete er das Veraltete, ein Album von Idiosynkrasieen, in denen der Glücksanspruch

12. "Nature becomes a discontinuum of solitary and terrible objects because they have only virtual links. No one chooses for them a privileged meaning or use or service. No one reduces them to mean a mental attitude or an intention, that is to say, in the last analysis, a tenderness. . . . These word objects without link, armed with all the violence of their explosive power . . . these poetic words exclude men. There is no poetic humanism in "modernity": this heady discourse is a discourse full of terror which means that it relates man not to other men, but to the most inhuman images of nature, heaven, hell, the sacred, childhood, madness, pure matter etc. *Ibid.*, p. 73 f.

verraucht, den die Menschen in ihrer eigenen technifizierten Welt verweigert finden.[13]

Or, the work of Bertolt Brecht preserves the *"promesse de bonheur"* contained in romance and Kitsch (moonshine and the blue sea; melody and sweet home; loyalty and love) by making it into political ferment. His characters sing of lost paradises and of unforgettable hope ("Siehst du den Mond über Soho, Geliebter?" "Jedoch eines Tages, und der Tag war blau." "Zuerst war es immer Sonntag." "Und ein Schiff mit acht Segeln." "Alter Bilbao Mond, Da wo noch Liebe lohnt")—and the song is one of cruelty and greed, exploitation, cheating, and lies. The deceived sing of their deception, but they learn (or have learned) its causes, and it is only in learning the causes (and how to cope with them) that they regain the truth of their dream.

The efforts to recapture the Great Refusal in the language of literature suffer the fate of being absorbed by what they refute. As modern classics, the avant-garde and the beatniks share in the function of entertaining without endangering the good conscience of the men of good will. This absorption is justified by technical progress; the refusal is refuted by the alleviation of misery in the advanced industrial society. The liquidation of high culture is a by-product of the conquest of nature, and of the progressing conquest of scarcity.

Invalidating the cherished images of transcendence by incorporating them into its omnipresent daily reality, this society testifies to the extent to which insoluble conflicts are becoming manageable—to which tragedy and romance, ar-

13. "[Surrealist paintings] . . . gathered together what functionalism covers with taboos because it betrays reality as reification and the irrational in its rationality. Surrealism recaptures what functionalism denies to man; the distortions demonstrate what the taboo did to the desired. Thus surrealism rescues the obsolete—an album of idiosyncrasies where the claim for happiness evaporates that which the technified world refuses to man." Theodor W. Adorno, *Noten zur Literatur.* (Berlin-Frankfurt, Suhrkamp, 1958), p. 160.

chetypal dreams and anxieties are being made susceptible to technical solution and dissolution. The psychiatrist takes care of the Don Juans, Romeos, Hamlets, Fausts, as he takes care of Oedipus—he cures them. The rulers of the world are losing their metaphysical features. Their appearance on television, at press conferences, in parliament, and at public hearings is hardly suitable for drama beyond that of the advertisement,[14] while the consequences of their actions surpass the scope of the drama.

The prescriptions for inhumanity and injustice are being administered by a rationally organized bureaucracy, which is, however, invisible at its vital center. The soul contains few secrets and longings which cannot be sensibly discussed, analyzed, and polled. Solitude, the very condition which sustained the individual against and beyond his society, has become technically impossible. Logical and linguistic analysis demonstrate that the old metaphysical problems are illusory problems; the quest for the "meaning" of things can be reformulated as the quest for the meaning of words, and the established universe of discourse and behavior can provide perfectly adequate criteria for the answer.

It is a rational universe which, by the mere weight and capabilities of its apparatus, blocks all escape. In its relation to the reality of daily life, the high culture of the past was many things—opposition and adornment, outcry and resignation. But it was also the appearance of the realm of freedom: the refusal to behave. Such refusal cannot be blocked without a compensation which seems more satisfying than the refusal. The conquest and unification of opposites, which finds its ideological glory in the transformation of higher into popular culture, takes place on a material ground of

14. The legendary revolutionary hero still exists who can defy even television and the press—his world is that of the "underdeveloped" countries.

increased satisfaction. This is also the ground which allows a sweeping *desublimation*.

Artistic alienation is sublimation. It creates the images of conditions which are irreconcilable with the established Reality Principle but which, as cultural images, become tolerable, even edifying and useful. Now this imagery is invalidated. Its incorporation into the kitchen, the office, the shop; its commercial release for business and fun is, in a sense, desublimation—replacing mediated by immediate gratification. But it is desublimation practiced from a "position of strength" on the part of society, which can afford to grant more than before because its interests have become the innermost drives of its citizens, and because the joys which it grants promote social cohesion and contentment.

The Pleasure Principle absorbs the Reality Principle; sexuality is liberated (or rather liberalized) in socially constructive forms. This notion implies that there are repressive modes of desublimation,[15] compared with which the sublimated drives and objectives contain more deviation, more freedom, and more refusal to heed the social taboos. It appears that such repressive desublimation is indeed operative in the sexual sphere, and here, as in the desublimation of higher culture, it operates as the by-product of the social controls of technological reality, which extend liberty while intensifying domination. The link between desublimation and technological society can perhaps best be illuminated by discussing the change in the social use of instinctual energy.

In this society, not all the time spent on and with mechanisms is labor time (i.e., unpleasurable but necessary toil), and not all the energy saved by the machine is labor power. Mechanization has also "saved" libido, the energy of the Life Instincts—that is, has barred it from previous modes of realization. This is the kernel of truth in the romantic con-

15. See my book *Eros and Civilization* (Boston: Beacon Press, 1954), esp. Chapter X.

trast between the modern traveler and the wandering poet or artisan, between assembly line and handicraft, town and city, factory-produced bread and the home-made loaf, the sailboat and the outboard motor, etc. True, this romantic pre-technical world was permeated with misery, toil, and filth, and these in turn were the background of all pleasure and joy. Still, there was a "landscape," a medium of libidinal experience which no longer exists.

With its disappearance (itself a historical prerequisite of progress), a whole dimension of human activity and passivity has been de-eroticized. The environment from which the individual could obtain pleasure—which he could cathect as gratifying almost as an extended zone of the body—has been rigidly reduced. Consequently, the "universe" of libidinous cathexis is likewise reduced. The effect is a localization and contraction of libido, the reduction of erotic to sexual experience and satisfaction.[16]

For example, compare love-making in a meadow and in an automobile, on a lovers' walk outside the town walls and on a Manhattan street. In the former cases, the environment partakes of and invites libidinal cathexis and tends to be eroticized. Libido transcends beyond the immediate erotogenic zones—a process of nonrepressive sublimation. In contrast, a mechanized environment seems to block such self-transcendence of libido. Impelled in the striving to extend the field of erotic gratification, libido becomes less "polymorphous," less capable of eroticism beyond localized sexuality, and the *latter* is intensified.

Thus diminishing erotic and intensifying sexual energy, the technological reality *limits the scope of sublimation.* It also reduces the *need* for sublimation. In the mental apparatus, the tension between that which is desired and that which

16. In accordance with the terminology used in the later works of Freud: sexuality as "specialized" partial drive; Eros as that of the entire organism.

is permitted seems considerably lowered, and the Reality Principle no longer seems to require a sweeping and painful transformation of instinctual needs. The individual must adapt himself to a world which does not seem to demand the denial of his innermost needs—a world which is not essentially hostile. The organism is thus being preconditioned for the spontaneous acceptance of what is offered. Inasmuch as the greater liberty involves a contraction rather than extension and development of instinctual needs, it works *for* rather than *against* the status quo of general repression—one might speak of "institutionalized desublimation." The latter appears to be a vital factor in the making of the authoritarian personality of our time.

It has often been noted that advanced industrial civilization operates with a greater degree of sexual freedom— "operates" in the sense that the latter becomes a market value and a factor of social mores. Without ceasing to be an instrument of labor, the body is allowed to exhibit its sexual features in the everyday work world and in work relations. This is one of the unique achievements of industrial society—rendered possible by the reduction of dirty and heavy physical labor; by the availability of cheap, attractive clothing, beauty culture, and physical hygiene; by the requirements of the advertising industry, etc. The sexy office and sales girls, the handsome, virile junior executive and floor walker are highly marketable commodities, and the possession of suitable mistresses—once the prerogative of kings, princes, and lords—facilitates the career of even the less exalted ranks in the business community.

Functionalism, going artistic, promotes this trend. Shops and offices open themselves through huge glass windows and expose their personnel; inside, high counters and non-transparent partitions are coming down. The corrosion of privacy in massive apartment houses and suburban homes breaks the barrier which formerly separated the individual from the public existence and exposes more easily the attractive qualities of other wives and other husbands.

This socialization is not contradictory but complementary to the de-erotization of the environment. Sex is integrated into work and public relations and is thus made more susceptible to (controlled) satisfaction. Technical progress and more comfortable living permit the systematic inclusion of libidinal components into the realm of commodity production and exchange. But no matter how controlled the mobilization of instinctual energy may be (it sometimes amounts to a scientific management of libido), no matter how much it may serve as a prop for the status quo—it is also gratifying to the managed individuals, just as racing the outboard motor, pushing the power lawn mower, and speeding the automobile are fun.

This mobilization and administration of libido may account for much of the voluntary compliance, the absence of terror, the pre-established harmony between individual needs and socially-required desires, goals, and aspirations. The technological and political conquest of the transcending factors in human existence, so characteristic of advanced industrial civilization, here asserts itself in the instinctual sphere: satisfaction in a way which generates submission and weakens the rationality of protest.

The range of socially permissible and desirable satisfaction is greatly enlarged, but through this satisfaction, the Pleasure Principle is reduced—deprived of the claims which are irreconcilable with the established society. Pleasure, thus adjusted, generates submission.

In contrast to the pleasures of adjusted desublimation, sublimation preserves the consciousness of the renunciations which the repressive society inflicts upon the individual, and thereby preserves the need for liberation. To be sure, all sublimation is enforced by the power of society, but the unhappy consciousness of this power already breaks through alienation. To be sure, all sublimation accepts the social barrier to instinctual gratification, but it also transgresses this barrier.

The Superego, in censoring the unconscious and in implanting conscience, also censors the censor because the developed conscience registers the forbidden evil act not only in the individual but also in his society. Conversely, loss of conscience due to the satisfactory liberties granted by an unfree society makes for a *happy consciousness* which facilitates acceptance of the misdeeds of this society. It is the token of declining autonomy and comprehension. Sublimation demands a high degree of autonomy and comprehension; it is mediation between the conscious and the unconscious, between the primary and secondary processes, between the intellect and instinct, renunciation and rebellion. In its most accomplished modes, such as in the artistic *oeuvre*, sublimation becomes the cognitive power which defeats suppression while bowing to it.

In the light of the cognitive function of this mode of sublimation, the desublimation rampant in advanced industrial society reveals its truly conformist function. This liberation of sexuality (and of aggressiveness) frees the instinctual drives from much of the unhappiness and discontent that elucidate the repressive power of the established universe of satisfaction. To be sure, there is pervasive unhappiness, and the happy consciousness is shaky enough—a thin surface over fear, frustration, and disgust. This unhappiness lends itself easily to political mobilization; without room for conscious development, it may become the instinctual reservoir for a new fascist way of life and death. But there are many ways in which the unhappiness beneath the happy consciousness may be turned into a source of strength and cohesion for the social order. The conflicts of the unhappy individual now seem far more amenable to cure than those which made for Freud's "discontent in civilization," and they seem more adequately defined in terms of the "neurotic personality of our time" than in terms of the eternal struggle between Eros and Thanatos.

The way in which controlled desublimation may weaken the instinctual revolt against the established Reality Principle may be illuminated by the contrast between the representation of sexuality in classical and romantic literature and in our contemporary literature. If one selects, from among the works which are, in their very substance and inner form, determined by the erotic commitment, such essentially different examples as Racine's *Phèdre*, Goethe's *Wahlverwandtschaften*, Baudelaire's *Les Fleurs du Mal*, Tolstoy's *Anna Karenina*, sexuality consistently appears in a highly sublimated, "mediated," reflective form—but in this form, it is absolute, uncompromising, unconditional. The dominion of Eros is, from the beginning, also that of Thanatos. Fulfillment is destruction, not in a moral or sociological but in an ontological sense. It is beyond good and evil, beyond social morality, and thus it remains beyond the reaches of the established Reality Principle, which this Eros refuses and explodes.

In contrast, desublimated sexuality is rampant in O'Neill's alcoholics and Faulkner's savages, in the *Streetcar Named Desire* and under the *Hot Tin Roof*, in *Lolita*, in all the stories of Hollywood and New York orgies, and the adventures of suburban housewives. This is infinitely more realistic, daring, uninhibited. It is part and parcel of the society in which it happens, but nowhere its negation. What happens is surely wild and obscene, virile and tasty, quite immoral—and, precisely because of that, perfectly harmless.

Freed from the sublimated form which was the very token of its irreconcilable dreams—a form which is the style, the language in which the story is told—sexuality turns into a vehicle for the bestsellers of oppression. It could not be said of any of the sexy women in contemporary literature what Balzac says of the whore Esther: that hers was the tenderness which blossoms only in infinity. This society turns everything it touches into a potential source of progress *and* of exploitation, of drudgery *and* satisfaction, of freedom *and* of oppression. Sexuality is no exception.

The concept of controlled desublimation would imply the possibility of a simultaneous release of repressed sexuality *and* aggressiveness, a possibility which seems incompatible with Freud's notion of the fixed quantum of instinctual energy available for distribution between the two primary drives. According to Freud, strengthening of sexuality (libido) would necessarily involve weakening of aggressiveness, and vice versa. However, if the socially permitted and encouraged release of libido would be that of partial and localized sexuality, it would be tantamount to an actual compression of erotic energy, and this desublimation would be compatible with the growth of unsublimated as well as sublimated forms of aggressiveness. The latter is rampant throughout contemporary industrial society.

Has it attained a degree of normalization where the individuals are getting used to the risk of their own dissolution and disintegration in the course of normal national preparedness? Or is this acquiescence entirely due to their impotence to do much about it? In any case, the risk of avoidable, man-made destruction has become normal equipment in the mental as well as material household of the people, so that it can no longer serve to indict or refute the established social system. Moreover, as part of their daily household, it may even tie them to this system. The economic and political connection between the absolute enemy and the high standard of living (and the desired level of employment!) is transparent enough, but also rational enough to be accepted.

Assuming that the Destruction Instinct (in the last analysis: the Death Instinct) is a large component of the energy which feeds the technical conquest of man and nature, it seems that society's growing capacity to manipulate technical progress also increases its *capacity to manipulate and control this instinct*, i.e., to satisfy it "productively." Then social cohesion would be strengthened at the deepest instinctual roots. The supreme risk, and even the fact of war would meet, not only with helpless acceptance, but also with instinctual approval on the part of the victims. Here too, we would have controlled desublimation.

Institutionalized desublimation thus appears to be an aspect of the "conquest of transcendence" achieved by the one-dimensional society. Just as this society tends to reduce, and even absorb opposition (the qualitative difference!) in the realm of politics and higher culture, so it does in the instinctual sphere. The result is the atrophy of the mental organs for grasping the contradictions and the alternatives and, in the one remaining dimension of technological rationality, the *Happy Consciousness* comes to prevail.

It reflects the belief that the real is rational, and that the established system, in spite of everything, delivers the goods. The people are led to find in the productive apparatus the effective agent of thought and action to which their personal thought and action can and must be surrendered. And in this transfer, the apparatus also assumes the role of a moral agent. Conscience is absolved by reification, by the general necessity of things.

In this general necessity, guilt has no place. One man can give the signal that liquidates hundreds and thousands of people, then declare himself free from all pangs of conscience, and live happily ever after. The antifascist powers who beat fascism on the battlefields reap the benefits of the

Nazi scientists, generals, and engineers; they have the historical advantage of the late-comer. What begins as the horror of the concentration camps turns into the practice of training people for abnormal conditions—a subterranean human existence and the daily intake of radioactive nourishment. A Christian minister declares that it does not contradict Christian principles to prevent with all available means your neighbor from entering your bomb shelter. Another Christian minister contradicts his colleague and says it does. Who is right? Again, the neutrality of technological rationality shows forth over and above politics, and again it shows forth as spurious, for in both cases, it serves the politics of domination.

"The world of the concentration camps . . . was not an exceptionally monstrous society. What we saw there was the image, and in a sense the quintessence, of the infernal society into which we are plunged every day." [17]

It seems that even the most hideous transgressions can be repressed in such a manner that, for all practical purposes, they have ceased to be a danger for society. Or, if their eruption leads to functional disturbances in the individual (as in the case of one Hiroshima pilot), it does not disturb the functioning of society. A mental hospital manages the disturbance.

The Happy Consciousness has no limits—it arranges games with death and disfiguration in which fun, team work, and strategic importance mix in rewarding social harmony. The Rand Corporation, which unites scholarship, research, the military, the climate, and the good life, reports such

17. E. Ionesco, in *Nouvelle Revue Française*, July 1956, as quoted in *London Times Literary Supplement*, March 4, 1960. Herman Kahn suggests in a 1959 RAND study (RM-2206-RC) that "a study should be made of the survival of populations in environments similar to overcrowded shelters (concentration camps, Russian and German use of crowded freight cars, troopships, crowded prisons . . . etc.). Some useful guiding principles might be found and adapted to the shelter program."

games in a style of absolving cuteness, in its "RANDom News," volume 9, number 1, under the heading BETTER SAFE THAN SORRY. The rockets are rattling, the H-bomb is waiting, and the space-flights are flying, and the problem is "how to guard the nation and the free world." In all this, the military planners are worried, for "the cost of taking chances, of experimenting and making a mistake, may be fearfully high." But here RAND comes in; RAND relieves, and "devices like RAND'S SAFE come into the picture." The picture into which they come is unclassified. It is a picture in which "the world becomes a map, missiles merely symbols [long live the soothing power of symbolism!], and wars just [just] plans and calculations written down on paper . . ." In this picture, RAND has transfigured the world into an interesting technological game, and one can relax—the "military planners can gain valuable 'synthetic' experience without risk."

PLAYING THE GAME

To understand the game one should participate, for understanding is "in the experience."

Because SAFE players have come from almost every department at RAND as well as the Air Force, we might find a physicist, an engineer, and an economist on the Blue team. The Red team will represent a similar cross-section.

The first day is taken up by a joint briefing on what the game is all about and a study of the rules. When the teams are finally seated around the maps in their respective rooms the game begins. Each team receives its policy statement from the Game Director. These statements, usually prepared by a member of the Control Group, give an estimate of the world situation at the time of playing, some information on the policy of the opposing team, the objectives to be met by the team, and the team's budget. (The policies are changed for each game to explore a wide range of strategic possibilities.)

> In our hypothetical game, Blue's objective is to maintain
> a deterrent capability throughout the game—that is, main-
> tain a force that is capable of striking back at Red so Red
> will be unwilling to risk an attack. (Blue also receives some
> information on the Red policy.)
>
> Red's policy is to achieve force superiority over Blue.
>
> The budgets of Blue and Red compare with actual de-
> fense budgets . . .

It is comforting to hear that the game has been played
since 1961 at RAND, "down in our labyrinthine basement—
somewhere under the Snack Bar," and that "Menus on the
walls of the Red and Blue rooms list available weapons and
hardware that the teams buy . . . About seventy items in
all." There is a "Game Director" who interprets game rules,
for although "the rule book complete with diagrams and
illustrations is 66 pages," problems inevitably arise during
the play. The Game Director also has another important
function: "without previously notifying the players," he "introduces war to get a measure of the effectiveness of the
military forces in being." But then, the caption announces
"Coffee, Cake, and Ideas." Relax! The "game continues
through the remaining periods—to 1972 when it ends. Then
the Blue and Red teams bury the missiles and sit down together for coffee and cake at the 'post mortem' session." But
don't relax too much: there is "one real-world situation that
can't be transposed effectively to SAFE," and that is—
"negotiation." We are grateful for it: the one hope that is
left in the real world situation is beyond the reaches of
RAND.

Obviously, in the realm of the Happy Consciousness,
guilt feeling has no place, and the calculus takes care of
conscience. When the whole is at stake, there is no crime
except that of rejecting the whole, or not defending it.
Crime, guilt, and guilt feeling become a private affair. Freud
revealed in the psyche of the individual the crimes of man-

kind, in the individual case history the history of the whole. This fatal link is successfully suppressed. Those who identify themselves with the whole, who are installed as the leaders and defenders of the whole can make mistakes, but they cannot do wrong—they are not guilty. They may become guilty again when this identification no longer holds, when they are gone.

4: The Closing of the
Universe of Discourse

"Dans l'état présent de l'Histoire, toute écriture politique ne peut que confirmer un univers policier, de même toute écriture intellectuelle ne peut qu'instituer une para-littérature, qui n'ose plus dire son nom."

"In the present state of history, all political writing can only confirm a police-universe, just as all intellectual writing can only produce para-literature which does not dare any longer to tell its name."

ROLAND BARTHES

The Happy Consciousness—the belief that the real is rational and that the system delivers the goods—reflects the new conformism which is a facet of technological rationality translated into social behavior. It is new because it is rational to an unprecedented degree. It sustains a society which has reduced—and in its most advanced areas eliminated—the more primitive irrationality of the preceding stages, which prolongs and improves life more regularly than before. The war of annihilation has not yet occurred; the Nazi extermination camps have been abolished. The Happy Consciousness repels the connection. Torture has been reintroduced as a normal affair, but in a colonial war which takes place at the margin of the civilized world. And there it is practiced with good conscience for war is war. And this war, too, is at the margin—it ravages only the "underdeveloped" countries. Otherwise, peace reigns.

The power over man which this society has acquired is daily absolved by its efficacy and productiveness. If it assimilates everything it touches, if it absorbs the opposition, if it plays with the contradiction, it demonstrates its cultural superiority. And in the same way the destruction of resources and the proliferation of waste demonstrate its opulence and the "high levels of well-being"; "the Community is too well off to care!" [1]

The Language of Total Administration

This sort of well-being, the productive superstructure over the unhappy base of society, permeates the "media" which mediate between the masters and their dependents. Its publicity agents shape the universe of communication in which the one-dimensional behavior expresses itself. Its language testifies to identification and unification, to the systematic promotion of positive thinking and doing, to the concerted attack on transcendent, critical notions. In the prevailing modes of speech, the contrast appears between two-dimensional, dialectical modes of thought and technological behavior or social "habits of thought."

In the expression of these habits of thought, the tension between appearance and reality, fact and factor, substance and attribute tend to disappear. The elements of autonomy, discovery, demonstration, and critique recede before designation, assertion, and imitation. Magical, authoritarian and ritual elements permeate speech and language. Discourse is deprived of the mediations which are the stages of the process of cognition and cognitive evaluation. The concepts which comprehend the facts and thereby transcend the facts are losing their authentic linguistic representation. Without these mediations, language tends to express and promote the immediate identification of reason and fact, truth and established truth, essence and existence, the thing and its function.

These identifications, which appeared as a feature of operationalism,[2] reappear as features of discourse in social

1. John K. Galbraith, *American Capitalism;* (Boston, Houghton Mifflin, 1956), p. 96.
2. See p. 12.

behavior. Here functionalization of language helps to repel non-conformist elements from the structure and movement of speech. Vocabulary and syntax are equally affected. Society expresses its requirements directly in the linguistic material but not without opposition; the popular language strikes with spiteful and defiant humor at the official and semi-official discourse Slang and colloquial speech have rarely been so creative. It is as if the common man (or his anonymous spokesman) would in his speech assert his humanity against the powers that be, as if the rejection and revolt, subdued in the political sphere, would burst out in the vocabulary that calls things by their names: "head-shrinker" and "egghead," "boob tube," "think tank," "beat it" and "dig it," and "gone, man, gone."

However, the defense laboratories and the executive offices, the governments and the machines, the time-keepers and managers, the efficiency experts and the political beauty parlors (which provide the leaders with the appropriate make-up) speak a different language and, for the time being, they seem to have the last word. It is the word that orders and organizes, that induces people to do, to buy, and to accept. It is transmitted in a style which is a veritable linguistic creation; a syntax in which the structure of the sentence is abridged and condensed in such a way that no tension, no "space" is left between the parts of the sentence. This linguistic form militates against a development of meaning. I shall presently try to illustrate this style.

The feature of operationalism—to make the concept synonymous with the corresponding set of operations[3]— recurs in the linguistic tendency "to consider the names of things as being indicative at the same time of their manner of functioning, and the names of properties and processes as symbolical of the apparatus used to detect or produce

3. See p. 13.

them." [4] This is technological reasoning, which tends "to identify things and their functions." [5]

As a habit of thought outside the scientific and technical language, such reasoning shapes the expression of a specific social and political behaviorism. In this behavioral universe, words and concepts tend to coincide, or rather the concept tends to be absorbed by the word. The former has no other content than that designated by the word in the publicized and standardized usage, and the word is expected to have no other response than the publicized and standardized behavior (reaction). The word becomes *cliché* and, as cliché, governs the speech or the writing; the communication thus precludes genuine development of meaning.

To be sure, any language contains innumerable terms which do not require development of their meaning, such as the terms designating the objects and implements of daily life, visible nature, vital needs and wants. These terms are generally understood so that their mere appearance produces a response (linguistic or operational) adequate to the pragmatic context in which they are spoken.

The situation is very different with respect to terms which denote things or occurrences beyond this noncontroversial context. Here, the functionalization of language expresses an abridgement of meaning which has a political connotation. The names of things are not only "indicative of their manner of functioning," but their (actual) manner of functioning also defines and "closes" the meaning of the thing, excluding other manners of functioning. The noun governs the sentence in an authoritarian and totalitarian fashion, and the sentence becomes a declaration to be accepted—it repels demonstration, qualification, negation of its codified and declared meaning.

4. Stanley Gerr, "Language and Science," in: *Philosophy of Science,* April 1942, p. 156.
  5. *Ibid.*

At the nodal points of the universe of public discourse, self-validating, analytical propositions appear which function like magic-ritual formulas. Hammered and re-hammered into the recipient's mind, they produce the effect of enclosing it within the circle of the conditions prescribed by the formula.

I have already referred to the self-validating hypothesis as propositional form in the universe of political discourse.[6] Such nouns as "freedom," "equality," "democracy," and "peace" imply, analytically, a specific set of attributes which occur invariably when the noun is spoken or written. In the West, the analytic predication is in such terms as free enterprise, initiative, elections, individual; in the East in terms of workers and peasants, building communism or socialism, abolition of hostile classes. On either side, transgression of the discourse beyond the closed analytical structure is incorrect or propaganda, although the means of enforcing the truth and the degree of punishment are very different. In this universe of public discourse, speech moves in synonyms and tautologies; actually, it never moves toward the qualitative difference. The analytic structure insulates the governing noun from those of its contents which would invalidate or at least disturb the accepted use of the noun in statements of policy and public opinion. The ritualized concept is made immune against contradiction.

Thus, the fact that the prevailing mode of freedom is servitude, and that the prevailing mode of equality is superimposed inequality is barred from expression by the closed definition of these concepts in terms of the powers which shape the respective universe of discourse. The result is the familiar Orwellian language ("peace is war" and "war is peace," etc.), which is by no means that of terroristic totalitarianism only. Nor is it any less Orwellian if the contradiction is not made explicit in the sentence but is enclosed in

6. See p. 14.

the noun. That a political party which works for the defense and growth of capitalism is called "Socialist," and a despotic government "democratic," and a rigged election "free" are familiar linguistic—and political—features which long pre-date Orwell.

Relatively new is the general acceptance of these lies by public and private opinion, the suppression of their monstrous content. The spread and the effectiveness of this language testify to the triumph of society over the contradictions which it contains; they are reproduced without exploding the social system. And it is the outspoken, blatant contradiction which is made into a device of speech and publicity. The syntax of abridgment proclaims the reconciliation of opposites by welding them together in a firm and familiar structure. I shall attempt to show that the "clean bomb" and the "harmless fall-out" are only the extreme creations of a normal style. Once considered the principal offense against logic, the contradiction now appears as a principle of the logic of manipulation—realistic caricature of dialectics. It is the logic of a society which can afford to dispense with logic and play with destruction, a society with technological mastery of mind and matter.

The universe of discourse in which the opposites are reconciled has a firm basis for such unification—its beneficial destructiveness. Total commercialization joins formerly antagonistic spheres of life, and this union expresses itself in the smooth linguistic conjunction of conflicting parts of speech. To a mind not yet sufficiently conditioned, much of the public speaking and printing appears utterly surrealistic. Captions such as "Labor is Seeking Missile Harmony," [7] and advertisements such as a "Luxury Fall-Out Shelter" [8] may still evoke the naïve reaction that "Labor," "Missile," and "Harmony" are irreconcilable contradictions, and that no

7. *New York Times*, December 1, 1960.
8. *Ibid.*, November 2, 1960.

logic and no language should be capable of correctly joining luxury and fall-out. However, the logic and the language become perfectly rational when we learn that a "nuclear-powered, ballistic-missile-firing submarine" "carries a price tag of $120,000,000" and that "carpeting, scrabble and TV" are provided in the $1,000 model of the shelter. The validation is not primarily in the fact that this language sells (it seems that the fall-out business was not so good) but rather that it promotes the immediate identification of the particular with the general interest, Business with National Power, prosperity with the annihilation potential. It is only a slip of the truth if a theater announces as a "Special Election Eve Perf., Strindberg's *Dance of Death*." [9] The announcement reveals the connection in a less ideological form than is normally admitted.

The unification of opposites which characterizes the commercial and political style is one of the many ways in which discourse and communication make themselves immune against the expression of protest and refusal. How can such protest and refusal find the right word when the organs of the established order admit and advertise that peace is really the brink of war, that the ultimate weapons carry their profitable price tags, and that the bomb shelter may spell coziness? In exhibiting its contradictions as the token of its truth, this universe of discourse closes itself against any other discourse which is not on its own terms. And, by its capacity to assimilate all other terms to its own, it offers the prospect of combining the greatest possible tolerance with the greatest possible unity. Nevertheless its language testifies to the repressive character of this unity. This language speaks in constructions which impose upon the recipient the slanted and abridged meaning, the blocked de-

9. *Ibid.*, November 7, 1960.

velopment of content, the acceptance of that which is offered in the form in which it is offered.

The analytic predication is such a repressive construction. The fact that a specific noun is almost always coupled with the same "explicatory" adjectives and attributes makes the sentence into a hypnotic formula which, endlessly repeated, fixes the meaning in the recipient's mind. He does not think of essentially different (and possibly true) explications of the noun. Later we shall examine other constructions in which the authoritarian character of this language reveals itself. They have in common a telescoping and abridgment of syntax which cuts off development of meaning by creating fixed images which impose themselves with an overwhelming and petrified concreteness. It is the well-known technique of the advertisement industry, where it is methodically used for "establishing an image" which sticks to the mind and to the product, and helps to sell the men and the goods. Speech and writing are grouped around "impact lines" and "audience rousers" which convey the image. This image may be "freedom" or "peace," or the "nice guy" or the "communist" or "Miss Rheingold." The reader or listener is expected to associate (and does associate) with them a fixated structure of institutions, attitudes, aspirations, and he is expected to react in a fixated, specific manner.

Beyond the relatively harmless sphere of merchandising, the consequences are rather serious, for such language is at one and the same time "intimidation and glorification." [10] Propositions assume the form of suggestive commands—they are evocative rather than demonstrative. Predication becomes prescription; the whole communication has a hypnotic character. At the same time it is tinged with a false familiarity—the result of constant repetition, and of the

10. Roland Barthes, *Le Degré zéro de l'écriture*, (Paris, Editions du Seuil, 1953), p. 33.

skillfully managed popular directness of the communication. This relates itself to the recipient immediately—without distance of status, education, and office—and hits him or her in the informal atmosphere of the living room, kitchen, and bedroom.

The same familiarity is established through personalized language, which plays a considerable role in advanced communication.[11] It is "your" congressman, "your" highway, "your" favorite drugstore, "your" newspaper; it is brought "to you," it invites "you," etc. In this manner, superimposed, standardized, and general things and functions are presented as "especially for you." It makes little difference whether or not the individuals thus addressed believe it. Its success indicates that it promotes the self-identification of the individuals with the functions which they and the others perform.

In the most advanced sectors of functional and manipulated communication, language imposes in truly striking constructions the authoritarian identification of person and function. *Time* magazine may serve as an extreme example of this trend. Its use of the inflectional genitive makes individuals appear to be mere appendices or properties of their place, their job, their employer, or enterprise. They are introduced as Virginia's Byrd, U. S. Steel's Blough, Egypt's Nasser. A hyphenated attributive construction creates a fixed syndrome:

"Georgia's high-handed, low-browed governor . . . had the stage all set for one of his wild political rallies last week."

The governor,[12] his function, his physical features, and his political practices are fused together into one indivisible and

---

11. See Leo Lowenthal, *Literature, Popular Culture, and Society* (Prentice-Hall, 1961), p. 109 ff. and Richard Hoggart, *The Uses of Literacy* Boston, Beacon Press, 1961), p. 161 ff.

12. The statement refers, not to the present Governor, but to Mr. Talmadge.

immutable structure which, in its natural innocence and immediacy, overwhelms the reader's mind. The structure leaves no space for distinction, development, differentiation of meaning: it moves and lives only as a whole. Dominated by such personalized and hypnotic images, the article can then proceed to give even essential information. The narrative remains safely within the well-edited framework of a more or less human interest story as defined by the publisher's policy.

Use of the hyphenized abridgment is widespread. For example, "brush-browed" Teller, the "father of the H-bomb," "bull-shouldered missileman von Braun," "science-military dinner" [13] and the "nuclear-powered, ballistic-missile-firing" submarine. Such constructions are, perhaps not accidentally, particularly frequent in phrases joining technology, politics, and the military. Terms designating quite different spheres or qualities are forced together into a solid, overpowering whole.

The effect is again a magical and hypnotic one—the projection of images which convey irresistible unity, harmony of contradictions. Thus the loved and feared Father, the spender of life, generates the H-bomb for the annihilation of life; "science-military" joins the efforts to reduce anxiety and suffering with the job of creating anxiety and suffering. Or, without the hyphen, the Freedom Academy of cold war specialists,[14] and the "clean bomb"—attributing to destruction moral and physical integrity. People who speak and accept such language seem to be immune to everything —and susceptible to everything. Hyphenation (explicit or not) does not always reconcile the irreconcilable; frequently,

13. The last three items quoted in *The Nation*, Feb. 22, 1958.
14. A suggestion of *Life* magazine, quoted in *The Nation*, August 20, 1960. According to David Sarnoff, a bill to establish such an Academy is before Congress. See John K. Jessup, Adlai Stevenson, and others, *The National Purpose* (produced under the supervision and with the help of the editorial staff of *Life* magazine, New York, Holt, Rinehart and Winston, 1960), p. 58.

the combine is quite gentle—as in the case of the "bull-shouldered missileman"—or it conveys a threat, or an inspiring dynamic. But the effect is similar. The imposing structure unites the actors and actions of violence, power, protection, and propaganda in one lightning flash. We see the man or the thing in operation and only in operation—it cannot be otherwise.

Note on abridgment. NATO, SEATO, UN, AFL-CIO, AEC, but also USSR, DDR, etc. Most of these abbreviations are perfectly reasonable and justified by the length of the unabbreviated designata. However, one might venture to see in some of them a "cunning of Reason"—the abbreviation may help to repress undesired questions. NATO does not suggest what North Atlantic Treaty Organization says, namely, a treaty among the nations on the North-Atlantic— in which case one might ask questions about the membership of Greece and Turkey. USSR abbreviates Socialism and Soviet; DDR: democratic. UN dispenses with undue emphasis on "united"; SEATO with those Southeast-Asian countries which do not belong to it. AFL-CIO entombs the radical political differences which once separated the two organizations, and AEC is just one administrative agency among many others. The abbreviations denote that and only that which is institutionalized in such a way that the transcending connotation is cut off. The meaning is fixed, doctored, loaded. Once it has become an official vocable, constantly repeated in general usage, "sanctioned" by the intellectuals, it has lost all cognitive value and serves merely for recognition of an unquestionable fact.

This style is of an overwhelming *concreteness*. The "thing identified with its function" is more real than the thing distinguished from its function, and the linguistic expression of this identification (in the functional noun, and in the many forms of syntactical abridgment) creates a basic vocabulary and syntax which stand in the way of differentiation, separation, and distinction. This language, which constantly imposes *images*, militates against the development and expression of *concepts*. In its immediacy and directness, it impedes conceptual thinking; thus, it impedes thinking. For the concept does *not* identify the thing and its function. Such identification may well be the legitimate and perhaps even the only meaning of the operational and technological concept, but operational and technological definitions are specific usages of concepts for specific purposes. Moreover, they dissolve concepts in operations and exclude the conceptual intent which is opposed to such dissolution. Prior to its operational usage, the concept *denies* the identification of the thing with its function; it distinguishes that which the thing *is* from the contingent functions of the thing in the established reality.

The prevalent tendencies of speech, which repulse these distinctions, are expressive of the changes in the modes of thought discussed in the earlier chapters—the functionalized, abridged and unified language is the language of one-dimensional thought. In order to illustrate its novelty, I shall contrast it briefly with a classical philosophy of grammar which transcends the behavioral universe and relates linguistic to ontological categories.

According to this philosophy, the grammatical subject of a sentence is first a "substance" and remains such in the various states, functions, and qualities which the sentence predicates of the subject. It is actively or passively related to its predicates but remains different from them. If it is not a proper noun, the subject is more than a noun: it names the *concept* of a thing, a universal which the sentence defines as in a particular state or function. The grammatical subject thus carries a meaning in *excess* of that expressed in the sentence.

In the words of Wilhelm von Humboldt: the noun as grammatical subject denotes something that "can enter into certain relationships," [15] but is not identical with these relationships. Moreover, it remains what it is in and "against" these relationships; it is their "universal" and substantive core. The propositional synthesis links the action (or state) with the subject in such a manner that the subject is designated as the actor (or bearer) and thus is distinguished from the state or function in which it happens to be. In saying: "lightning strikes," one "thinks not merely of the striking lightning, but of the lightning itself which strikes," of a subject which "passed into action." And if a sentence gives a definition of its subject, it does not dissolve the subject in its states and functions, but defines it as being in this state, or exercising this function. Neither disappearing in its predicates nor existing as an entity before and outside its predicates, the subject constitutes itself in its predicates—the result of a process of mediation which is expressed in the sentence.[16]

I have alluded to the philosophy of grammar in order to illuminate the extent to which the linguistic abridgments indicate an abridgment of thought which they in turn fortify and promote. Insistence on the philosophical elements in grammar, on the link between the grammatical, logical, and ontological "subject," points up the contents which are suppressed in the functional language, barred from expression and communication. Abridgment of the concept in fixed images; arrested development in self-validating, hypnotic formulas; immunity against contradiction; identification of the thing (and of the person) with its function—these tend-

15. W. v. Humboldt, *Über die Verschiedenheit des menschlichen Sprachbaues*, reprint Berlin 1936, p. 254.

16. See for this philosophy of grammar in dialectical logic Hegel's concept of the "substance as subject" and of the "speculative sentence" in the Preface to the *Phaenomenology of the Spirit*.

encies reveal the one-dimensional mind in the language it speaks.

If the linguistic behavior blocks conceptual development, if it militates against abstraction and mediation, if it surrenders to the immediate facts, it repels recognition of the factors behind the facts, and thus repels recognition of the facts, and of their historical content. In and for the society, this organization of functional discourse is of vital importance; it serves as a vehicle of coordination and subordination. The unified, functional language is an irreconcilably anti-critical and anti-dialectical language. In it, operational and behavioral rationality absorbs the transcendent, negative, oppositional elements of Reason.

I shall discuss[17] these elements in terms of the tension between the "is" and the "ought," between essence and appearance, potentiality and actuality—ingression of the negative in the positive determinations of logic. This sustained tension permeates the two-dimensional universe of discourse which is the universe of critical, abstract thought. The two dimensions are antagonistic to each other; the reality partakes of both of them, and the dialectical concepts develop the real contradictions. In its own development, dialectical thought came to comprehend the historical character of the contradictions and the process of their mediation as historical process. Thus the "other" dimension of thought appeared to be *historical* dimension—the potentiality as historical possibility, its realization as historical event.

The suppresssion of this dimension in the societal universe of operational rationality is a *suppression of history,* and this is not an academic but a political affair. It is suppression of the society's own past—and of its future, inasmuch as this future invokes the qualitative change, the negation of the present. A universe of discourse in which the categories of freedom have become interchangeable and

17. In chapter V below.

even identical with their opposites is not only practicing Orwellian or Aesopian language but is repulsing and forgetting the historical reality—the horror of fascism; the idea of socialism; the preconditions of democracy; the content of freedom. If a bureaucratic dictatorship rules and defines communist society, if fascist regimes are functioning as partners of the Free World, if the welfare program of enlightened capitalism is successfully defeated by labeling it "socialism," if the foundations of democracy are harmoniously abrogated in democracy, then the old historical concepts are invalidated by up-to-date operational redefinitions. The redefinitions are falsifications which, imposed by the powers that be and the powers of fact, serve to transform falsehood into truth.

The functional language is a radically anti-historical language: operational rationality has little room and little use for historical reason.[18] Is this fight against history part of the fight against a dimension of the mind in which centrifugal faculties and forces might develop—faculties and forces that might hinder the total coordination of the individual with the society? Remembrance of the past may give rise to dangerous insights, and the established society seems to be apprehensive of the subversive contents of memory. Remembrance is a mode of dissociation from the given facts, a mode of "mediation" which breaks, for short moments, the omnipresent power of the given facts. Memory recalls the terror and the hope that passed. Both come to life again, but whereas in reality, the former recurs in ever new forms, the latter remains hope. And in the personal events which reappear in the individual memory, the fears and aspirations of mankind assert themselves—the universal

18. This does not mean that history, private or general, disappears from the universe of discourse. The past is evoked often enough: be it as the Founding Fathers, or Marx-Engels-Lenin, or as the humble origins of a presidential candidate. However these too, are ritualized invocations which do not allow development of the content recalled; frequently, the mere invocation serves to block such development, which would show its historical impropriety.

in the particular. It is history which memory preserves. It succumbs to the totalitarian power of the behavioral universe:

Das "Schreckbild einer Menschheit ohne Erinnerung . . . ist kein blosses Verfallsprodukt . . . sondern es ist mit der Fortschritt-lichkeit des bürgerlichen Prinzips notwendig verknüpft." "Oeko-nomen und Soziologen wie Werner Sombart und Max Weber haben das Prinzip des Traditionalismus den feudalen Gesell-schaftsformen zugeordnet und das der Rationalität den bürger-lichen. Das sagt aber nicht weniger, als dass Erinnerung, Zeit, Gedächtnis von der fortschreitenden bürgerlichen Gesellschaft selber als eine Art irrationaler Rest liquidiert wird . . ." [19]

If the progressing rationality of advanced industrial society tends to liquidate, as an "irrational rest," the disturbing elements of Time and Memory, it also tends to liquidate the disturbing rationality contained in this irrational rest. Recognition and relation to the past as present counteracts the functionalization of thought by and in the established reality. It militates against the closing of the universe of discourse and behavior; it renders possible the development of concepts which de-stabilize and transcend the closed universe by comprehending it as historical universe. Confronted with the given society as object of its reflection, critical thought becomes historical consciousness; as such, it is essentially judgment.[20] Far from necessitating an indifferent relativism, it searches in the real history of man for

19. "The spectre of man without memory . . . is more than an aspect of decline—it is necessarily linked with the principle of progress in bourgeois society." "Economists and sociologists such as Werner Sombart and Max Weber correlated the principle of tradition to feudal, and that of rationality to bourgeois, forms of society. This means no less than that the advancing bourgeois society liquidates Memory, Time, Recollection as irrational leftovers of the past . . . ." Th. W. Adorno, "Wes bedeutet Aufar-beitung der Vergangenheit?", in: Bericht über die Erzieherkonferenz am 6 und 7. November in Wiesbaden; Frankfurt 1960, p. 14. The struggle against history will be further discussed in chapter VII.
20. See p. x, and chapter V.

the criteria of truth and falsehood, progress and regression.[21] The mediation of the past with the present discovers the factors which made the facts, which determined the way of life, which established the masters and the servants; it projects the limits and the alternatives. When this critical consciousness speaks, it speaks "le langage de la connaissance" (Roland Barthes) which breaks open a closed universe of discourse and its petrified structure. The key terms of this language are not hypnotic nouns which evoke endlessly the same frozen predicates. They rather allow of an open development; they even unfold their content in contradictory predicates.

The Communist Manifesto provides a classical example. Here the two key terms, Bourgeoisie and Proletariat, each "govern" contrary predicates. The "bourgeoisie" is the subject of technical progress, liberation, conquest of nature, creation of social wealth, *and* of the perversion and destruction of these achievements. Similarly, the "proletariat" carries the attributes of total oppression *and* of the total defeat of oppression.

Such dialectical relation of opposites in and by the proposition is rendered possible by the recognition of the subject as an historical agent whose identity constitutes itself in *and against* its historical practice, in *and against* its social reality. The discourse develops and states the conflict between the thing and its function, and this conflict finds linguistic expression in sentences which join contradictory predicates in a logical unit—conceptual counterpart of the objective reality. In contrast to all Orwellian language, the contradiction is demonstrated, made explicit, explained, and denounced.

I have illustrated the contrast between the two languages by referring to the style of Marxian theory, but the critical, cognitive qualities are not the exclusive character-

21. For a further discussion of these criteria see chapter VIII.

istics of the Marxian style. They can also be found (though in different modes) in the style of the great conservative and liberal critique of the unfolding bourgeois society. For example, the language of Burke and Tocqueville on the one side, of John Stuart Mill on the other is a highly demonstrative, conceptual, "open" language, which has not yet succumbed to the hypnotic-ritual formulas of present-day neo-conservatism and neo-liberalism.

However, the authoritarian ritualization of discourse is more striking where it affects the dialectical language itself. The requirements of competitive industrialization, and the total subjection of man to the productive apparatus appears in the authoritarian transformation of the Marxist into the Stalinist and post-Stalinist language. These requirements, as interpreted by the leadership which controls the apparatus, define what is right and wrong, true and false. They leave no time and no space for a discussion which would project disruptive alternatives. This language no longer lends itself to "discourse" at all. It pronounces and, by virtue of the power of the apparatus, establishes facts—it is self-validating enunciation. Here,[22] it must suffice to quote and paraphrase the passage in which Roland Barthes describes its magic-authoritarian features: "il n'y a plus aucun sursis entre la dénomination et le jugement, et la clôture du langage est parfaite . . ."[23]

The closed language does not demonstrate and explain —it communicates decision, dictum, command. Where it defines, the definition becomes "separation of good from evil"; it establishes unquestionable rights and wrongs, and one value as justification of another value. It moves in tautologies, but the tautologies are terribly effective "sentences." They pass judgment in a "prejudged form"; they pronounce

22. See my *Soviet Marxism*, loc. cit., p. 87 ff.
23. "there is no longer any delay between the naming and the judgment, and the closing of the lauguage is complete."

condemnation. For example, the "objective content," that is, the definition of such terms as "deviationist," "revisionist," is that of the penal code, and this sort of validation promotes a consciousness for which the language of the powers that be is the language of truth.[24]

Unfortunately, this is not all. The productive growth of the established communist society also condemns the libertarian communist opposition; the language which tries to recall and preserve the original truth succumbs to its ritualization. The orientation of discourse (and action) on terms such as "the proletariat," "workers' councils," the "dictatorship of the Stalinist apparatus," becomes orientation on ritual formulas where the "proletariat" no longer or not yet exists, where direct control "from below" would interfere with the progress of mass production, and where the fight against the bureaucracy would weaken the efficacy of the only real force that can be mobilized against capitalism on an international scale. Here the past is rigidly retained but not mediated with the present. One opposes the concepts which comprehended a historical situation without developing them into the present situation—one blocks their dialectic.

The ritual-authoritarian language spreads over the contemporary world, through democratic and non-democratic, capitalist and non-capitalist countries.[25] According to Roland Barthes, it is the language "propre à tous les régimes d'autorité," and is there today, in the orbit of advanced industrial civilization, a society which is not under an authoritarian regime? As the substance of the various regimes no

24. Roland Barthes, *loc. cit.*, pp. 37-40.
25. For West Germany see the intensive studies undertaken by the Institut für Sozialforschung, Frankfurt am Main, in 1950-1951: *Gruppen Experiment*, ed. F. Pollock (Frankfurt, Europaeische Verlagsanstalt, 1955) esp. p. 545 f. Also Karl Korn, *Sprache in der verwalteten Welt* (Frankfurt, Heinrich Scheffler, 1958), for both parts of Germany.

longer appears in alternative modes of life, it comes to rest in alternative techniques of manipulation and control. Language not only reflects these controls but becomes itself an instrument of control even where it does not transmit orders but information; where it demands, not obedience but choice, not submission but freedom.

This language controls by reducing the linguistic forms and symbols of reflection, abstraction, development, contradiction; by substituting images for concepts. It denies or absorbs the transcendent vocabulary; it does not search for but establishes and imposes truth and falsehood. But this kind of discourse is not terroristic. It seems unwarranted to assume that the recipients believe, or are made to believe, what they are being told. The new touch of the magic-ritual language rather is that people don't believe it, or don't care, and yet act accordingly. One does not "believe" the statement of an operational concept but it justifies itself in action—in getting the job done, in selling and buying, in refusal to listen to others, etc.

If the language of politics tends to become that of advertising, thereby bridging the gap between two formerly very different realms of society, then this tendency seems to express the degree to which domination and administration have ceased to be a separate and independent function in the technological society. This does not mean that the power of the professional politicians has decreased. The contrary is the case. The more global the challenge they build up in order to meet it, the more normal the vicinity of total destruction, the greater their freedom from effective popular sovereignty. But their domination has been incorporated into the daily performances and relaxation of the citizens, and the "symbols" of politics are also those of business, commerce, and fun.

The vicissitudes of the language have their parallel in the vicissitudes of political behavior. In the sale of equipment for relaxing entertainment in bomb shelters, in the television show of competing candidates for national leadership, the juncture between politics, business, and fun is complete. But the juncture is fraudulent and fatally premature—business and fun are still the politics of domination. This is not the satire-play after the tragedy; it is not *finis tragoediae*—the tragedy may just begin. And again, it will not be the hero but the people who will be the ritual victims.

The Research of Total Administration

Functional communication is only the outer layer of the one-dimensional universe in which man is trained to forget—to translate the negative into the positive so that he can continue to function, reduced but fit and reasonably well. The institutions of free speech and freedom of thought do not hamper the mental coordination with the established reality. What is taking place is a sweeping redefinition of thought itself, of its function and content. The coordination of the individual with his society reaches into those layers of the mind where the very concepts are elaborated which are designed to comprehend the established reality. These concepts are taken from the intellectual tradition and translated into operational terms—a translation which has the effect of reducing the tension between thought and reality by weakening the negative power of thought.

This is a philosophical development, and in order to elucidate the extent to which it breaks with the tradition, the analysis will have to become increasingly abstract and ideological. It is the sphere farthest removed from the concreteness of society which may show most clearly the extent of the conquest of thought by society. Moreover, the analysis will have to go back into the history of the philosophic tradition and try to identify the tendencies which led to the break.

However, before entering into the philosophic analysis, and as a transition to the more abstract and theoretical realm, I shall discuss briefly two (representative in my view) examples in the intermediary field of empirical research, directly concerned with certain conditions characteristic of advanced industrial society. Questions of language or of thought, of words or of concepts; linguistic or epistemological analysis—the matter to be discussed militates against such clean academic distinctions. The separation of a purely linguistic from a conceptual analysis is itself an expression of the redirection of thought which the next chapters will try to explain. Inasmuch as the following critique of empirical research is undertaken in preparation for the subsequent philosophic analysis—and in the light of it—a preliminary statement on the use of the term "concept" which guides the critique may serve as an introduction.

"Concept" is taken to designate the mental representation of something that is understood, comprehended, known as the result of a process of reflection. This something may be an object of daily practice, or a situation, a society, a novel. In any case, if they are comprehended (*begriffen; auf ihren Begriff gebracht*), they have become objects of thought, and as such, their content and meaning are identical with and yet different from the real objects of immediate experience. "Identical" in as much as the concept denotes the same thing; "different" in as much as the concept is the result of a reflection which has understood the thing in the context (and in the light) of other things which did not appear in the immediate experience and which "explain" the thing (mediation).

If the concept never denotes one particular concrete thing, if it is always abstract and general, it is so because the concept comprehends more and other than a particular thing—some universal condition or relation which is essential to the particular thing, which determines the form in which it appears as a concrete object of experience. If the concept of anything concrete is the product of mental classification, organization, and abstraction, these mental processes lead to comprehension only inasmuch as they reconstitute the particular thing in its universal condition and relation, thus transcending its immediate appearance toward its reality.

By the same token, all cognitive concepts have a *transitive meaning*: they go beyond descriptive reference to particular facts. And if the facts are those of society, the cognitive concepts also go beyond any particular context of facts—into the processes and conditions on which the respective society rests, and which enter into all particular facts, making, sustaining, and destroying the society. By virtue of their reference to this historical totality, cognitive concepts transcend all operational context, but their transcendence is empirical because it renders the facts recognizable as that which they really are.

The "excess" of meaning over and above the operational concept illuminates the limited and even deceptive form in which the facts are allowed to be experienced. Therefore the tension, the discrepancy, the conflict between the concept and the immediate fact—the thing concrete; between the word that refers to the concept and that which refers to the things. Therefore the notion of the "reality of the universal." Therefore also the uncritical, accommodating character of those modes of thought which treat concepts as mental devices and translate universal concepts into terms with particular, objective referents.

Where these reduced concepts govern the analysis of the human reality, individual or social, mental or material, they arrive at a false concreteness—a concreteness isolated from the conditions which constitute its reality. In this context, the operational treatment of the concept assumes a political function. The individual and his behavior are analyzed in a therapeutic sense—adjustment to his society. Thought and expression, theory and practice are to be brought in line with the facts of his existence without leaving room for the conceptual critique of these facts.

The therapeutic character of the operational concept shows forth most clearly where conceptual thought is methodically placed into the service of exploring and improving the existing social conditions, within the framework of the existing societal institutions—in industrial sociology, motivation research, marketing and public opinion studies.

If the given form of society is and remains the ultimate frame of reference for theory and practice, there is nothing wrong with this sort of sociology and psychology. It is more human and more productive to have good labor-management relations than bad ones, to have pleasant rather than unpleasant working conditions, to have harmony instead of conflict between the desires of the customers and the needs of business and politics.

But the rationality of this kind of social science appears in a different light if the given society, while remaining the frame of reference, becomes the object of a critical theory which aims at the very structure of this society, present in all particular facts and conditions and determining their place and their function. Then their ideological and political character becomes apparent, and the elaboration of adequately cognitive concepts demands going beyond the fallacious concreteness of positivist empiricism. The therapeutic and operational concept becomes false to the extent to which it insulates and atomizes the facts, stabilizes them within the repressive whole, and accepts the terms of this whole as the terms of the analysis. The methodological translation of the universal into the operational concept then becomes repressive reduction of thought.[26]

I shall take as an example a "classic" of industrial sociology: the study of labor relations in the Hawthorne Works of the Western Electric Company.[27] It is an old study, undertaken about a quarter of a century ago, and methods have since been much refined. But in my opinion, their substance and function have remained the same. Moreover, this mode of thought has since not only spread into other branches of social science and into philosophy, but it has also helped to shape the human subjects with whom it is concerned. The operational concepts terminate in methods of improved social control: they become part of the science of management, Department of Human Relations. In *Labor Looks At Labor* are these words of an automobile worker:

The managements "couldn't stop us on the picket line; they couldn't stop us by straight-arm tactics, and so they have been studying 'human relations' in the economic, social, and political fields to find out how to stop unions."

26. In the theory of functionalism, the therapeutic and ideological character of the analysis does not appear; it is obscured by the abstract generality of the concepts ("system," "part," "unit," "item," "multiple consequences," "function"). They are in principle applicable to whatever "system" the sociologist chooses as object of his analysis—from the smallest group to society as such. Functional analysis is enclosed in the selected system which itself is not subject to a critical analysis transcending the boundaries of the system toward the historical continuum, in which its functions and dysfunctions become what they are. Functional theory thus displays the fallacy of misplaced abstractness. The generality of its concepts is attained by abstracting from the very qualities which make the system an historical one and which give critical-transcendent meaning to its functions and dysfunctions.

27. The quotations are from Roethlisberger and Dickson, *Management and the Worker*. (Cambridge: Harvard University Press, 1947). See the excellent discussion in Loren Baritz, *The Servants of Power. A History of the Use of Social Science in American Industry*. (Middletown, Wesleyan University P._~~. 1960), chapters 5 and 6.

In investigating the workers' complaints about working conditions and wages, the researchers hit upon the fact that most of these complaints were formulated in statements which contained "vague, indefinite terms," lacked the "objective reference" to "standards which are generally accepted," and had characteristics "essentially different from the properties generally associated with common facts." [28] In other words, the complaints were formulated in such general statements as "the washrooms are unsanitary," "the job is dangerous," "rates are too low."

Guided by the principle of operational thinking, the researchers set out to translate or reformulate these statements in such a manner that their vague generality could be reduced to particular referents, terms designating the particular situation in which the complaint originated and thus picturing "accurately the conditions in the company." The general form was dissolved into statements identifying the particular operations and conditions from which the complaint was derived, and the complaint was taken care of by changing these particular operations and conditions.

For example, the statement "the washrooms are unsanitary" was translated into "on such and such occasion I went into this washroom, and the washbowl had some dirt in it." Inquiries then ascertained that this was "largely due to the carelessness of some employées," a campaign against throwing papers, spitting on the floor, and similar practices was instituted, and an attendant was assigned to constant duty in the washrooms. "It was in this way that many of the complaints were re-interpreted and used to effect improvements." [29]

Another example: a worker B makes the general statement that the piece rates on his job are too low. The inter-

28. Roethlisberger and Dickson. *Loc. cit.*, p. 255 f.
29. *Ibid.*, p. 256.

view reveals that "his wife is in the hospital and that he is worried about the doctor's bills he has incurred. In this case the latent content of the complaint consists of the fact that B's present earnings, due to his wife's illness, are insufficient to meet his current financial obligations." [30]

Such translation changes significantly the meaning of the actual proposition. The untranslated statement formulates a general condition in its generality ("wages are too low"). It goes beyond the particular condition in the particular factory and beyond the worker's particular situation. In this generality, and only in this generality, the statement expresses a sweeping indictment which takes the particular case as a manifestation of a universal state of affairs, and insinuates that the latter might not be changed by the improvement of the former.

Thus the untranslated statement established a concrete relation between the particular case and the whole of which it is a case—and this whole includes the conditions outside the respective job, outside the respective plant, outside the respective personal situation. This whole is eliminated in the translation, and it is this operation which makes the cure possible. The worker may not be aware of it, and for him his complaint may indeed have that particular and personal meaning which the translation brings out as its "latent content." But then the language he uses asserts its objective validity against his consciousness—it expresses conditions that *are*, although they are not "for him." The concreteness of the particular case which the translation achieves is the result of a series of abstractions from its *real* concreteness, which is in the universal character of the case.

The translation relates the general statement to the personal experience of the worker who makes it, but stops at the point where the individual worker would experience

30. *Ibid.*, p. 267.

himself as "the worker," and where his job would appear as "the job" of the working class. Is it necessary to point out that, in his translations, the operational researcher merely follows the process of reality, and probably even the worker's own translations? The arrested experience is not his doing, and his function is not to think in terms of a critical theory but to train supervisors "in more human and effective methods of dealing with their workers" [31] (only the term "human" seems non-operational and wanting of analysis).

But as this managerial mode of thought and research spreads into other dimensions of the intellectual effort, the services which it renders become increasingly inseparable from its scientific validity. In this context, functionalization has a truly therapeutic effect. Once the personal discontent is isolated from the general unhappiness, once the universal concepts which militate against functionalization are dissolved into particular referents, the case becomes a treatable and tractable incident.

To be sure, the case remains incident of a universal—no mode of thought can dispense with universals—but of a genus very different from that meant in the untranslated statement. The worker B, once his medical bills have been taken care of, will recognize that, generally speaking, wages are *not* too low, and that they were a hardship only in his individual situation (which may be similar to other individual situations). His case has been subsumed under another genus—that of personal hardship cases. He is no longer a "worker" or "employee" (member of a class), but the worker or employee B in the Hawthorne plant of the Western Electric Company.

The authors of *Management and the Worker* were well aware of this implication. They say that one of the fundamental functions to be performed in an industrial organiza-

31. *Loc. cit.*, p. VIII.

tion is "the specific function of personnel work," and this function requires that, in dealing with employer-employee relations, one must be "thinking of what is on some particular employee's mind in terms of a worker who has had a particular personal history," or "in terms of an employee whose job is in some particular place in the factory which brings him into association with particular persons and groups of people . . ." In contrast, the authors reject, as incompatible with the "specific function of personnel work," an attitude addressing itself to the "average" or "typical" employee or "what is on the worker's mind in general." [32]

We may summarize these examples by contrasting the original statements with their translation into the functional form. We take the statements in both forms at their face value, leaving aside the problem of their verification.

1) "Wages are too low." The subject of the proposition is "wages," not the particular remuneration of a particular worker on a particular job. The man who makes the statement might only think of his individual experience but, in the form he gives his statement, he transcends this individual experience. The predicate "too low" is a relational adjective, requiring a referent which is not designated in the proposition—too low for whom or for what? This referent might again be the individual who makes the statement, or his co-workers on the job, but the general noun (wages) carries the entire movement of thought expressed by the proposition and makes the other propositional elements share the general character. The referent remains indeterminate—"too low, in general," or "too low for everyone who is a wage-earner like the speaker." The proposition is abstract. It refers to universal conditions for which no particular case can be substituted; its meaning is "transitive" as against any indi-

32. *Loc. cit.*, p. 591.

vidual case. The proposition calls indeed for its "translation" into a more concrete context, but one in which the universal concepts cannot be defined by any *particular* set of operations (such as the personal history of the worker B, and his special function in the plant W). The concept "wages" refers to the group "wage-earners," integrating all personal histories and special jobs into one concrete universal.

2) "B's present earnings, due to his wife's illness, are insufficient to meet his current obligations." Note that in this translation of (1), the subject has been shifted. The universal concept "wages" is replaced by "B's present earnings," the meaning of which is fully defined by the particular set of operations B has to perform in order to buy for his family food, clothing, lodging, medicine etc. The "transitiveness" of meaning has been abolished; the grouping "wage-earners" has disappeared together with the subject "wages," and what remains is a particular case which, stripped of its transitive meaning, becomes susceptible to the accepted standards of treatment by the company whose case it is.

What is wrong with it? Nothing. The translation of the concepts and of the proposition as a whole is validated by the society to which the researcher addresses himself. The therapy works because the plant or the government can afford to bear at least a considerable part of the costs, because they are willing to do so, and because the patient is willing to submit to a treatment which promises to be a success. The vague, indefinite, universal concepts which appeared in the untranslated complaint were indeed remnants of the past; their persistence in speech and thought were indeed a block (though a minor one) to understanding and collaboration. Insofar as operational sociology and psychology have contributed to alleviating subhuman conditions, they are parts of progress, intellectual and material.

But they also testify to the ambivalent rationality of progress, which is satisfying in its repressive power, and repressive in its satisfactions.

The elimination of transitive meaning has remained a feature of empirical sociology. It characterizes even a large number of studies which are not designed to fulfill a therapeutic function in some particular interest. Result: once the "unrealistic" excess of meaning is abolished, the investigation is locked within the vast confine in which the established society validates and invalidates propositions. By virtue of its methodology, this empiricism is ideological. In order to illustrate its ideological character, let us look at a study of political activity in the United States.

In their paper "Competitive Pressure and Democratic Consent," Morris Janowitz and Dwaine Marvick want to "judge the extent to which an election is an effective expression of the democratic process." Such judgment implies evaluation of the election process "in terms of the requirements for maintaining a democratic society," and this in turn requires a definition of "democratic." The authors offer the choice between two alternative definitions; the "mandate" and the "competitive" theories of democracy:

"The 'mandate' theories, which find their origin in the classical conceptions of democracy, postulate that the process of representation derives from a clear-cut set of directives which the electorate imposes on its representatives. An election is a procedure of convenience and a method for insuring that representatives comply with directives from constituents." [33]

Now this "preconception" was "rejected in advance as unrealistic because it assumed a level of articulated opinion and ideology on the campaign issues not likely to be found in the United States." This rather frank statement of fact

33. H. Eulau, S. J. Eldersveld, M. Janowitz (edts), *Political Behavior* (Glencoe Free Press, 1956), p. 275.

is somehow alleviated by the comforting doubt "whether such a level of articulated opinion has existed in any democratic electorate since the extension of the franchise in the nineteenth century." In any case, the authors accept instead of the rejected preconception the "competitive" theory of democracy, according to which a democratic election is a process "of selecting and rejecting candidates" who are "in competition for public office." This definition, in order to be really operational, requires "criteria" by which the character of political competition is to be assessed. When does political competition produce a "process of consent," and when does it produce a "process of manipulation"? A set of three criteria is offered:

(1) a democratic election requires competition between opposing candidates which pervades the entire constituency. The electorate derives power from its ability to choose between at least two competitively oriented candidates, either of whom is believed to have a reasonable chance to win.

(2) a democratic election requires both [!] parties to engage in a balance of efforts to maintain established voting blocs, to recruit independent voters, and to gain converts from the opposition parties.

(3) a democratic election requires both [!] parties to be engaged vigorously in an effort to win the current election; but, win or lose, both parties must also be seeking to enhance their chances of success in the next and subsequent elections . . .[34]

I think these definitions describe pretty accurately the factual state of affairs in the American elections of 1952, which is the subject of the analysis. In other words, the criteria for judging a given state of affairs are those offered by (or, since they are those of a well-functioning and firmly established social system, imposed by) the given state of affairs. The analysis is "locked"; the range of judgment is

34. *Ibid.*, p. 276.

confined within a context of facts which excludes judging the context in which the facts are made, man-made, and in which their meaning, function, and development are determined.

Committed to this framework, the investigation becomes circular and self-validating. If "democratic" is defined in the limiting but realistic terms of the actual process of election, then this process is democratic prior to the results of the investigation. To be sure, the operational framework still allows (and even calls for) distinction between consent and manipulation; the election can be more or less democratic according to the ascertained degree of consent and manipulation. The authors arrive at the conclusion that the 1952 election "was characterized by a process of genuine consent to a greater extent than impressionistic estimates might have implied" [35]—although it would be a "grave error" to overlook the "barriers" to consent and to deny that "manipulative pressures were present." [36] Beyond this hardly illuminating statement the operational analysis cannot go. In other words, it cannot raise the decisive question whether the consent itself was not the work of manipulation—a question for which the actual state of affairs provides ample justification. The analysis cannot raise it because it would transcend its terms toward transitive meaning—toward a concept of democracy which would reveal the democratic election as a rather limited democratic process.

Precisely such a non-operational concept is the one rejected by the authors as "unrealistic" because it defines democracy on too articulate a level as the clear-cut control of representation by the electorate—popular control as popular sovereignty. And this non-operational concept is by no means extraneous. It is by no means a figment of the imagina-

35. *Ibid.*, p. 284.
36. *Ibid.*, p. 285.

tion or speculation but rather defines the historical intent of democracy, the conditions for which the struggle for democracy was fought, and which are still to be fulfilled.

Moreover, this concept is impeccable in its semantic exactness because it means exactly what it says—namely, that it is really the electorate which imposes its directives on the representatives, and not the representatives who impose their directives on the electorate which then selects and re-elects the representatives. An autonomous electorate, free because it is free from indoctrination and manipulation, would indeed be on a "level of articulate opinion and ideology" which is not likely to be found. Therefore, the concept has to be rejected as "unrealistic"—has to be if one accepts the factually prevailing level of opinion and ideology as prescribing the valid criteria for sociological analysis. And if indoctrination and manipulation have reached the stage where the prevailing level of opinion has become a level of falsehood, where the actual state of affairs is no longer recognized as that which it is, then an analysis which is methodologically committed to reject transitive concepts commits itself to a false consciousness. Its very empiricism is ideological.

The authors are well aware of the problem. "Ideological rigidity" presents a "serious implication" in assessing the degree of democratic consent. Indeed, consent to what? To the political candidates and their policy naturally. But this is not enough, because then consent to a fascist regime (and one may speak of genuine consent to such a regime) would be a democratic process. Thus, the consent itself has to be assessed—assessed in terms of its content, its objectives, its "values"—and this step seems to involve transitiveness of meaning. However, such an "unscientific" step can be avoided if the ideological orientation to be assessed is no other than that of the existing and "effectively" competing two parties, plus the "ambivalent-neutralized" orientation of the voters.[37]

The table giving the results of the polling of ideological orientation shows three degrees of adherence to the Republican and to the Democratic party ideologies and the "ambivalent and neutralized" opinions.[38] The established parties themselves, their policies, and their machinations are not questioned, nor is the actual difference between them questioned as far as the vital issues are concerned (those of atomic policy and total preparedness), questions which seem essential for the assessment of the democratic processes, unless the analysis operates with a concept of democracy which merely assembles the features of the *established form* of democracy. Such an operational concept is not altogether inadequate to the subject matter of the investigation. It points up clearly enough the qualities which, in the contemporary period, distinguish democratic and non-democratic systems (for example, effective competition between candidates representing different parties; freedom of the electorate to choose between these candidates), but this adequacy does not suffice if the task of theoretical analysis is more and other than a descriptive one—if the task is to *comprehend*, to *recognize* the facts for what they are, what they "mean" for those who have been given them as facts and who have to live with them. In social theory, recognition of facts is critique of facts.

But operational concepts do not even suffice for *describing* the facts. They only attain certain aspects and segments of facts which, if taken for the whole, deprive the description of its objective, empirical character. As an example let us look at the concept of "political activity" in Julian L. Woodward's and Elmo Roper's study of "Political Activity

37. *Ibid.*, p. 280.
38. *Ibid.*, p. 138 ff.

of American Citizens." [39] The authors present an "operational
definition of the term 'political activity' " constituted by "five
ways of behaving": (1) voting at the polls; (2) supporting
possible pressure groups . . . (3) personally communicating
directly with legislators (4) participating in political party
activity . . . (5) engaging in habitual dissemination of political opinions through word-of-mouth communication . . .

Certainly these are "channels of possible influence on
legislators and government officials," but can their measurement really provide "a method for separating the people
who are relatively active in relation to national political
issues from those who are relatively inactive?" Do they include such decisive activities "in relation to national issues"
as the technical and economic contacts between corporate
business and the government, and among the key corporations themselves? Do they include the formulation and dissemination of "unpolitical" opinion, information, entertainment by the big publicity media? Do they take account of
the very different political weights of the various organizations that take a stand on public issues?

If the answer is negative (and I believe it is), then the
facts of political activity are not adequately described and
ascertained. Many, and I think the determining, constitutive
facts remain outside the reach of the operational concept.
And by virtue of this limitation—this methodological in-
junction against transitive concepts which might show the
facts in their true light and call them by their true name—
the descriptive analysis of the facts blocks the apprehension
of facts and becomes an element of the ideology that sustains
the facts. Proclaiming the existing social reality as its own
norm, this sociology fortifies in the individuals the "faithless
faith" in the reality whose victims they are: "Nothing remains of ideology but the recognition of that which is—

39. *Ibid.*, p. 133.

model of a behavior which submits to the overwhelming power of the established state of affairs."[40] Against this ideological empiricism, the plain contradiction reasserts its right: "... that which is cannot be true."[41]

40. Theodor W. Adorno, "Ideologie," in: Kurt Lenk (ed.) *Ideologie* (Neuwied, Luchterhand, 1961), p. 262 f.
41. Ernst Bloch, *Philosophische Grundfragen I* (Frankfurt, Suhrkamp, 1961), p. 65.

One-Dimensional Thought

5: Negative Thinking:
The Defeated Logic of Protest

". . . that which is cannot be true." To our well-trained ears and eyes, this statement is flippant and ridiculous, or as outrageous as that other statement which seems to say the opposite: "what is real is rational." And yet, in the tradition of Western thought, both reveal, in provocatively abridged formulation, the idea of Reason which has guided its logic. Moreover, both express the same concept, namely, the antagonistic structure of reality, and of thought trying to understand reality. The world of immediate experience—the world in which we find ourselves living—must be comprehended, transformed, even subverted in order to become that which it really is.

In the equation Reason = Truth = Reality, which joins the subjective and objective world into one antagonistic unity, Reason is the subversive power, the "power of the negative" that establishes, as theoretical and practical Reason, the truth for men and things—that is, the conditions in which men and things become what they really are. The attempt to demonstrate that this truth of theory and practice is not a subjective but an objective condition was the original concern of Western thought and the origin of its logic—logic not in the sense of a special discipline of philosophy but as the mode of thought appropriate for comprehending the real as rational.

The totalitarian universe of technological rationality is the latest transmutation of the idea of Reason. In this and the following chapter, I shall try to identify some of the main stages in the development of this idea—the process by which logic became the logic of domination. Such ideological analysis can contribute to the understanding of the real development inasmuch as it is focused on the union (and separation) of theory and practice, thought and action, in the historical process—an unfolding of theoretical and practical Reason in one.

The closed operational universe of advanced industrial civilization with its terrifying harmony of freedom and oppression, productivity and destruction, growth and regression is pre-designed in this idea of Reason as a specific historical project. The technological and the pre-technological stages share certain basic concepts of man and nature which express the continuity of the Western tradition. Within this continuum, different modes of thought clash with each other; they belong to different ways of apprehending, organizing, changing society and nature. The stabilizing tendencies conflict with the subversive elements of Reason, the power of positive with that of negative thinking, until the achievements of advanced industrial civilization lead to the triumph of the one-dimensional reality over all contradiction.

This conflict dates back to the origins of philosophic thought itself and finds striking expression in the contrast between Plato's dialectical logic and the formal logic of the Aristotelian Organon. The subsequent sketch of the classical model of dialectical thought may prepare the ground for an analysis of the contrasting features of technological rationality.

In classical Greek philosophy, Reason is the cognitive faculty to distinguish what is true and what is false insofar as truth (and falsehood) is primarily a condition of Being, of Reality—and only on this ground a property of *propositions*. True discourse, logic, reveals and expresses that which really *is*—as distinguished from that which *appears* to be (real). And by virtue of this equation between Truth and (real) Being, Truth is a value, for Being is better than Non-Being. The latter is not simply Nothing; it is a potentiality of and a threat to Being—destruction. The struggle for truth is a struggle against destruction, for the "salvation" (σώζειν) of Being (an effort which appears itself to be destructive if it assails an established reality as "untrue": Socrates against the Athenian city state). Inasmuch as the struggle for truth "saves" reality from destruction, truth commits and engages human existence. It is the essentially human project. If man has learned to see and know what really *is*, he will act in accordance with truth. Epistemology is in itself ethics, and ethics is epistemology.

This conception reflects the experience of a world antagonistic in itself—a world afflicted with want and negativity, constantly threatened with destruction, but also a world which is a *cosmos*, structured in accordance with final causes. To the extent to which the experience of an antagonistic world guides the development of the philosophical categories, philosophy moves in a universe which is broken in itself (*déchirement ontologique*)—two-dimensional. Appearance and reality, untruth and truth, (and, as we shall see, unfreedom and freedom) are ontological conditions.

The distinction is not by virtue or by fault of abstract thought; it is rather rooted in the experience of the universe of which thought partakes in theory and practice. In this universe, there are modes of being in which men and things are "by themselves" and "as themselves," and modes in which they are *not*—that is, in which they exist in distortion, limitation, or denial of their nature (essence). To overcome these negative conditions is the process of being and of thought. Philosophy originates in dialectic; its universe of discourse responds to the facts of an antagonistic reality.

What are the criteria for this distinction? On what ground is the status of "truth" assigned to one mode or condition rather than to another? Classical Greek philosophy relies largely on what was later termed (in a rather derogative sense) "intuition," i.e., a form of cognition in which the object of thought appears clearly as that which it really is (in its essential qualities), and in antagonistic relation to its contingent, immediate situation. Indeed this evidence of intuition is not too different from the Cartesian one. It is not a mysterious faculty of the mind, not a strange immediate experience, nor is it divorced from conceptual analysis. Intuition is rather the (preliminary) terminus of such an analysis—the result of methodic intellectual mediation. As such, it is the mediation of concrete experience.

The notion of the essence of man may serve as an illustration. Analyzed in the condition in which he finds himself in his universe, man seems to be in possession of certain faculties and powers which would enable him to lead a "good life," i.e., a life which is as much as possible free from toil, dependence, and ugliness. To attain such a life is to attain the "best life": to live in accordance with the essence of nature or man.

To be sure, this is still the dictum of the philosopher; it is he who analyzes the human situation. He subjects experience to his critical judgment, and this contains a value judgment—namely, that freedom from toil is preferable to toil, and an intelligent life is preferable to a stupid life. It so happened that philosophy was born with these values. Scientific thought had to break this union of value judgment and analysis, for it became increasingly clear that the philosophic values did not guide the organization of society nor the transformation of nature. They were ineffective, unreal. Already the Greek conception contains the historical element—the essence of man is different in the slave and in the free citizen, in the Greek and in the Barbarian. Civilization has overcome the ontological stabilization of this difference (at least in theory). But this development does not yet invalidate the distinction between essential and contingent nature, between true and false modes of existence—provided only that the distinction derives from a logical analysis of the empirical situation, and understands its potential as well as its contingency.

To the Plato of the later dialogues and to Aristotle, the modes of Being are modes of movement—transition from potentiality to actuality, realization. Finite Being is incomplete realization, subject to change. Its generation is corruption; it is permeated with negativity. Thus it is not true reality—Truth. The philosophic quest proceeds from the finite world to the construction of a reality which is not subject to the painful difference between potentiality and actuality, which has mastered its negativity and is complete and independent in itself—*free*.

This discovery is the work of Logos and Eros. The two key terms designate two modes of negation; erotic as well as logical cognition break the hold of the established, contingent reality and strive for a truth incompatible with it. Logos and Eros are subjective and objective in one. The ascent from the "lower" to the "higher" forms of reality is movement of matter as well as mind. According to Aristotle, the perfect reality, the god, attracts the world below ὡς ἐρώμενον; he is the final cause of all being. Logos and Eros are in themselves the unity of the positive and the negative, creation and destruction. In the exigencies of thought and in the madness of love is the destructive refusal of the established ways of life. Truth transforms the modes of thought and existence. Reason and Freedom converge.

However, this dynamic has its inherent limits insofar as the antagonistic character of reality, its explosion in true and untrue modes of existence, appears to be an immutable ontological condition. There are modes of existence which can never be "true" because they can never *rest* in the realization of their potentialities, in the *joy* of being. In the human reality, all existence that spends itself in procuring the prerequisites of existence is thus an "untrue" and unfree existence. Obviously this reflects the not at all ontological condition of a society based on the proposition that freedom is incompatible with the activity of procuring the necessities of life, that this activity is the "natural" function of a specific class, and that cognition of the truth and true existence imply freedom from the entire dimension of such activity. This is indeed the pre- and anti-technological constellation *par excellence.*

But the real dividing line between pre-technological and technological rationality is not that between a society based on unfreedom, and one based on freedom. Society still is organized in such a way that procuring the necessities of life constitutes the full-time and life-long occupation of specific social classes, which are *therefore* unfree and prevented from a human existence. In this sense, the classical proposition according to which truth is incompatible with enslavement by socially necessary labor is still valid.

The classical concept implies the proposition that freedom of thought and speech must remain a class privilege as long as this enslavement prevails. For thought and speech are of a thinking and speaking subject, and if the life of the latter depends on the performance of a superimposed function, it depends on fulfilling the requirements of this function—thus it depends on those who control these requirements. The dividing line between the pre-technological and the technological project rather is in the manner in which the subordination to the necessities of life—to "earning a living"—is organized and, in the new modes of freedom and unfreedom, truth and falsehood which correspond to this organization.

Who is, in the classical conception, the subject that comprehends the ontological condition of truth and untruth? It is the master of pure contemplation (theoria), and the master of a practice guided by theoria, i.e., the philosopher-statesman. To be sure, the truth which he knows and expounds is potentially accessible to everyone. Led by the philosopher, the slave in Plato's *Meno* is capable of grasping the truth of a geometrical axiom, i.e., a truth *beyond* change and corruption. But since truth is a state of Being as well as of thought, and since the latter is the expression and manifestation of the former, access to truth remains mere potentiality as long as it is not living in and with the truth. And this mode of existence is closed to the slave—and to anyone who has to spend his life procuring the necessities of life. Consequently, if men no longer had to spend their lives in the realm of necessity, truth and a true human existence would be in a strict and real sense *universal*. Philosophy envisages the *equality* of man but, at the same time, it submits to the factual denial of equality. For in the given reality, procurement of the necessities is the life-long job of the majority, and the necessities *have* to be procured and served so that truth (which is freedom from material necessities) can be.

Here, the historical barrier arrests and distorts the quest for truth; the societal division of labor obtains the dignity of an ontological condition. If truth presupposes freedom from toil, and if this freedom is, in the social reality, the prerogative of a minority, then the reality allows such a truth only in approximation and for a privileged group. This state of affairs contradicts the universal character of truth, which defines and "prescribes" not only a theoretical goal, but the best life of man qua man, with respect to the essence of man. For philosophy, the contradiction is insoluble, or else it does not appear as a contradiction because it is the structure of the slave or serf society which this philosophy does not transcend. Thus it leaves history behind, unmastered, and elevates truth safely above the historical reality. There, truth is preserved intact, not as an achievement of

heaven or in heaven, but as an achievement of thought—
intact because its very notion expresses the insight that those
who devote their lives to earning a living are incapable of
living a human existence.

The ontological concept of truth is in the center of a
logic which may serve as a model of pre-technological rationality. It is the rationality of a two-dimensional universe
of discourse which contrasts with the one-dimensional modes
of thought and behavior that develop in the execution of the
technological project.

Aristotle uses the term "apophantic logos" in order to
distinguish a specific type of Logos (speech, communication)—that which discovers truth and falsehood and is, in
its development, determined by the difference between
truth and falsehood (*De Interpretatione*, 16b-17a). It is the
logic of judgment, but in the emphatic sense of a (judicial)
sentence: attributing (p) to (S) because and inasfar as it
pertains to (S), as a property of (S); or denying (p) to (S)
because and inasfar as it does not pertain to (S); etc. From
this ontological basis, the Aristotelian philosophy proceeds
to establish the "pure forms" of all possible true (and false)
predications; it becomes the formal logic of judgments.

When Husserl revived the idea of an apophantic logic,
he emphasized its original *critical* intent. And he found this
intent precisely in the idea of a logic of *judgments*—that is,
in the fact that thought was not directly concerned with
Being (*das Seiende selbst*) but rather with "pretensions,"
propositions on Being.[1] Husserl sees in this orientation on
judgments a restriction and a prejudice with respect to the
task and scope of logic.

The classical idea of logic shows indeed an ontological

1. Husserl, *Formale und Transzendentale Logik* (Halle, Niemeyer,
1929), esp. pp. 42 f. and 115 f.

prejudice—the structure of the judgment (proposition) refers to a divided reality. The discourse moves between the
experience of Being and Non-being, essence and fact, generation and corruption, potentiality and actuality. The Aristotelian Organon abstracts from this unity of opposites the
general forms of propositions and of their (correct or incorrect) connections; still, decisive parts of this formal logic
remain committed to Aristotelian metaphysics.[2]

Prior to this formalization, the experience of the divided
world finds its logic in the Platonic dialectic. Here, the
terms "Being," "Non-being," "Movement," "the One and the
Many," "Identity," and "Contradiction" are methodically
kept open, ambiguous, not fully defined. They have an open
horizon, an entire universe of meaning which is gradually
structured in the process of communication itself, but which
is never closed. The propositions are submitted, developed,
and tested in a dialogue, in which the partner is led to question the normally unquestioned universe of experience and
speech, and to enter a new dimension of discourse—otherwise he is *free* and the discourse is addressed to his freedom.
He is supposed to go beyond that which is given to him—as
the speaker, in his proposition, goes beyond the initial setting of the terms. These terms have many meanings because
the conditions to which they refer have many sides, implications, and effects which cannot be insulated and stabilized.
Their logical development responds to the process of reality,
or *Sache selbst*. The laws of thought are laws of reality, or
rather *become* the laws of reality if thought understands the
truth of immediate experience as the appearance of another
truth, which is that of the true Forms of reality—of the
Ideas. Thus there is contradiction rather than correspondence between dialectical thought and the given reality; the

2. Carl Prantl, *Geschichte der Logik im Abendlande*, Darmstadt 1957,
Vol. I, p. 135, 211. For the argument against this interpretation, see p. 136
below.

true judgment judges this reality not in its own terms, but in terms which envisage its subversion. And in this subversion, reality comes into its own truth.

In the classical logic, the judgment which constituted the original core of dialectical thought was formalized in the propositional form, "S is p." But this form conceals rather than reveals the basic dialectical proposition, which states the negative character of the empirical reality. Judged in the light of their essence and idea, men and things exist as other than they are; consequently thought contradicts that which is (given), opposes its truth to that of the given reality. The truth envisaged by thought is the Idea. As such it is, in terms of the given reality, "mere" Idea, "mere" essence—potentiality.

But the essential potentiality is not like the many possibilities which are contained in the given universe of discourse and action; the essential potentiality is of a very different order. Its realization involves subversion of the established order, for thinking in accordance with truth is the commitment to exist in accordance with truth. (In Plato, the extreme concepts which illustrate this subversion are: death as the beginning of the philosopher's life, and the violent liberation from the Cave.) Thus, the subversive character of truth inflicts upon thought an *imperative* quality. Logic centers on judgments which are, as demonstrative propositions, imperatives,—the predicative "is" implies an *"ought."*

This contradictory, two-dimensional style of thought is the inner form not only of dialectical logic but of all philosophy which comes to grips with reality. The propositions which define reality affirm as true something that is *not* (immediately) the case; thus they contradict that which is the case, and they deny its truth. The affirmative judgment contains a negation which disappears in the propositional form (S is p). For example, "virtue is knowledge"; "justice is that state in which everyone performs the function for which his nature is best suited"; "the perfectly real is the perfectly knowable"; "verum est id, quod est"; "man is free"; "the State is the reality of Reason."

If these propositions are to be true, then the copula "is" states an "ought," a desideratum. It judges conditions in which virtue is *not* knowledge, in which men do *not* perform the function for which their nature best suits them, in which they are not free, etc. Or, the categorical S-p form states that (S) is *not* (S); (S) is defined as other-than-itself. Verification of the proposition involves a *process* in fact as well as in thought: (S) must *become* that which it is. The categorical statement thus turns into a categorical *imperative;* it does not state a fact but the necessity to *bring about* a fact. For example, it could be read as follows: man *is not* (in fact) free, endowed with inalienable rights, etc., but he *ought to be,* because he is free in the eyes of God, by nature, etc.[3]

Dialectical thought understands the critical tension between "is" and "ought" first as an ontological condition, pertaining to the structure of Being itself. However, the recognition of this state of Being—its theory—intends from the beginning a concrete *practice.* Seen in the light of a truth which appears in them falsified or denied, the given facts themselves appear false and negative.

Consequently, thought is led, by the situation of its

3. But why does the proposition not *say* "ought" if it *means* "ought"? Why does the negation disappear in the affirmation? Did the metaphysical origins of logic perhaps determine the propositional form? Pre-Socratic as well as Socratic thought predates the separation of logic from ethics. If only that which is true (the Logos; the Idea) really *is,* then the reality of immediate experience partakes of the μὴ ὄν, of that which is *not.* And yet, this μὴ ὄν *is,* and for the immediate experience (which is the unique reality for the vast majority of men) it is the only reality which *is.* The twofold meaning of "is" would thus express the two-dimensional structure of the one world.

objects, to measure their truth in terms of another logic, another universe of discourse. And this logic projects another mode of existence: the realization of the truth in the words and deeds of man. And inasmuch as this project involves man as "societal animal," the *polis*, the movement of thought has a political content. Thus, the Socratic discourse is political discourse inasmuch as it contradicts the established political institutions. The search for the correct definition, for the "concept" of virtue, justice, piety, and knowledge becomes a subversive undertaking, for the concept intends a new *polis*.

Thought has no power to bring about such a change unless it transcends itself into practice, and the very dissociation from the material practice, in which philosophy originates, gives philosophic thought its abstract and ideological quality. By virtue of this dissociation, critical philosophic thought is necessarily transcendent and *abstract*. Philosophy shares this abstractness with all genuine thought, for nobody really thinks who does not abstract from that which is given, who does not relate the facts to the factors which have made them, who does not—in his mind—undo the facts. Abstractness is the very life of thought, the token of its authenticity.

But there are false and true abstractions. Abstraction is a historical event in a historical continuum. It proceeds on historical grounds, and it remains related to the very basis from which it moves away: the established societal universe. Even where the critical abstraction arrives at the negation of the established universe of discourse, the basis survives in the negation (subversion) and limits the possibilities of the new position.

At the classical origins of philosophic thought, the transcending concepts remained committed to the prevailing separation between intellectual and manual labor—to the established society of enslavement. Plato's "ideal" state retains and reforms enslavement while organizing it in accordance with an eternal truth. And in Aristotle, the philosopher-king (in whom theory and practice were still combined) gives way to the supremacy of the *bios theoreticos,* which can hardly claim a subversive function and content. Those who bore the brunt of the untrue reality and who, therefore, seemed to be most in need of attaining its subversion were not the concern of philosophy. It abstracted from them and continued to abstract from them.

In this sense, "idealism" was germane to philosophic thought, for the notion of the supremacy of thought (consciousness) also pronounces the impotence of thought in an empirical world which philosophy transcends and corrects —in thought. The rationality in the name of which philosophy passed its judgments obtained that abstract and general "purity" which made it immune against the world in which one had to live. With the exception of the materialistic "heretics," philosophic thought was rarely afflicted by the afflictions of human existence.

Paradoxically, it is precisely the critical intent in philosophic thought which leads to the idealistic purification—a critical intent which aims at the empirical world as a whole, and not merely at certain modes of thinking or behaving within it. Defining its concepts in terms of potentialities which are of an essentially different order of thought and existence, the philosophic critique finds itself blocked by the reality from which it dissociates itself, and proceeds to construct a realm of Reason purged from empirical contingency. The two dimensions of thought—that of the essential and that of the apparent truths—no longer interfere with each other, and their concrete dialectical relation becomes an abstract epistemological or ontological relation. The judgments passed on the given reality are replaced by propositions defining the general forms of thought, objects of thought, and relations between thought and its objects. The subject of thought becomes the pure and universal form of subjectivity, from which all particulars are removed.

For such a formal subject, the relation between ὄν and μὴ ὄν, change and permanence, potentiality and actuality, truth and falsehood is no longer an existential concern;[4] it is rather a matter of pure philosophy. The contrast is striking between Plato's dialectical and Aristotle's formal logic.

In the Aristotelian Organon, the syllogistic "term" (*horos*) is "so void of substantial meaning that a letter of the alphabet is a fully equivalent substitute." It is thus entirely different from the "metaphysical" term (also *horos*) which designates the result of the essential definition, the answer to the question: "τί ἐστίν?"[5] Kapp maintains against Prantl that the "two different significations are entirely independent of one another and were never mixed up by Aristotle himself." In any case, in formal logic, thought is organized in a manner very different from that of the Platonic dialogue.

In this formal logic, thought is indifferent toward its objects. Whether they are mental or physical, whether they pertain to society or to nature, they become subject to the same general laws of organization, calculation, and conclusion—but they do so as fungible signs or symbols, in abstraction from their particular "substance." This general quality (quantitative quality) is the precondition of law and order—in logic as well as in society—the price of universal control.

4. To avoid a misunderstanding: I do not believe that the *Frage nach dem Sein* and similar questions are or ought to be an existential concern. What was meaningful at the origins of philosophic thought may well have become meaningless at its end, and the loss of meaning may not be due to the incapacity to think. The history of mankind has given definite answers to the "question of Being," and has given them in very concrete terms, which have proved their efficacy. The technological universe is one of them. For a further discussion see chapter VI.

5. Ernst Kapp, *Greek Foundations of Traditional Logic* (New York, Columbia University Press, 1942), p. 29.

Die Allgemeinheit der Gedanken, wie die diskursive Logik sie entwickelt, erhebt sich auf dem Fundament der Herrschaft in der Wirklichkeit.[6]

Aristotle's *Metaphysics* states the connection between concept and control: the knowledge of "first causes" is— as knowledge of the universal—the most effective and certain knowledge, for disposing over the causes is disposing over their effects. By virtue of the universal concept, thought attains mastery over the particular cases. However, the most formalized universe of logic still refers to the most general structure of the given, experienced world; the pure form is still that of the content which it formalizes. The idea of formal logic itself is a historical event in the development of the mental and physical instruments for universal control and calculability. In this undertaking, man had to create theoretical harmony out of actual discord, to purge thought from contradictions, to hypostatize identifiable and fungible units in the complex process of society and nature.

Under the rule of formal logic, the notion of the conflict between essence and appearance is expendable if not meaningless; the material content is neutralized; the principle of identity is separated from the principle of contradiction (contradictions are the fault of incorrect thinking); final causes are removed from the logical order. Well defined in their scope and function, concepts become instruments of prediction and control. Formal logic is thus the first step on the long road to scientific thought—the first step only, for a much higher degree of abstraction and mathematization is still required to adjust the modes of thought to technological rationality.

The methods of logical procedure are very different in

6. "The general concept which discursive logic had developed has its foundation in the reality of domination." M. Horkheimer and T. W. Adorno, *Dialektik der Aufklärung* (Amsterdam 1947), p. 25.

ancient and modern logic, but behind all difference is the construction of a universally valid order of thought, neutral with respect to material content. Long before technological man and technological nature emerged as the objects of rational control and calculation, the mind was made susceptible to abstract generalization. Terms which could be organized into a coherent logical system, free from contradiction or with manageable contradiction, were separated from those which could not. Distinction was made between the universal, calculable, "objective" and the particular, incalculable, subjective dimension of thought; the latter entered into science only through a series of reductions.

Formal logic foreshadows the reduction of secondary to primary qualities in which the former become the measurable and controllable properties of physics. The elements of thought can then be scientifically organized—as the human elements can be organized in the social reality. Pretechnological and technological rationality, ontology and technology are linked by those elements of thought which adjust the rules of thought to the rules of control and domination. Pre-technological and technological modes of domination are fundamentally different—as different as slavery is from free-wage labor, paganism from Christianity, the city state from the nation, the slaughter of the population of a captured city from the Nazi concentration camps. However, history is still the history of domination, and the logic of thought remains the logic of domination.

Formal logic intended universal validity for the laws of thought. And indeed, without universality, thought would be a private, non-committal affair, incapable of understanding the smallest sector of existence. Thought is always more and other than individual thinking; if I start thinking of individual persons in a specific situation, I find them in a supra-individual context of which they partake, and I think in general concepts. All objects of thought are universals. But it is equally true that the supra-individual meaning, the universality of a concept, is never merely a formal one; it is constituted in the interrelationship between the (thinking and acting) subjects and their world.[7] Logical abstraction is also sociological abstraction. There is a logical *mimesis* which formulates the laws of thought in protective accord with the laws of society, but it is only one mode of thought among others.

The sterility of Aristotelian formal logic has often been noted. Philosophic thought developed alongside and even outside this logic. In their main efforts, neither the idealist nor the materialist, neither the rationalist nor the empiricist schools seem to owe anything to it. Formal logic was non-transcendent in its very structure. It canonized and organized thought within a set framework beyond which no syllogism can pass—it remained "analytics." Logic continued as a special discipline alongside the substantive development of philosophic thought, essentially unchanging in spite of the new concepts and new contents which marked this development.

Indeed, neither the Schoolmen nor the rationalism and the empiricism of the early modern period had any reason to object to the mode of thought which had canonized its general forms in the Aristotelian logic. Its intent at least was in accord with scientific validity and exactness, and the rest did not interfere with the conceptual elaboration of the new experience and the new facts.

The contemporary mathematical and symbolic logic is certainly very different from its classical predecessor, but they share the radical opposition to dialectical logic. In terms of this opposition, the old and the new formal logic express

7. See T. W. Adorno, *Zur Metakritik der Erkenntnistheorie*, Stuttgart 1956, chapter I, *Kritik der logischen Absolutismus*.

the same mode of thought. It is purged from that "negative" which loomed so large at the origins of logic and of philosophic thought—the experience of the denying, deceptive, falsifying power of the established reality. And with the elimination of this experience, the conceptual effort to sustain the tension between "is" and "ought," and to subvert the established universe of discourse in the name of its own truth is likewise eliminated from all thought which is to be objective, exact, and scientific. For the *scientific* subversion of the immediate experience which establishes the truth of science as against that of immediate experience does not develop the concepts which carry in themselves the protest and the refusal. The new scientific truth which they oppose to the accepted one does not contain in itself the judgment that condemns the established reality.

In contrast, dialectical thought is and remains unscientific to the extent to which it *is* such judgment, and the judgment is imposed upon dialectical thought by the nature of its *object*—by its objectivity. This object is the reality in its true concreteness; dialectical logic precludes all abstraction which leaves the concrete content alone and behind, uncomprehended. Hegel detects in the critical philosophy of his time the "fear of the object" (*Angst vor dem Objekt*), and he demands that a genuinely scientific thought overcome this position of fear and comprehend the "logical and the pure-rational" (*das Logische, das Rein-Vernünftige*) in the very concreteness of its objects.[8] Dialectical logic cannot be formal because it is determined by the real, which is concrete. And this concreteness, far from militating against a system of general principles and concepts, requires such a system of logic because it moves under general laws which make for the rationality of the real. It is the rationality of contradiction, of the opposition of forces, tendencies, ele-

8. *Wissenschaft der Logik*, ed. Lasson (Leipzig, Meiner, 1923), vol. I, p. 32.

ments, which constitutes the movement of the real and, if comprehended, the concept of the real.

Existing as the living contradiction between essence and appearance, the objects of thought are of that "inner negativity" [9] which is the specific quality of their concept. The dialectical definition defines the movement of things from that which they are not to that which they are. The development of contradictory elements, which determines the structure of its object, also determines the structure of dialectical thought. The object of dialectical logic is neither the abstract, general form of objectivity, nor the abstract, general form of thought—nor the data of immediate experience. Dialectical logic undoes the abstractions of formal logic and of transcendental philosophy, but it also denies the concreteness of immediate experience. To the extent to which this experience comes to rest with the things as they appear and happen to be, it is a limited and even false experience. It attains its truth if it has freed itself from the deceptive objectivity which conceals the factors behind the facts —that is, if it understands its world as a *historical* universe, in which the established facts are the work of the historical practice of man. This practice (intellectual and material) is the reality in the data of experience; it is also the reality which dialectical logic comprehends.

When historical content enters into the dialectical concept and determines methodologically its development and function, dialectical thought attains the concreteness which links the structure of thought to that of reality. Logical truth becomes historical truth. The ontological tension between essence and appearance, between "is" and "ought" becomes historical tension, and the "inner negativity" of the object-world is understood as the work of the historical subject—man in his struggle with nature and society. Reason becomes historical Reason. It contradicts the established

9. *Ibid.*, p. 38.

order of men and things on behalf of existing societal forces that reveal the irrational character of this order—for "rational" is a mode of thought and action which is geared to reduce ignorance, destruction, brutality, and oppression.

The transformation of ontological into historical dialectic retains the two-dimensionality of philosophic thought as critical, negative thinking. But now essence and appearance, "is" and "ought," confront each other in the conflict between actual forces and capabilities in the society. And they confront each other, not as Reason and Unreason, Right and Wrong—for both are part and parcel of the same established universe, both partaking of Reason and Unreason, Right and Wrong. The slave is capable of abolishing the masters and of cooperating with them; the masters are capable of improving the life of the slave and of improving his exploitation. The idea of Reason pertains to the movement of thought and of action. It is a theoretical and a practical exigency.

If dialectical logic understands contradiction as "necessity" belonging to the very "nature of thought" (*zur Natur der Denkbestimmungen*),[10] it does so because contradiction belongs to the very nature of the *object* of thought, to reality, where Reason is still Unreason, and the irrational still the rational. Conversely, all established reality militates against the logic of contradictions—it favors the modes of thought which sustain the established forms of life and the modes of behavior which reproduce and improve them. The given reality has its own logic and its own truth; the effort to comprehend them as such and to transcend them presupposes a different logic, a contradicting truth. They belong to modes of thought which are non-operational in their very structure; they are alien to scientific as well as common-sense operationalism; their historical concreteness militates against quantification and mathematization on the one hand, and

10. *Ibid.*

against positivism and empiricism on the other. Thus these modes of thought appear to be a relic of the past, like all non-scientific and non-empirical philosophy. They recede before a more effective theory and practice of Reason.

6: From Negative to Positive Thinking:
Technological Rationality
and the Logic of Domination

In the social reality, despite all change, the domination of man by man is still the historical continuum that links pre-technological and technological Reason. However, the society which projects and undertakes the technological transformation of nature alters the base of domination by gradually replacing personal dependence (of the slave on the master, the serf on the lord of the manor, the lord on the donor of the fief, etc.) with dependence on the "objective order of things" (on economic laws, the market etc.). To be sure, the "objective order of things" is itself the result of domination, but it is nevertheless true that domination now generates a higher rationality—that of a society which sustains its hierarchic structure while exploiting ever more efficiently the natural and mental resources, and distributing the benefits of this exploitation on an ever-larger scale. The limits of this rationality, and its sinister force, appear in the progressive enslavement of man by a productive apparatus which perpetuates the struggle for existence and extends it to a total international struggle which ruins the lives of those who build and use this apparatus.

At this stage, it becomes clear that something must be wrong with the rationality of the system itself. What is wrong is the way in which men have organized their societal labor. This is no longer in question at the present time when, on the one side, the great entrepreneurs themselves are willing to sacrifice the blessings of private enterprise and "free" competition to the blessings of government orders and regulations, while, on the other side, socialist construction continues to proceed through progressive domination. However, the question cannot come to rest here. The wrong organization of society demands further explanation in view of the situation of *advanced* industrial society, in which the integration of the formerly negative and transcending social forces with the established system seems to create a new social structure.

This transformation of negative into positive opposition points up the problem: the "wrong" organization, in becoming totalitarian on internal grounds, refutes the alternatives. Certainly it is quite natural, and does not seem to call for an explanation in depth, that the tangible benefits of the system are considered worth defending—especially in view of the repelling force of present day communism which appears to be the historical alternative. But it is natural only to a mode of thought and behavior which is unwilling and perhaps even incapable of comprehending what is happening and why it is happening, a mode of thought and behavior which is immune against any other than the established rationality. To the degree to which they correspond to the given reality, thought and behavior express a false consciousness, responding to and contributing to the preservation of a false order of facts. And this false consciousness has become embodied in the prevailing technical apparatus which in turn reproduces it.

We live and die rationally and productively. We know that destruction is the price of progress as death is the price of life, that renunciation and toil are the prerequisites for gratification and joy, that business must go on, and that the alternatives are Utopian. This ideology belongs to the established societal apparatus; it is a requisite for its continuous functioning and part of its rationality.

However, the apparatus defeats its own purpose if its purpose is to create a humane existence on the basis of a humanized nature. And if this is not its purpose, its rationality is even more suspect. But it is also more logical for, from the beginning, the negative is in the positive, the inhuman in the humanization, enslavement in liberation. This dynamic is that of reality and not of the mind, but of a reality in which the scientific mind had a decisive part in joining theoretical and practical reason.

Society reproduced itself in a growing technical ensemble of things and relations which included the technical utilization of men—in other words, the struggle for existence and the exploitation of man and nature became ever more scientific and rational. The double meaning of "rationalization" is relevant in this context. Scientific management and scientific division of labor vastly increased the productivity of the economic, political, and cultural enterprise. Result: the higher standard of living. At the same time and on the same ground, this rational enterprise produced a pattern of mind and behavior which justified and absolved even the most destructive and oppressive features of the enterprise. Scientific-technical rationality and manipulation are welded together into new forms of social control. Can one rest content with the assumption that this unscientific outcome is the result of a specific societal *application* of science? I think that the general direction in which it came to be applied was inherent in pure science even where no practical purposes were intended, and that the point can be identified where theoretical Reason turns into social practice. In this attempt, I shall briefly recall the methodological origins of the new rationality, contrasting it with the features of the pre-technological model discussed in the previous chapter.

The quantification of nature, which led to its explication in terms of mathematical structures, separated reality from all inherent ends and, consequently, separated the true from the good, science from ethics. No matter how science may now define the objectivity of nature and the interrelations among its parts, it cannot scientifically conceive it in terms of "final causes." And no matter how constitutive may be the role of the subject as point of observation, measurement, and calculation, this subject cannot play its scientific role as ethical or aesthetic or political agent. The tension between Reason on the one hand, and the needs and wants of the underlying population (which has been the object but rarely the subject of Reason) on the other, has been there from the beginning of philosophic and scientific thought. The "nature of things," including that of society, was so defined as to justify repression and even suppression as perfectly rational. True knowledge and reason demand domination over—if not liberation from—the senses. The union of Logos and Eros led already in Plato to the supremacy of Logos; in Aristotle, the relation between the god and the world moved by him is "erotic" only in terms of analogy. Then the precarious ontological link between Logos and Eros is broken, and scientific rationality emerges as essentially neutral. What nature (including man) may be striving for is scientifically rational only in terms of the general laws of motion—physical, chemical, or biological.

Outside this rationality, one lives in a world of values, and values separated out from the objective reality become subjective. The only way to rescue some abstract and harmless validity for them seems to be a metaphysical sanction (divine and natural law). But such sanction is not verifiable and thus not really objective. Values may have a higher dignity (morally and spiritually), but they are not *real* and thus count less in the real business of life—the less so the higher they are elevated *above* reality.

The same de-realization affects all ideas which, by their very nature, cannot be verified by scientific method. No matter how much they may be recognized, respected, and sanctified, in their own right, they suffer from being non-objective. But precisely their lack of objectivity makes them into factors of social cohesion. Humanitarian, religious, and moral ideas are only "ideal"; they don't disturb unduly the established way of life, and are not invalidated by the fact that they are contradicted by a behavior dictated by the daily necessities of business and politics.

If the Good and the Beautiful, Peace and Justice cannot be derived either from ontological or scientific-rational conditions, they cannot logically claim universal validity and realization. In terms of scientific reason, they remain matters of preference, and no resuscitation of some kind of Aristotelian or Thomistic philosophy can save the situation, for it is *a priori* refuted by scientific reason. The unscientific character of these ideas fatally weakens the opposition to the established reality; the ideas become mere *ideals*, and their concrete, critical content evaporates into the ethical or metaphysical atmosphere.

Paradoxically, however, the objective world, left equipped only with quantifiable qualities, comes to be more and more dependent in its objectivity on the subject. This long process begins with the algebraization of geometry which replaces "visible" geometric figures with purely mental operations. It finds its extreme form in some conceptions of contemporary scientific philosophy, according to which all matter of physical science tends to dissolve in mathematical or logical relations. The very notion of an objective substance, pitted against the subject, seems to disintegrate. From very different directions, scientists and philosophers of science arrive at similar hypotheses on the exclusion of particular sorts of entities.

For example, physics "does not measure the objective qualities of the external and material world—these are only the results obtained by the accomplishment of such operations."[1] Objects continue to persist only as "convenient intermediaries," as obsolescent "cultural posits."[2] The density and opacity of things evaporate: the objective world loses its "objectionable" character, its opposition to the subject. Short of its interpretation in terms of Pythagorean-Platonic metaphysics, the mathematized Nature, the scientific reality appears to be ideational reality.

These are extreme statements, and they are rejected by more conservative interpretations, which insist that propositions in contemporary physics still refer to "physical things."[3] But the physical things turn out to be "physical events," and then the propositions refer to (and refer *only* to) attributes and relationships that characterize various kinds of physical things and processes.[4] Max Born states:

". . . the theory of relativity . . . has never abandoned all attempts to assign properties to matter . . ." But "often a measurable quantity is not a property of a thing, but a property of its *relation* to other things . . . Most measurements in physics are not directly concerned with the things which interest us, but with some kind of projection, the word taken in the widest possible sense."[5]

And W. Heisenberg:

1. Herbert Dingler, in *Nature*, vol. 168 (1951), p. 630.
2. W. V. O. Quine, *From a Logical Point of View*, Cambridge, Harvard Univ. Press (1953), p. 44. Quine speaks of the "myth of physical objects" and says that "in point of epistemological footing the physical objects and the gods [of Homer] differ only in degree and not in kind" (*ibid.*). But the myth of physical objects is epistemologically superior "in that it has proved more efficacious than other myths as a device for working a manageable structure into the flux of experience." The evaluation of the scientific concept in terms of "efficacious," "device," and "manageable" reveals its manipulative-technological elements.
3. H. Reichenbach, in Philipp G. Frank (ed.), *The Validation of Scientific Theories* (Boston, Beacon Press, 1954), p. 85 f. (quoted by Adolf Grünbaum)
4. Adolf Grünbaum, *ibid.*, p. 87 f.
5. *Ibid.*, p. 88 f. (my italics).

"Was wir mathematisch festlegen, ist nur zum kleinen Teil ein 'objectives Faktum,' zum grösseren Teil eine Uebersicht über Möglichkeiten." [6]

Now "events," "relations," "projections," "possibilities" can be meaningfully objective only for a subject—not only in terms of observability and measurability, but in terms of the very structure of the event or relationship. In other words, the subject here involved is a *constituting* one—that is, a possible subject for which some *data* must be, or can be conceivable as event or relation. If this is the case, Reichenbach's statement would still hold true: that propositions in physics can be formulated without reference to an *actual* observer, and the "disturbance by means of observation," is due, not to the human observer, but to the instrument as "physical thing." [7]

To be sure, we may assume that the equations established by mathematical physics express (formulate) the actual constellation of atoms, i.e., the objective structure of matter. Regardless of any observing and measuring "outside" subject A may "include" B, "precede" B, "result in" B; B may be "between" C, "larger than" C, etc.—it would still be true that these relations imply location, distinction, and identity in the difference of A, B, C. They thus imply the capacity of *being* identical in difference, of *being* related to . . . in a specific mode, of *being* resistant to other relations, etc. Only this capacity would be in matter itself, and then matter itself would be objectively of the structure of mind—an interpretation which contains a strong idealistic element:

". . . inanimate objects, without hesitation, without error, simply by their existence, are integrating the equations of which they

6. "What we establish mathematically is 'objective fact' only in small part, in larger part it is a survey of possibilities." "Über den Begriff 'Abgeschlossene Theorie,'" in: *Dialectica*, vol. II, no. 1, 1948, p. 333.
7. Philipp G. Frank, *loc. cit.*, p. 85.

know nothing. Subjectively, nature is not of the mind—she does not think in mathematical terms. But objectively, nature is of the mind—she can be thought in mathematical terms." [8]

A less idealistic interpretation is offered by Karl Popper,[9] who holds that, in its historical development, physical science uncovers and defines different layers of one and the same objective reality. In this process, the historically surpassed concepts are being cancelled and their intent is being integrated into the succeeding ones—an interpretation which seems to imply progress toward the real core of reality, that is, the absolute truth. Or else reality may turn out to be an onion without a core, and the very concept of scientific truth may be in jeopardy.

I do not suggest that the philosophy of contemporary physics denies or even questions the reality of the external world but that, in one way or another, it suspends judgment on what reality itself may be, or considers the very question meaningless and unanswerable. Made into a methodological principle, this suspenion has a twofold consequence: (a) it strengthens the shift of theoretical emphasis from the metaphysical "What is . . . ?" ($\tau\iota$ $\dot{\epsilon}\sigma\tau\iota\nu$) to the functional "How . . . ?", and (b) it establishes a practical (though by no means absolute) certainty which, in its operations with matter, is with good conscience free from commitment to any substance outside the operational context. In other words, theoretically, the transformation of man and nature has no other objective limits than those offered by the brute factuality of matter, its still unmastered resistance to knowledge and control. To the degree to which this conception

8. C. F. von Weizsäcker, *The History of Nature* (Chicago: University of Chicago Press, 1949), p. 20.
9. In: *British Philosophy in the Mid-Century* (N.Y.: Macmillan, 1957), ed. C. A. Mace, p. 155 ff. Similarly: Mario Bunge, *Metascientific Queries* (Springfield, Ill.: Charles C. Thomas, 1959), p. 108 ff.

becomes applicable and effective in reality, the latter is approached as a (hypothetical) system of instrumentalities; the metaphysical "being-as-such" gives way to "being-instrument." Moreover, proved in its effectiveness, this conception works as an *a priori*—it predetermines experience, it *projects* the direction of the transformation of nature, it organizes the whole.

We just saw that contemporary philosophy of science seemed to be struggling with an idealistic element and, in its extreme formulations, moving dangerously close to an idealistic concept of nature. However, the new mode of thought again puts idealism "on its feet." Hegel epitomized the idealistic ontology: if Reason is the common denominator of subject and object, it is so as the synthesis of *opposites*. With this idea, ontology comprehended the *tension* between subject and object; it was saturated with concreteness. The reality of Reason was the playing out of this tension in nature, history, philosophy. Even the most extremely monistic system thus maintained the idea of a substance which unfolds itself in subject and object—the idea of an antagonistic reality. The scientific spirit has increasingly weakened this antagonism. Modern scientific philosophy may well begin with the notion of the two substances, *res cogitans* and *res extensa*—but as the extended matter becomes comprehensible in mathematical equations which, translated into technology, "remake" this matter, the *res extensa* loses its character as independent substance.

"The old division of the world into objective processes in space and time and the mind in which these processes are mirrored—in other words, the Cartesian difference between *res cogitans* and *res extensa*—is no longer a suitable starting point for our understanding of modern science." [10]

10. W. Heisenberg, *The Physicist's Conception of Nature* (London, Hutchinson, 1958), p. 29. In his *Physics and Philosophy* (London: Allen and Unwin, 1959), p. 83, Heisenberg writes: "The 'thing-in-itself' if for the

The Cartesian division of the world has also been questioned on its own grounds. Husserl pointed out that the Cartesian *Ego* was, in the last analysis, not really an independent substance but rather the "residue" or limit of quantification; it seems that Galileo's idea of the world as a "universal and absolutely pure" *res extensa* dominated *a priori* the Cartesian conception.[11] In which case the Cartesian dualism would be deceptive, and Descartes' thinking ego-substance would be akin to the *res extensa*, anticipating the scientific subject of quantifiable observation and measurement. Descartes' dualism would already imply its negation; it would clear rather than block the road toward the establishment of a one-dimensional scientific universe in which nature is "objectively of the mind," that is, of the subject. And this subject is related to its world in a very special way:

"... la nature est mise sous le signe de l'homme actif, de l'homme inscrivant la technique dans la nature." [12]

The science of nature develops under the *technological a priori* which projects nature as potential instrumentality, stuff of control and organization. And the apprehension of nature as (hypothetical) instrumentality *precedes* the development of all particular technical organization:

"Modern man takes the entirety of Being as raw material for production and subjects the entirety of the object-world to the sweep and order of production (*Herstellen*)." "... the use of

atomic physicist, if he uses this concept at all, finally a mathematical structure; but this structure is—contrary to Kant—indirectly deduced from experience."

11. *Die Krisis der Europäischen Wissenschaften und die transzendentale Phänomenologie*, ed. W. Biemel (Haag, Nijhoff, 1954), p. 81.

12. "Nature is placed under the sign of active man, of the man who inscribes technique in nature." Gaston Bachelard, *L'Activité rationaliste de la physique contemporaine* (Paris, Presses Universitaires, 1951) p. 7, with reference to Marx and Engels, *Die Deutsche Ideologie* (trad. Molitor, p. 163 f).

machinery and the production of machines is not technics itself but merely an adequate instrument for the realization (*Einrichtung*) of the essence of technics in its objective raw material." [13]

The technological *a priori* is a political *a priori* inasmuch as the transformation of nature involves that of man, and inasmuch as the "man-made creations" issue from and re-enter a societal ensemble. One may still insist that the machinery of the technological universe is "as such" indifferent towards political ends—it can revolutionize or retard a society. An electronic computer can serve equally a capitalist or socialist administration; a cyclotron can be an equally efficient tool for a war party or a peace party. This neutrality is contested in Marx's controversial statement that the "hand-mill gives you society with the feudal lord; the steam-mill society with the industrial capitalist." [14] And this statement is further modified in Marxian theory itself: the social mode of production, not technics is the basic historical factor. However, when technics becomes the universal form of material production, it circumscribes an entire culture; it projects a historical totality—a "world."

Can we say that the evolution of scientific method merely "reflects" the transformation of natural into technical reality in the process of industrial civilization? To formulate the relation between science and society in this way is assuming two separate realms and events that meet each other, namely, (1) science and scientific thought, with their internal concepts and their internal truth, and (2) the use and application of science in the social reality. In other words, no matter how close the connection between the two developments may be, they do not imply and define

13. Martin Heidegger, *Holzwege* (Frankfurt, Klostermann, 1950), p. 266 ff. (My translation). See also his *Vorträge and Aufsätze* (Pfüllingen, Günther Neske, 1954), p. 22, 29.
14. *The Poverty of Philosophy*, chapter II, "Second Observation"; in: *A Handbook of Marxism*, ed. E. Burns, New York, 1935, p. 355.

each other. Pure science is not applied science; it retains its identity and validity apart from its utilization. Moreover, this notion of the essential *neutrality* of science is also extended to technics. The machine is indifferent toward the social uses to which it is put, provided those uses remain within its technical capabilities.

In view of the internal instrumentalist character of scientific method, this interpretation appears inadequate. A closer relationship seems to prevail between scientific thought and its application, between the universe of scientific discourse and that of ordinary discourse and behavior— a relationship in which both move under the same logic and rationality of domination.

In a paradoxical development, the scientific efforts to establish the rigid objectivity of nature led to an increasing de-materialization of nature:

"The idea of infinite nature existing as such, this idea that we have to give up, is the myth of modern science. Science has started out by destroying the myth of the Middle Ages. And now science is forced by its own consistency to realize that it has merely raised another myth instead." [15]

The process which begins with the elimination of independent substances and final causes arrives at the ideation of objectivity. But it is a very specific ideation, in which the object constitutes itself in a quite *practical* relation to the subject:

"And what is matter? In atomic physics, matter is defined by its possible reactions to human experiments, and by the mathematical—that is, intellectual—laws it obeys. We are *defining* matter as a possible object of man's manipulation." [16]

And if this is the case, then science has become in itself technological:

15. C. F. von Weizsäcker, *The History of Nature,* loc. cit., p. 71.
16. *Ibid.,* p. 142 (my emphasis).

"Pragmatic science has the view of nature that is fitting for a technical age." [17]

To the degree to which this operationalism becomes the center of the scientific enterprise, rationality assumes the form of methodical construction; organization and handling of matter as the mere stuff of control, as instrumentality which lends itself to all purposes and ends—instrumentality *per se,* "in itself."

The "correct" attitude toward instrumentality is the *technical* approach, the correct logos is *techno-logy,* which projects and responds to a *technological reality.* [18] In this reality, matter as well as science is "neutral"; objectivity has neither a telos in itself nor is it structured toward a telos. But it is precisely its neutral character which relates objectivity to a specific historical Subject—namely, to the consciousness that prevails in the society by which and for which this neutrality is established. It operates in the very abstractions which constitute the new rationality—as an internal rather than external factor. Pure and applied operationalism, theoretical and practical reason, the scientific and the business enterprise execute the reduction of secondary to primary qualities, quantification and abstraction from "particular sorts of entities."

True, the rationality of pure science is value-free and does not stipulate any practical ends, it is "neutral" to any extraneous values that may be imposed upon it. But this neutrality is a *positive* character. Scientific rationality makes for a specific societal organization precisely because it

17. *Ibid.,* p. 71.
18. I hope I will not be misunderstood as suggesting that the concepts of mathematical physics are designed as "tools," that they have a technical, practical intent. Techno-logical is rather the *a priori* "intuition" or apprehension of the universe in which science moves, in which it constitutes itself as *pure* science. Pure science remains committed to the *a priori* from which it abstracts. It might be clearer to speak of the instrumentalist *horizon* of mathematical physics. See Suzanne Bachelard, *La Conscience de rationalité* (Paris, Presses Universitaires, 1958), p. 31.

projects mere form (or mere matter—here, the otherwise opposite terms converge) which can be bent to practically all ends. Formalization and functionalization are, *prior* to all application, the "pure form" of a concrete societal practice. While science freed nature from inherent ends and stripped matter of all but quantifiable qualities, society freed men from the "natural" hierarchy of personal dependence and related them to each other in accordance with quantifiable qualities—namely, as units of abstract labor power, calculable in units of time. "By virtue of the rationalization of the modes of labor, the elimination of qualities is transferred from the universe of science to that of daily experience." [19]

Between the two processes of scientific and societal quantification, is there parallelism and causation, or is their connection simply the work of sociological hindsight? The preceding discussion proposed that the new scientific rationality was in itself, in its very abstractness and purity, operational inasmuch as it developed under an instrumentalist horizon. Observation and experiment, the methodical organization and coordination of data, propositions, and conclusions never proceed in an unstructured, neutral, theoretical space. The project of cognition involves operations on objects, or abstractions from objects which occur in a given universe of discourse and action. Science observes, calculates, and theorizes from a position in this universe. The stars which Galileo observed were the same in classical antiquity, but the different universe of discourse and action—in short, the different social reality—opened the new direction and range of observation, and the possibilities of ordering the observed data. I am not concerned here with the historical relation between scientific and societal rationality in the beginning of the modern period. It is my purpose to demonstrate the *internal* instrumentalist character of this scientific

19. M. Horkheimer and T. W. Adorno, *Dialektik der Aufklärung*, loc. cit., p. 50 (my translation).

rationality by virtue of which it is *a priori* technology, and the *a priori* of a *specific* technology—namely, technology as form of social control and domination.

Modern scientific thought, inasmuch as it is pure, does not project particular practical goals nor particular forms of domination. However, there is no such thing as domination *per se*. As theory proceeds, it abstracts from, or rejects, a factual teleological context—that of the given, concrete universe of discourse and action. It is within this universe itself that the scientific project occurs or does not occur, that theory conceives or does not conceive the possible alternatives, that its hypotheses subvert or extend the pre-established reality.

The principles of modern science were *a priori* structured in such a way that they could serve as conceptual instruments for a universe of self-propelling, productive control; theoretical operationalism came to correspond to practical operationalism. The scientific method which led to the ever-more-effective domination of nature thus came to provide the pure concepts as well as the instrumentalities for the ever-more-effective domination of man by man *through* the domination of nature. Theoretical reason, remaining pure and neutral, entered into the service of practical reason. The merger proved beneficial to both. Today, domination perpetuates and extends itself not only through technology but *as* technology, and the latter provides the great legitimation of the expanding political power, which absorbs all spheres of culture.

In this universe, technology also provides the great rationalization of the unfreedom of man and demonstrates the "technical" impossibility of being autonomous, of determining one's own life. For this unfreedom appears neither as irrational nor as political, but rather as submission to the technical apparatus which enlarges the comforts of life and increases the productivity of labor. Technological rationality thus protects rather than cancels the legitimacy of domination, and the instrumentalist horizon of reason opens on a rationally totalitarian society:

"On pourrait nommer philosophie autocratique des techniques celle qui prend l'ensemble technique comme un lieu où l'on utilise les machines pour obtenir de la puissance. La machine est seulement un moyen; la fin est la conquête de la nature, la domestication des forces naturelles au moyen d'un premier asservissement: la machine est un esclave qui sert à faire d'autres esclaves. Une pareille inspiration dominatrice et esclavagiste peut se rencontrer avec une requête de liberté pour l'homme. Mais il est difficile de se libérer en transférant l'esclavage sur d'autres êtres, hommes, animaux ou machines; régner sur un peuple de machines asservissant le monde entier, c'est encore régner, et tout règne suppose l'acceptation des schèmes d'asservissement." [20]

The incessant dynamic of technical progress has become permeated with political content, and the Logos of technics has been made into the Logos of continued servitude. The liberating force of technology—the instrumentalization of things—turns into a fetter of liberation; the instrumentalization of man.

This interpretation would tie the scientific project (method and theory), *prior* to all application and utilization, to a specific societal project, and would see the tie precisely in the inner form of scientific rationality, i.e., in the functional character of its concepts. In other words, the scientific

20. "One might call autocratic a philosophy of technics which takes the technical whole as a place where machines are used to obtain power. The machine is only a means; the end is the conquest of nature, the domestication of natural forces through a primary enslavement: The machine is a slave which serves to make other slaves. Such a domineering and enslaving drive may go together with the quest for human freedom. But it is difficult to liberate oneself by transferring slavery to other beings, men, animals, or machines; to rule over a population of machines subjecting the whole world means still to rule, and all rule implies acceptance of schemata of subjection." Gilbert Simondon, *Du Mode d'existence des objets techniques* (Paris, Aubier, 1958), p. 127.

universe (that is, not the specific propositions on the structure of matter, energy, their interrelation, etc., but the projection of nature as quantifiable matter, as guiding the hypothetical approach to—and the mathematical-logical expression of—objectivity) would be the horizon of a concrete societal practice which would be *preserved* in the development of the scientific project.

But, even granting the internal instrumentalism of scientific rationality, this assumption would not yet establish the *socio*-logical validity of the scientific project. Granted that the formation of the most abstract scientific concepts still preserves the interrelation between subject and object in a given universe of discourse and action, the link between theoretical and practical reason can be understood in quite different ways.

Such a different interpretation is offered by Jean Piaget in his "genetic epistemology." Piaget interprets the formation of scientific concepts in terms of different abstractions from a general interrelation between subject and object. Abstraction proceeds neither from the mere object, so that the subject functions only as the neutral point of observation and measurement, nor from the subject as the vehicle of pure cognitive Reason. Piaget distinguishes between the process of cognition in mathematics and in physics. The former is abstraction "à l'intérieur de l'action comme telle":

"Contrairement à ce que l'on dit souvent, les êtres mathématiques ne résultent donc pas d'une abstraction à partir des objets, mais bien d'une abstraction effectuée au sein des actions comme telles. Réunir, ordonner, déplacer, etc. sont des actions plus générales que penser, pousser, etc. parce qu'elles tiennent à la coordination même de toutes les actions particulières et entrent en chacune d'elles à titre de facteur coordinateur . . ." [21]

21. "Contrary to what is often said, mathematical entities are not therefore the result of an abstraction based on objects but rather of an abstraction made in the midst of actions as such. To assemble, to order, to

Mathematical propositions thus express "une accomodation générale à l'objet"—in contrast to the particular adaptations which are characteristic of true propositions in physics. Logic and mathematical logic are "une action sur l'objet quelconque, c'est-à-dire une action accomodée de façon générale";[22] and this "action" is of general validity in as much as

"cette abstraction ou différenciation porte jusqu'au sein des coordinations héréditaires, puisque les mécanismes coordinateurs de l'action tiennent toujours, en leur source, à des coordinations réflexes et instinctives."[23]

In physics, abstraction proceeds from the object but is due to specific actions on the part of the subject, thus abstraction assumes necessarily a logic-mathematical form because

"des actions particulières ne donnent lieu à une connaissance que coordonnées entre elles et que cette coordination est, par sa nature même, logico-mathématique."[24]

Abstraction in physics leads necessarily back to logico-mathematical abstraction and the latter is, as pure coordination, the general form of action—"action as such" (*l'action comme telle*). And this coordination constitutes objectivity because it retains hereditary, "reflexive and instinctive" structures.

---

move, etc., are more general actions than to think, to push, etc., because they insist on the coordination itself of all particular actions and because they enter into each of them as coordinating factor." *Introduction à l'épistémologie génétique*, tome III (Presses Universitaires, Paris, 1950), p. 287.

22. *Ibid.*, p. 288.

23. "This abstraction or differentiation extends to the very center of hereditary coordinations because the coordinating mechanisms of the action are always attached, at their source, to coordinations by reflex and instinct." *Ibid.*, p. 289.

24. "Particular actions result only in knowledge if they are coordinated among them and if this coordination is in its very nature logical-mathematical." *Ibid.*, p. 291.

Piaget's interpretation recognizes the internal practical character of theoretical reason, but derives it from a general structure of action which, in the last analysis, is a hereditary, biological structure. Scientific method would ultimately rest on a biological foundation, which is supra- (or rather infra-) historical. Moreover, granted that all scientific knowledge presupposes coordination of particular actions, I do not see why such coordination is "by its very nature" logico-mathematical—unless the "particular actions" are the scientific operations of modern physics, in which case the interpretation would be circular.

In contrast to Piaget's rather psychological and biological analysis, Husserl has offered a genetic epistemology which is focused on the socio-historical structure of scientific reason. I shall here refer to Husserl's work[25] only insofar as it emphasizes the extent to which modern science is the "methodology" of a pre-given historical reality within whose universe it moves.

Husserl starts with the fact that the mathematization of nature resulted in valid practical knowledge: in the construction of an "ideational" reality which could be effectively "correlated" with the *empirical* reality (p. 19; 42). But the scientific achievement referred back to a *pre*-scientific practice, which constituted the original basis (the *Sinnesfundament*) of Galilean science. This pre-scientific basis of science in the world of practice (*Lebenswelt*), which determined the theoretical structure, was not questioned by Galileo; moreover, it was concealed (*verdeckt*) by the further development of science. The result was the illusion that the mathematization of nature created an "autonomous (*eigenständige*) absolute truth" (p. 49 f.), while in reality, it remained a specific method and technique for the *Lebens-*

25. *Die Krisis der Europäischen Wissenschaften und die transcendentale Phänomenologie, loc. cit.*

welt. The ideational *veil* (*Ideenkleid*) of mathematical science is thus a veil of *symbols* which represents and at the same time masks (*vertritt* and *verkleidet*) the world of practice (p. 52).

What is the original, pre-scientific intent and content that is preserved in the conceptual structure of science? *Measurement* in practice discovers the possibility of using certain basic forms, shapes, and relations, which are universally "available as identically the same, for exactly determining and calculating empirical objects and relations" (p. 25). Through all abstraction and generalization, scientific method retains (and masks) its pre-scientific-technical structure; the development of the former represents (and masks) the development of the latter. Thus classical geometry "idealizes" the practice of surveying and measuring the land (*Feldmesskunst*). Geometry is the theory of practical objectification.

To be sure, algebra and mathematical logic construct an absolute ideational reality, freed from the incalculable uncertainties and particularities of the *Lebenswelt* and of the subjects living in it. However, this ideational construction *is* the theory and technic of "idealizing" the new *Lebenswelt*:

"In the mathematical practice, we attain what is denied to us in the empirical practice, i.e., *exactness*. For it is possible to determine the ideal forms in terms of *absolute identity* . . . As such, they become universally available and disposable . . ." (p. 24).

The coordination (*Zuordnung*) of the ideational with the empirical world enables us to "project the anticipated regularities of the practical Lebenswelt":

"Once one possesses the formulas, one possesses the *foresight* which is desired in practice"

—the foresight of that which is to be expected in the experience of concrete life (p. 43).

Husserl emphasizes the pre-scientific, technical connotations of mathematical exactness and fungibility. These central notions of modern science emerge, not as mere by-products of a pure science, but as pertaining to its inner conceptual structure. The scientific abstraction from concreteness, the quantification of qualities which yield exactness as well as universal validity, involve a specific concrete experience of the *Lebenswelt*—a specific mode of "seeing" the world. And this "seeing," in spite of its "pure," disinterested character, is seeing within a purposive, practical context. It is anticipating (*Voraussehen*) and projecting (*Vorhaben*). Galilean science is the science of methodical, systematic anticipation and projection. But—and this is decisive—of a specific anticipation and projection—namely, that which experiences, comprehends, and shapes the world in terms of calculable, predictable relationships among exactly identifiable units. In this project, universal quantifiability is a prerequisite for the *domination* of nature. Individual, non-quantifiable qualities stand in the way of an organization of men and things in accordance with the measurable power to be extracted from them. But this is a specific, socio-historical project, and the consciousness which undertakes this project is the hidden subject of Galilean science; the latter is the technic, the art of anticipation extended in infinity (*ins Unendliche erweiterte Voraussicht:* p. 51).

Now precisely because Galilean science is, in the formation of its concepts, the technic of a specific *Lebenswelt,* it does not and cannot *transcend* this Lebenswelt. It remains essentially within the basic experiential framework and within the universe of ends set by this reality. In Husserl's formulation; in Galilean science, the "concrete universe of causality becomes applied mathematics" (p. 112)—but the world of perception and experience, "in which we live our whole practical life, remains as that which it is, in its essential structure, in its own concrete causality *unchanged . . .*" (p. 51; my italics).

A provocative statement, which is easily minimized, and I take the liberty of a possible overinterpretation. The statement does not refer simply to the fact that, in spite of non-Euclidean geometry, we still perceive and act in three-dimensional space; or that, in spite ot the "statistical" concept of causality, we still act, in common sense, in accord with the "old" laws of causality. Nor does the statement contradict the perpetual changes in the world of daily practice as the result of "applied mathematics." Much more may be at stake: namely, the inherent limit of the established science and scientific method, by virtue of which they extend, rationalize, and insure the prevailing *Lebenswelt* without altering its existential structure—that is *without envisaging a qualitatively new mode of "seeing"* and qualitatively new relations between men and between man and nature.

With respect to the institutionalized forms of life, science (pure as well as applied) would thus have a stabilizing, static, conservative function. Even its most revolutionary achievements would only be construction and destruction in line with a specific experience and organization of reality. The continuous self-correction of science—the revolution of its hypotheses which is built into its method—itself propels and extends the same historical universe, the same basic experience. It retains the same formal *a priori*, which makes for a very material, practical content. Far from minimizing the fundamental change which occurred with the establishment of Galilean science, Husserl's interpretation points up the radical break with the pre-Galilean tradition; the instrumentalist horizon of thought was indeed a new horizon. It created a new world of theoretical and practical Reason, but it has remained committed to a specific historical world which has its evident limits—in theory as well as in practice, in its pure as well as applied methods.

The preceding discussion seems to suggest not only the inner limitations and prejudices of scientific method but also its historical subjectivity. Moreover, it seems to imply the need for some sort of "qualitative physics," revival of teleological philosophies, etc. I admit that this suspicion is justified, but at this point, I can only assert that no such obscurantist ideas are intended.[26]

No matter how one defines truth and objectivity, they remain related to the human agents of theory and practice, and to their ability to comprehend and change their world. This ability in turn depends on the extent to which matter (whatever it may be) is recognized and understood as that which it *is* itself in all particular forms. In these terms, contemporary science is of immensely greater objective validity than its predecessors. One might even add that, at present, the scientific method is the only method that can claim such validity; the interplay of hypotheses and observable facts validates the hypotheses and establishes the facts. The point which I am trying to make is that science, *by virtue of its own method* and concepts, has projected and promoted a universe in which the domination of nature has remained linked to the domination of man—a link which tends to be fatal to this universe as a whole. Nature, scientifically comprehended and mastered, reappears in the technical apparatus of production and destruction which sustains and improves the life of the individuals while subordinating them to the masters of the apparatus. Thus the rational hierarchy merges with the social one. If this is the case, then the change in the direction of progress, which might sever this fatal link, would also affect the very structure of science— the scientific project. Its hypotheses, without losing their rational character, would develop in an essentially different

26. See chapter IX and X below.

experimental context (that of a pacified world); consequently, science would arrive at essentially different concepts of nature and establish essentially different facts. The rational society subverts the idea of Reason.

I have pointed out that the elements of this subversion, the notions of another rationality, were present in the history of thought from its beginning. The ancient idea of a state where Being attains fulfillment, where the tension between "is" and "ought" is resolved in the cycle of an eternal return, partakes of the metaphysics of domination. But it also pertains to the metaphysics of liberation—to the reconciliation of Logos and Eros. This idea envisages the coming-to-rest of the repressive productivity of Reason, the end of domination in gratification.

The two contrasting rationalities cannot simply be correlated with classical and modern thought respectively, as in John Dewey's formulation "from contemplative enjoyment to active manipulation and control"; and "from knowing as an esthetic enjoyment of the properties of nature . . . to knowing as a means of secular control."[27] Classical thought was sufficiently committed to the logic of secular control, and there is a sufficient component of indictment and refusal in modern thought to vitiate John Dewey's formulation. Reason, as conceptual thought and behavior, is necessarily mastery, domination. Logos is law, rule, order by virtue of knowledge. In subsuming particular cases under a universal, in subjecting it to their universal, thought attains mastery over the particular cases. It becomes capable not only of comprehending but also of acting upon them, controlling them. However, while all thought stands under the rule of logic, the unfolding of this logic is different in the various modes of thought. Classical formal and modern symbolic logic, transcendental and dialectical logic—each rules

27. John Dewey, *The Quest for Certainty* (New York, Minton, Balch and Co., 1929), p. 95, 100.

over a different universe of discourse and experience. They all developed within the historical continuum of domination to which they pay tribute. And this continuum bestows upon the modes of positive thinking their conformist and ideological character; upon those of negative thinking their speculative and utopian character.

By way of summary, we may now try to identify more clearly the hidden subject of scientific rationality and the hidden ends in its pure form. The scientific concept of a universally controllable nature projected nature as endless matter-in-function, the mere stuff of theory and practice. In this form, the object-world entered the construction of a technological universe—a universe of mental and physical instrumentalities, means in themselves. Thus it is a truly "hypothetical" system, depending on a validating and verifying subject.

The processes of validation and verification may be purely theoretical ones, but they never occur in a vacuum and they never terminate in a private, individual mind. The hypothetical system of forms and functions becomes dependent on another system—a pre-established universe of ends, in which and *for* which it develops. What appeared extraneous, foreign to the theoretical project, shows forth as part of its very structure (method and concepts); pure objectivity reveals itself as *object for a subjectivity* which provides the Telos, the ends. In the construction of the technological reality, there is no such thing as a purely rational scientific order; the process of technological rationality is a political process.

Only in the medium of technology, man and nature become fungible objects of organization. The universal effectiveness and productivity of the apparatus under which they are subsumed veil the particular interests that organize the apparatus. In other words, technology has become the great vehicle of *reification*—reification in its most mature and effective form. The social position of the individual and his relation to others appear not only to be determined by objective qualities and laws, but these qualities and laws seem to lose their mysterious and uncontrollable character; they appear as calculable manifestations of (scientific) rationality. The world tends to become the stuff of total administration, which absorbs even the administrators. The web of domination has become the web of Reason itself, and this society is fatally entangled in it. And the transcending modes of thought seem to transcend Reason itself.

Under these conditions, scientific thought (scientific in the larger sense, as opposed to muddled, metaphysical, emotional, illogical thinking) outside the physical sciences assumes the form of a pure and self-contained formalism (symbolism) on the one hand, and a total empiricism on the other. (The contrast is not a conflict. See the very empirical application of mathematics and symbolic logic in electronic industries.) In relation to the established universe of discourse and behavior, non-contradiction and non-transcendence is the common denominator. Total empiricism reveals its ideological function in contemporary philosophy. With respect to this function, some aspects of linguistic analysis will be discussed in the following chapter. This discussion is to prepare the ground for the attempt to show the barriers which prevent this empiricism from coming to grips with reality, and establishing (or rather re-establishing) the concepts which may break these barriers.

7: The Triumph of Positive Thinking: One-Dimensional Philosophy

The redefinition of thought which helps to coordinate mental operations with those in the social reality aims at a therapy. Thought is on the level with reality when it is cured from transgression beyond a conceptual framework which is either purely axiomatic (logic, mathematics) or coextensive with the established universe of discourse and behavior. Thus, linguistic analysis claims to cure thought and speech from confusing metaphysical notions—from "ghosts" of a less mature and less scientific past which still haunt the mind although they neither designate nor explain. The emphasis is on the *therapeutic* function of philosophical analysis—correction of abnormal behavior in thought and speech, removal of obscurities, illusions, and oddities, or at least their exposure.

In chapter IV, I discussed the therapeutic empiricism of sociology in exposing and correcting abnormal behavior in industrial plants, a procedure which implied the exclusion of critical concepts capable of relating such behavior to the society as a whole. By virtue of this restriction, the theoretical procedure becomes immediately practical. It designs methods of better management, safer planning, greater efficiency, closer calculation. The analysis, via correction and improvement, terminates in affirmation; empiricism proves itself as positive thinking.

The philosophical analysis is of no such immediate application. Compared with the realizations of sociology and psychology, the therapeutic treatment of thought remains academic. Indeed, exact thinking, the liberation from metaphysical spectres and meaningless notions may well be considered ends in themselves. Moreover, the treatment of thought in linguistic analysis is its own affair and its own right. Its ideological character is not to be prejudged by correlating the struggle against conceptual transcendence beyond the established universe of discourse with the struggle against political transcendence beyond the established society.

Like any philosophy worthy of the name, linguistic analysis speaks for itself and defines its own attitude to reality. It identifies as its chief concern the debunking of transcendent concepts; it proclaims as its frame of reference the common usage of words, the variety of prevailing behavior. With these characteristics, it circumscribes its position in the philosophic tradition—namely, at the opposite pole from those modes of thought which elaborated their concepts in tension with, and even in contradiction to, the prevailing universe of discourse and behavior.

In terms of the established universe, such contradicting modes of thought are negative thinking. "The power of the negative" is the principle which governs the development of concepts, and contradiction becomes the distinguishing quality of Reason (Hegel). This quality of thought was not confined to a certain type of rationalism; it was also a decisive element in the empiricist tradition. Empiricism is not necessarily positive; its attitude to the established reality depends on the particular *dimension* of experience which functions as the source of knowledge and as the basic frame of reference. For example, it seems that sensualism and materialism are *per se* negative toward a society in which vital instinctual and material needs are unfulfilled. In contrast, the empiricism of linguistic analysis moves within a framework which does not allow such contradiction—the self-imposed restriction to the prevalent behavioral universe makes for an intrinsically positive attitude. In spite of the rigidly neutral approach of the philosopher, the pre-bound analysis succumbs to the power of positive thinking.

Before trying to show this intrinsically ideological character of linguistic analysis, I must attempt to justify my apparently arbitrary and derogatory play with the terms "positive" and "positivism" by a brief comment on their origin. Since its first usage, probably in the school of Saint-Simon, the term "positivism" has encompassed (1) the validation of cognitive thought by experience of facts; (2) the orientation of cognitive thought to the physical sciences as a model of certainty and exactness; (3) the belief that progress in knowledge depends on this orientation. Consequently, positivism is a struggle against all metaphysics, transcendentalisms, and idealisms as obscurantist and regressive modes of thought. To the degree to which the given reality is scientifically comprehended and transformed, to the degree to which society becomes industrial and technological, positivism finds in the society the medium for the realization (and validation) of its concepts—harmony between theory and practice, truth and facts. Philosophic thought turns into affirmative thought; the philosophic critique criticizes *within* the societal framework and stigmatizes non-positive notions as mere speculation, dreams or fantasies.[1]

The universe of discourse and behavior which begins to speak in Saint-Simon's positivism is that of technological reality. In it, the object-world is being transformed into an instrumentality. Much of that which is still outside the instrumental world—unconquered, blind nature—now appears within the reaches of scientific and technical progress.

1. The conformist attitude of positivism vis-à-vis radically non-conformist modes of thought appears perhaps for the first time in the positivist denunciation of Fourier. Fourier himself (in *La Fausse Industrie*, 1835, vol. I, p. 409) has seen the total commercialism of bourgeois society as the fruit of "our progress in rationalism and positivism." Quoted in André Lalande, *Vocabulaire Technique et Critique de la Philosophie* (Paris, Presses Universitaires de France, 1956), p. 792. For the various connotations of the term "positive" in the new social science, and in opposition to "negative" see *Doctrine de Saint-Simon*, ed. Bouglé and Halévy (Paris, Rivière, 1924), p. 181 f.

The metaphysical dimension, formerly a genuine field of rational thought, becomes irrational and unscientific. On the ground of its own realizations, Reason repels transcendence. At the later stage in contemporary positivism, it is no longer scientific and technical progress which motivates the repulsion; however, the contraction of thought is no less severe because it is self-imposed—philosophy's own method. The contemporary effort to reduce the scope and the truth of philosophy is tremendous, and the philosophers themselves proclaim the modesty and inefficacy of philosophy. It leaves the established reality untouched; it abhors transgression.

Austin's contemptuous treatment of the alternatives to the common usage of words, and his defamation of what we "think up in our armchairs of an afternoon"; Wittgenstein's assurance that philosophy "leaves everything as it is"—such statements[2] exhibit, to my mind, academic sado-masochism, self-humiliation, and self-denunciation of the intellectual whose labor does not issue in scientific, technical or like achievements. These affirmations of modesty and dependence seem to recapture Hume's mood of righteous contentment with the limitations of reason which, once recognized and accepted, protect man from useless mental adventures but leave him perfectly capable of orienting himself in the given environment. However, when Hume debunked substances, he fought a powerful ideology, while his successors today provide an intellectual justification for that which society has long since accomplished—namely, the defamation of alternative modes of thought which contradict the established universe of discourse.

The style in which this philosophic behaviorism presents

2. For similar declarations see Ernest Gellner, *Words And Things* (Boston, Beacon Press, 1959), p. 100, 256 ff. The proposition that philosophy leaves everything as it is may be true in the context of Marx's Theses on Feuerbach (where it is at the same time denied), or as self-characterization of neo-positivism, but as a general proposition on philosophic thought it is incorrect.

itself would be worthy of analysis. It seems to move between the two poles of pontificating authority and easy-going chumminess. Both trends are perfectly fused in Wittgenstein's recurrent use of the imperative with the intimate or condescending "*du*" ("thou");[3] or in the opening chapter of Gilbert Ryle's *The Concept of Mind,* where the presentation of "Descartes' Myth" as the "official doctrine" about the relation of body and mind is followed by the preliminary demonstration of its "absurdity," which evokes John Doe, Richard Roe, and what they think about the "Average Taxpayer."

Throughout the work of the linguistic analysts, there is this familiarity with the chap on the street whose talk plays such a leading role in linguistic philosophy. The chumminess of speech is essential inasmuch as it excludes from the beginning the high-brow vocabulary of "metaphysics"; it militates against intelligent non-conformity; it ridicules the egghead. The language of John Doe and Richard Roe is the language which the man on the street actually speaks; it is the language which expresses his behavior; it is therefore the token of concreteness. However, it is also the token of a false concreteness. The language which provides most of the material for the analysis is a purged language, purged not only of its "unorthodox" vocabulary, but also of the means for expressing any other contents than those furnished to the individuals by their society. The linguistic analyst finds this purged language an accomplished fact, and he takes the impoverished language as he finds it, insulating it from that which is not expressed in it although it enters the established universe of discourse as element and factor of meaning.

3. *Philosophical Investigations* (New York: Macmillan, 1960): "Und deine Skrupel sind Missverständnisse. Deine Fragen beziehen sich auf Wörter . . ." (p. 49). "Denk doch einmal garnicht an das Verstehen als 'seelischen Vorgang'!—Denn das ist die Redeweise, die dich verwirrt. Sondern frage dich . . ." (p. 61). "Überlege dir folgenden Fall . . ." (p. 62), and passim.

Paying respect to the prevailing variety of meanings and usages, to the power and common sense of ordinary speech, while blocking (as extraneous material) analysis of what this speech says about the society that speaks it, linguistic philosophy suppresses once more what is continually suppressed in this universe of discourse and behavior. The authority of philosophy gives its blessing to the forces which *make* this universe. Linguistic analysis abstracts from what ordinary language reveals in speaking as it does—the mutilation of man and nature.

Moreover, all too often it is not even the ordinary language which guides the analysis, but rather blown-up atoms of language, silly scraps of speech that sound like baby talk such as "This looks to me now like a man eating poppies," "He saw a robin," "I had a hat." Wittgenstein devotes much acumen and space to the analysis of "My broom is in the corner." I quote, as a representative example, an analysis from J. L. Austin's "Other Minds":[4]

"Two rather different ways of being hesitant may be distinguished.

(a) Let us take the case where we are tasting a certain taste. We may say 'I simply don't know what it is: I've never tasted anything remotely like it before . . . No, it's no use: the more I think about it the more confused I get: it's perfectly distinct and perfectly distinctive, quite unique in my experience!' This illustrates the case where I can find nothing in my past experience with which to compare the current case: I'm certain it's not appreciably like anything I ever tasted before, not sufficiently like anything I know to merit the same description. This case, though distinguishable enough, shades off into the more common type of case where I'm not quite certain, or only fairly certain, or prac-

---

4. In: *Logic and Language*, Second Series, ed. A. Flew (Oxford, Blackwell, 1959), p. 137 f. (Austin's footnotes are omitted). Here too, philosophy demonstrates its loyal conformity to ordinary usage by using the colloquial abridgments of ordinary speech: "Don't . . ." "isn't . . ."

tically certain, that it's the taste of, say, laurel. In all such cases, I am endeavouring to recognize the current item by searching in my past experience for something like it, some likeness in virtue of which it deserves, more or less positively, to be described by the same descriptive word, and I am meeting with varying degrees of success.

(b) The other case is different, though it very naturally combines itself with the first. Here, what I try to do is to *savour* the current experience, to *peer* at it, to *sense* it vividly. I'm not sure it *is* the taste of pineapple: isn't there perhaps just *something* about it, a tang, a bite, a lack of bite, a cloying sensation, which isn't *quite* right for pineapple? Isn't there perhaps just a peculiar hint of green, which would rule out mauve and would hardly do for heliotrope? Or perhaps it is faintly odd: I must look more intently, scan it over and over: maybe just possibly there is a suggestion of an unnatural shimmer, so that it doesn't look quite like ordinary water. There is a lack of sharpness in what we actually sense, which is to be cured not, or not merely, by thinking, but by acuter discernment, by sensory discrimination (though it is of course true that thinking of other, and more pronounced, cases in our past experience can and does assist our powers of discrimination)."

What can be objectionable in this analysis? In its exactness and clarity, it is probably unsurpassable—it is correct. But that is all it is, and I argue that not only is it not enough, but it is destructive of philosophic thought, and of critical thought as such. From the philosophic point of view, two questions arise: (1) can the explication of concepts (or words) ever orient itself to, and terminate, in the actual universe of ordinary discourse? (2) are exactness and clarity ends in themselves, or are they committed to other ends?

I answer the first question in the affirmative as far as its first part is concerned. The most banal examples of speech may, precisely because of their banal character, elucidate the empirical world in its reality, and serve to explain our think-

ing and talking about it—as do Sartre's analyses of a group
of people waiting for a bus, or Karl Kraus' analysis of daily
newspapers. Such analyses elucidate because they transcend
the immediate concreteness of the situation and its expression. They transcend it toward the factors which *make* the
situation and the behavior of the people who speak (or are
silent) in that situation. (In the examples just cited, these
transcendent factors are traced to the social division of labor.) Thus the analysis does not terminate in the universe of
ordinary discourse, it goes beyond it and opens a qualitatively different universe, the terms of which may even contradict
the ordinary one.

   To take another illustration: sentences such as "my
broom is in the corner" might also occur in Hegel's Logic,
but there they would be revealed as inappropriate or even
false examples. They would only be rejects, to be surpassed
by a discourse which, in its concepts, style, and syntax, is of
a different order—a discourse for which it is by no means
"clear that every sentence in our language 'is in order as it
is.'" [5] Rather the exact opposite is the case—namely, that
every sentence is as little in order as the world is which this
language communicates.

   The almost masochistic reduction of speech to the
humble and common is made into a program: "if the words
'language,' 'experience,' 'world,' have a use, it must be
as humble a one as that of the words 'table,' 'lamp,' 'door.'" [6]
We must "stick to the subjects of our every-day thinking,
and not go astray and imagine that we have to describe
extreme subtleties . . ." [7]—as if this were the only alternative, and as if the "extreme subleties" were not the suitable
term for Wittgenstein's language games rather than for Kant's
Critique of Pure Reason. Thinking (or at least its expression)

5. Wittgenstein, *Philosophical Investigations*, loc. cit., p. 45.
6. *Ibid.*, p. 44.
7. *Ibid.*, p. 46.

is not only pressed into the straitjacket of common usage, but also enjoined not to ask and seek solutions beyond those that are already there. "The problems are solved, not by giving new information, but by arranging what we have always known." [8]

The self-styled poverty of philosophy, committed with all its concepts to the given state of affairs, distrusts the possibilities of a new experience. Subjection to the rule of the established facts is total—only linguistic facts, to be sure, but the society speaks in its language, and we are told to obey. The prohibitions are severe and authoritarian: "Philosophy may in no way interfere with the actual use of language." [9] "And we may not advance any kind of theory. There must not be anything hypothetical in our considerations. We must do away with all *explanation,* and description alone must take its place." [10]

One might ask what remains of philosophy? What remains of thinking, intelligence, without anything hypothetical, without any explanation? However, what is at stake is not the definition or the dignity of philosophy. It is rather the chance of preserving and protecting the right, the *need* to think and speak in terms other than those of common usage—terms which are meaningful, rational, and valid precisely because they are other terms. What is involved is the spread of a new ideology which undertakes to describe what is happening (and meant) by eliminating the concepts capable of understanding what is happening (and meant).

To begin with, an irreducible difference exists between the universe of everyday thinking and language on the one side, and that of philosophic thinking and language on the other. In normal circumstances, ordinary language is indeed behavioral—a practical instrument. When somebody actual-

8. *Ibid.,* p. 47. The translation is not exact; the German text has Beibringen neuer Erfahrung for "giving new information."
9. *Ibid.,* p. 49.
10. *Ibid.,* p. 47.

ly says "My broom is in the corner," he probably intends that
somebody else who had actually asked about the broom is
going to take it or leave it there, is going to be satisfied, or
angry. In any case, the sentence has fulfilled its function by
causing a behavioral reaction: "the effect devours the cause;
the end absorbs the means." [11]

In contrast, if, in a philosophic text or discourse, the
word "substance," "idea," "man," "alienation" becomes the
subject of a proposition, no such transformation of meaning
into a behavioral reaction takes place or is intended to take
place. The word remains, as it were, unfulfilled—except in
thought, where it may give rise to other thoughts. And
through a long series of mediations within a historical continuum, the proposition may help to form and guide a
practice. But the proposition remains unfulfilled even then
—only the hubris of absolute idealism asserts the thesis
of a final identity between thought and its object. The words
with which philosophy is concerned can therefore never have
a use "as humble . . . as that of the words 'table,' 'lamp,'
'door.'"

Thus, exactness and clarity in philosophy cannot be
attained within the universe of ordinary discourse. The
philosophic concepts aim at a dimension of fact and meaning
which elucidates the atomized phrases or words of ordinary
discourse "from without" by showing this "without" as essential to the understanding of ordinary discourse. Or, if the
universe of ordinary discourse itself becomes the object of
philosophic analysis, the language of philosophy becomes a
"meta-language." [12] Even where it moves in the humble terms
of ordinary discourse, it remains antagonistic. It dissolves the
established experiential context of meaning into that of its

11. Paul Valéry, "Poésie et pensée abstraite," in: *Oeuvres*, loc. cit., p.
1331. Also "Les Droits du poète sur la langue," in: *Pièces sur l'art* (Paris,
Gallimard, 1934), p. 47 f.
12. See p. 195.

reality; it abstracts from the immediate concreteness in order to attain true concreteness.

Viewed from this position, the examples of linguistic analysis quoted above become questionable as valid objects of philosophic analysis. Can the most exact and clarifying description of tasting something that may or may not taste like pineapple ever contribute to philosophic cognition? Can it ever serve as a critique in which controversial human conditions are at stake—other than conditions of medical or psychological taste-testing, surely not the intent of Austin's analysis. The object of analysis, withdrawn from the larger and denser context in which the speaker speaks and lives, is removed from the universal medium in which concepts are formed and become words. What is this universal, larger context in which people speak and act and which gives their speech its meaning—this context which does not appear in the positivist analysis, which is *a priori* shut off by the examples as well as by the analysis itself?

This larger context of experience, this real empirical world, today is still that of the gas chambers and concentration camps, of Hiroshima and Nagasaki, of American Cadillacs and German Mercedes, of the Pentagon and the Kremlin, of the nuclear cities and the Chinese communes, of Cuba, of brainwashing and massacres. But the real empirical world is also that in which all these things are taken for granted or forgotten or repressed or unknown, in which people are free. It is a world in which the broom in the corner or the taste of something like pineapple are quite important, in which the daily toil and the daily comforts are perhaps the only items that make up all experience. And this second, restricted empirical universe is part of the first; the powers that rule the first also shape the restricted experience.

To be sure, establishing this relation is not the job of ordinary thought in ordinary speech. If it is a matter of finding the broom or tasting the pineapple, the abstraction is justified and the meaning can be ascertained and described without any transgression into the political universe. But in philosophy, the question is not that of finding the broom or tasting the pineapple—and even less so today should an empirical philosophy base itself on abstract experience. Nor is this abstractness corrected if linguistic analysis is applied to political terms and phrases. A whole branch of analytic philosophy is engaged in this undertaking, but the method already shuts off the concepts of a political, i.e., critical analysis. The operational or behavioral translation assimilates such terms as "freedom," "government," "England," with "broom" and "pineapple," and the reality of the former with that of the latter.

Ordinary language in its "humble use" may indeed be of vital concern to critical philosophic thought, but in the medium of this thought words lose their plain humility and reveal that "hidden" something which is of no interest to Wittgenstein. Consider the analysis of the "here" and "now" in Hegel's Phaenomenology, or (*sit venia verbo!*) Lenin's suggestion on how to analyze adequately "this glass of water" on the table. Such an analysis uncovers the *history*[13] in everyday speech as a hidden dimension of meaning—the rule of society over its language. And this discovery shatters the natural and reified form in which the given universe of discourse first appears. The words reveal themselves as genuine terms not only in a grammatical and formal-logical but also material sense; namely, as the limits which define the meaning and its development—the terms which society imposes on discourse, and on behavior. This historical dimension of meaning can no longer be elucidated by examples such as "my broom is in the corner" or "there is cheese on the table." To be sure, such statements can reveal many ambiguities,

13. See p. 79.

puzzles, oddities, but they are all in the same realm of language games and academic boredom.

Orienting itself on the reified universe of everyday discourse, and exposing and clarifying this discourse in terms of this reified universe, the analysis abstracts from the negative, from that which is alien and antagonistic and cannot be understood in terms of the established usage. By classifying and distinguishing meanings, and keeping them apart, it purges thought and speech of contradictions, illusions, and transgressions. But the transgressions are not those of "pure reason." They are not metaphysical transgressions beyond the limits of possible knowledge, they rather open a realm of knowledge beyond common sense and formal logic.

In barring access to this realm, positivist philosophy sets up a self-sufficient world of its own, closed and well protected against the ingression of disturbing external factors. In this respect, it makes little difference whether the validating context is that of mathematics, of logical propositions, or of custom and usage. In one way or another, all possibly meaningful predicates are prejudged. The prejudging judgment might be as broad as the spoken English language, or the dictionary, or some other code or convention. Once accepted, it constitutes an empirical *a priori* which cannot be transcended.

But this radical acceptance of the empirical violates the empirical, for in it speaks the mutilated, "abstract" individual who experiences (and expresses) only that which is *given* to him (given in a literal sense), who has only the facts and not the factors, whose behavior is one-dimensional and manipulated. By virtue of the factual repression, the experienced world is the result of a restricted experience, and the positivist cleaning of the mind brings the mind in line with the restricted experience.

In this expurgated form, the empirical world becomes the object of positive thinking. With all its exploring, exposing, and clarifying of ambiguities and obscurities, neo-positivism is not concerned with the great and general ambiguity and obscurity which is the established universe of experience. And it must remain unconcerned because the method adopted by this philosophy discredits or "translates" the concepts which could guide the understanding of the established reality in its repressive and irrational structure—the concepts of negative thinking. The transformation of critical into positive thinking takes place mainly in the therapeutic treatment of universal concepts; their translation into operational and behavioral terms parallels closely the sociological translation discussed above.

The therapeutic character of the philosophic analysis is strongly emphasized—to cure from illusions, deceptions, obscurities, unsolvable riddles, unanswerable questions, from ghosts and spectres. Who is the patient? Apparently a certain sort of intellectual, whose mind and language do not conform to the terms of ordinary discourse. There is indeed a goodly portion of psychoanalysis in this philosophy—analysis without Freud's fundamental insight that the patient's trouble is rooted in a *general* sickness which cannot be cured by analytic therapy. Or, in a sense, according to Freud, the patient's disease is a protest reaction against the sick world in which he lives. But the physician must disregard the "moral" problem. He has to restore the patient's health, to make him capable of functioning normally in his world.

The philosopher is not a physician; his job is not to cure individuals but to comprehend the world in which they live —to understand it in terms of what it has done to man, and what it can do to man. For philosophy is (historically, and its history is still valid) the contrary of what Wittgenstein made it out to be when he proclaimed it as the renunciation of all theory, as the undertaking that "leaves everything as it is." And philosophy knows of no more useless "discovery" than that which "gives philosophy peace, so that it is no longer tormented by questions which bring *itself* in question." [14] And there is no more unphilosophical motto than Bishop Butler's pronouncement which adorns G. E. Moore's *Principia Ethica:* "Everything is what it is, and not another thing"—unless the "is" is understood as referring to the qualitative difference between that which things really are and that which they are made to be.

The neo-positivist critique still directs its main effort against metaphysical notions, and it is motivated by a notion of exactness which is either that of formal logic or empirical description. Whether exactness is sought in the analytic purity of logic and mathematics, or in conformity with ordinary language—on both poles of contemporary philosophy is the same rejection or devaluation of those elements of thought and speech which transcend the accepted system of validation. This hostility is most sweeping where it takes the form of toleration—that is, where a certain truth value is granted to the transcendent concepts in a separate dimension of meaning and significance (poetic truth, metaphysical truth). For precisely the setting aside of a special reservation in which thought and language are permitted to be legitimately inexact, vague, and even contradictory is the most effective way of protecting the normal universe of discourse from being seriously disturbed by unfitting ideas. Whatever truth may be contained in literature is a "poetic" truth, whatever truth may be contained in critical idealism is a "metaphysical" truth—its validity, if any, commits neither ordinary discourse and behavior, nor the philosophy adjusted to them. This new form of the doctrine of the "double truth" sanctions a false consciousness by denying the relevance of the transcendent language to the universe of ordinary language, by proclaiming total non-interference.

14. *Philosophical Investigations,* loc. cit., p. 51.

Whereas the truth value of the former consists precisely in its relevance to and interference with the latter.

Under the repressive conditions in which men think and live, thought—any mode of thinking which is not confined to pragmatic orientation within the status quo—can recognize the facts and respond to the facts only by "going behind" them. Experience takes place before a curtain which conceals and, if the world is the appearance of something behind the curtain of immediate experience, then, in Hegel's terms, it is we ourselves who are behind the curtain. We ourselves not as the subjects of common sense, as in linguistic analysis, nor as the "purified" subjects of scientific measurement, but as the subjects and objects of the historical struggle of man with nature and with society. Facts are what they are as occurrences in this struggle. Their factuality is historical, even where it is still that of brute, unconquered nature.

This intellectual dissolution and even subversion of the given facts is the historical task of philosophy and the philosophic dimension. Scientific method, too, goes beyond the facts and even against the facts of immediate experience. Scientific method develops in the tension between appearance and reality. The mediation between the subject and object of thought, however, is essentially different. In science, the medium is the observing, measuring, calculating, experimenting subject divested of all other qualities; the abstract subject projects and defines the abstract object.

In contrast, the objects of philosophic thought are related to a consciousness for which the concrete qualities enter into the concepts and into their interrelation. The philosophic concepts retain and explicate the pre-scientific mediations (the work of everyday practice, of economic organization, of political action) which have made the object-world that which it actually is—a world in which all facts are events, occurrences in a historical continuum.

The separation of science from philosophy is itself a historical event. Aristotelian physics was a part of philosophy and, as such, preparatory to the "first science"—ontology. The Aristotelian concept of matter is distinguished from the Galilean and post-Galilean not only in terms of different stages in the development of scientific method (and in the discovery of different "layers" of reality), but also, and perhaps primarily, in terms of different historical projects, of a different historical enterprise which established a different nature as well as society. Aristotelian physics becomes *objectively* wrong with the new experience and apprehension of nature, with the historical establishment of a new subject and object-world, and the falsification of Aristotelian physics then extends backward into the past and surpassed experience and apprehension.[15]

But whether or not they are integrated into science, philosophic concepts remain antagonistic to the realm of ordinary discourse, for they continue to include contents which are not fulfilled in the spoken word, the overt behavior, the perceptible conditions or dispositions, or the prevailing propensities. The philosophic universe thus continues to contain "ghosts," "fictions," and "illusions" which may be more rational than their denial insomuch as they are concepts that recognize the limits and the deceptions of the prevailing rationality. They express the experience which Wittgenstein rejects—namely, that "contrary to our preconceived ideas, it is possible to think 'such-and-such'—whatever that may mean." [16]

The neglect or the clearing up of this specific philosophic dimension has led contemporary positivism to move in a synthetically impoverished world of academic concreteness, and to create more illusory problems than it has destroyed. Rarely has a philosophy exhibited a more tortuous

15. See chapter VI above, especially p. 165.
16. Wittgenstein, *loc. cit.*, p. 47.

esprit de sérieux than that displayed in such analyses as the interpretation of Three Blind Mice in a study of "Metaphysical and Ideographic Language," with its discussion of an "artificially constructed Triple principle-Blindness-Mousery asymmetric sequence constructed according to the pure principles of ideography."[17]

Perhaps this example is unfair. However it is fair to say that the most abstruse metaphysics has not exhibited such artificial and jargonic worries as those which have arisen in connection with the problems of reduction, translation, description, denotation, proper names, etc. Examples are skillfully held in balance between seriousness and the joke: the differences between Scott and the author of *Waverly;* the baldness of the present king of France; Joe Doe meeting or not meeting the "average taxpayer" Richard Roe on the street; my seeing here and now a patch of red and saying "this is red"; or the revelation of the fact that people often describe feelings as thrills, twinges, pangs, throbs, wrenches, itches, prickings, chills, glows, loads, qualms, hankerings, curdlings, sinkings, tensions, gnawings and shocks.[18]

This sort of empiricism substitutes for the hated world of metaphysical ghosts, myths, legends, and illusions a world of conceptual or sensual scraps, of words and utterances which are then organized into a philosophy. And all this is not only legitimate, it is even correct, for it reveals the extent to which non-operational ideas, aspirations, memories and images have become expendable, irrational, confusing, or meaningless.

In cleaning up this mess, analytic philosophy conceptualizes the behavior in the present technological organization of reality, but it also accepts the verdicts of this organization; the debunking of an old ideology becomes part of a

17. Margaret Masterman, in: *British Philosophy in the Mid-Century,* ed. C. A. Mace (London, Allen and Unwin, 1957), p. 323.
18. Gilbert Ryle, *The Concept of Mind,* loc. cit., p. 83 f.

new ideology. Not only the illusions are debunked but also the truth in those illusions. The new ideology finds its expression in such statements as "philosophy only states what everyone admits," or that our common stock of words embodies "all the distinctions men have found worth drawing." What is this "common stock"? Does it include Plato's "idea," Aristotle's "essence," Hegel's *Geist*, Marx's *Verdinglichung* in whatever adequate translation? Does it include the key words of poetic language? Of surrealist prose? And if so, does it contain them in their negative connotation— that is, as invalidating the universe of common usage? If not, then a whole body of distinctions which men have found worth drawing is rejected, removed into the realm of fiction or mythology; a mutilated, false consciousness is set up as the true consciousness that decides on the meaning and expression of that which is. The rest is denounced—and endorsed—as fiction or mythology.

It is not clear, however, which side is engaged in mythology. To be sure, mythology is primitive and immature thought. The process of civilization invalidates myth (this is almost a definition of progress), but it may also return rational thought to mythological status. In the latter case, theories which identify and project historical possibilities may become irrational, or rather appear irrational because they contradict the rationality of the established universe of discourse and behavior.

Thus, in the process of civilization, the myth of the Golden Age and the Millennium is subjected to progressive rationalization. The (historically) impossible elements are separated from the possible ones—dream and fiction from science, technology, and business. In the nineteenth century, the theories of socialism translated the primary myth into sociological terms—or rather discovered in the given historical possibilities the rational core of the myth. Then, however, the reverse movement occurred. Today, the rational and realistic notions of yesterday again appear to be mythological when confronted with the actual conditions. The reality of the laboring classes in advanced industrial society makes the Marxian "proletariat" a mythological concept; the reality of present-day socialism makes the Marxian idea a dream. The reversal is caused by the contradiction between theory and facts—a contradiction which, by itself, does not yet falsify the former. The unscientific, speculative character of critical theory derives from the specific character of its concepts, which designate and define the irrational in the rational, the mystification in the reality. Their mythological quality reflects the mystifying quality of the given facts—the deceptive harmonization of the societal contradictions.

The technical achievement of advanced industrial society, and the effective manipulation of mental and material productivity have brought about a *shift in the locus of mystification*. If it is meaningful to say that the ideology comes to be embodied in the process of production itself, it may also be meaningful to suggest that, in this society, the rational rather than the irrational becomes the most effective vehicle of mystification. The view that the growth of repression in contemporary society manifested itself, in the ideological sphere, first in the ascent of irrational pseudo-philosophies (*Lebensphilosophie;* the notions of Community against Society; Blood and Soil, etc.) was refuted by Fascism and National Socialism. These regimes denied these and their own irrational "philosophies" by the all-out technical rationalization of the apparatus. It was the total mobilization of the material and mental machinery which did the job and installed its mystifying power over the society. It served to make the individuals incapable of seeing "behind" the machinery those who used it, those who profited from it, and those who paid for it.

Today, the mystifying elements are mastered and employed in productive publicity, propaganda, and politics. Magic, witchcraft, and ecstatic surrender are practiced in the daily routine of the home, the shop, and the office, and the rational accomplishments conceal the irrationality of the whole. For example, the scientific approach to the vexing problem of mutual annihilation—the mathematics and calculations of kill and over-kill, the measurement of spreading or not-quite-so-spreading fallout, the experiments of endurance in abnormal situations—is mystifying to the extent to which it promotes (and even demands) behavior which accepts the insanity. It thus counteracts a truly rational behavior—namely, the refusal to go along, and the effort to do away with the conditions which produce the insanity.

Against this new mystification, which turns rationality into its opposite, the distinction must be upheld. The rational is *not* irrational, and the difference between an exact recognition and analysis of the facts, and a vague and emotional speculation is as essential as ever before. The trouble is that the statistics, measurements, and field studies of empirical sociology and political science are not rational enough. They become mystifying to the extent to which they are isolated from the truly concrete context which makes the facts and determines their function. This context is larger and other than that of the plants and shops investigated, of the towns and cities studied, of the areas and groups whose public opinion is polled or whose chance of survival is calculated. And it is also more real in the sense that it creates and determines the facts investigated, polled, and calculated. This real context in which the particular subjects obtain their real significance is definable only within a *theory* of society. For the factors in the facts are not immediate data of observation, measurement, and interrogation. They become data only in an analysis which is capable of identifying the structure that holds together the parts and processes of society and that determines their interrelation.

To say that this meta-context is the Society (with a capital "S") is to hypostatize the whole over and above the parts. But this hypostatization takes place in reality, *is* the reality, and the analysis can overcome it only by recognizing it and by comprehending its scope and its causes. Society is indeed the whole which exercises its independent power over the individuals, and this Society is no unidentifiable "ghost." It has its empirical hard core in the system of institutions, which are the established and frozen relationships among men. Abstraction from it falsifies the measurements, interrogations, and calculations—but falsifies them in a dimension which does not appear in the measurements, interrogations, and calculations, and which therefore does not conflict with them and does not disturb them. They retain their exactness, and are mystifying in their very exactness.

In its exposure of the mystifying character of transcendent terms, vague notions, metaphysical universals, and the like, linguistic analysis mystifies the terms of ordinary language by leaving them in the repressive context of the established universe of discourse. It is within this repressive universe that the behavioral explication of meaning takes place—the explication which is to exorcize the old linguistic "ghosts" of the Cartesian and other obsolete myths. Linguistic analysis maintains that if Joe Doe and Richard Roe speak of what they have in mind, they simply refer to the specific perceptions, notions, or dispositions which they happen to have; the mind is a verbalized ghost. Similarly, the will is not a real faculty of the soul, but simply a specific mode of specific dispositions, propensities, and aspirations. Similarly with "consciousness," "self," "freedom"—they are all explicable in terms designating particular ways or modes of conduct and behavior. I shall subsequently return to this treatment of universal concepts.

Analytic philosophy often spreads the atmosphere of denunciation and investigation by committee. The intellectual is called on the carpet. What do you mean when you say. . . ? Don't you conceal something? You talk a language which is suspect. You don't talk like the rest of us, like the man in the street, but rather like a foreigner who does not belong here. We have to cut you down to size, expose your tricks, purge you. We shall teach you to say what you have in mind, to "come clear," to "put your cards on the table." Of course, we do not impose on you and your freedom of thought and speech; you may think as you like. But once you speak, you have to communicate your thoughts to us—in our language or in yours. Certainly, you may speak your own language, but it must be translatable, and it will be translated. You may speak poetry—that is all right. We love poetry. But we want to understand your poetry, and we can do so only if we can interpret your symbols, metaphors, and images in terms of ordinary language.

The poet might answer that indeed he wants his poetry to be understandable and understood (that is why he writes it), but if what he says could be said in terms of ordinary language he would probably have done so in the first place. He might say: Understanding of my poetry presupposes the collapse and invalidation of precisely that universe of discourse and behavior into which you want to translate it. My language can be learned like any other language (in point of fact, it is also your own language), then it will appear that my symbols, metaphors, etc. are *not* symbols, metaphors, etc. but mean exactly what they say. Your tolerance is deceptive. In reserving for me a special niche of meaning and significance, you grant me exemption from sanity and reason, but in my view, the madhouse is somewhere else.

The poet may also feel that the solid sobriety of linguistic philosophy speaks a rather prejudiced and emotional language—that of the angry old or young men. Their vocabulary abounds with the "improper," "queer," "absurd," "puzzling," "odd," "gabbling," and "gibbering." Improper and puzzling oddities have to be removed if sensible understanding is to prevail. Communication ought not to be over the head of the people; contents that go beyond common and scientific sense should not disturb the academic and the ordinary universe of discourse.

But critical analysis must dissociate itself from that which it strives to comprehend; the philosophic terms must be other than the ordinary ones in order to elucidate the full meaning of the latter.[19] For the established universe of discourse bears throughout the marks of the specific modes of domination, organization, and manipulation to which the members of a society are subjected. People depend for their living on bosses and politicians and jobs and neighbors who make them speak and mean as they do; they are compelled, by societal necessity, to identify the "thing" (including their own person, mind, feeling) with its functions. How do we know? Because we watch television, listen to the radio, read the newspapers and magazines, talk to people.

Under these circumstances, the spoken phrase is an expression of the individual who speaks it, *and* of those who make him speak as he does, *and* of whatever tension or contradiction may interrelate them. In speaking their own language, people also speak the language of their masters, benefactors, advertisers. Thus they do not only express *themselves*, their own knowledge, feelings, and aspirations, but also something other than themselves. Describing "by themselves" the political situation, either in their home town or in the international scene, they (and "they" includes *us*,

19. Contemporary analytic philosophy has in its own way recognized this necessity as the problem of *metalanguage;* see p. 179 above and 195 below.

the intellectuals who know it and criticize it) describe what "their" media of mass communication tell them—and this merges with what they really think and see and feel.

Describing to each other our loves and hatreds, sentiments and resentments, we must use the terms of our advertisements, movies, politicians and best sellers. We must use the same terms for describing our automobiles, foods and furniture, colleagues and competitors—and we understand each other perfectly. This must necessarily be so, for language is nothing private and personal, or rather the private and personal is mediated by the available linguistic material, which is societal material. But this situation disqualifies ordinary language from fulfilling the validating function which it performs in analytic philosophy. "What people mean when they say . . ." is related to what they *don't* say. Or, what they mean cannot be taken at face value —not because they lie, but because the universe of thought and practice in which they live is a universe of manipulated contradictions.

Circumstances like these may be irrelevant for the analysis of such statements as "I itch," or "he eats poppies," or "this now looks red to me," but they may become vitally relevant where people really say something ("she just loved him," "he has no heart," "this is not fair," "what can I do about it?"), and they are vital for the linguistic analysis of ethics, politics, etc. Short of it, linguistic analysis can achieve no other empirical exactness than that exacted from the people by the given state of affairs, and no other clarity than that which is permitted them in this state of affairs—that is, it remains within the limits of mystified and deceptive discourse.

Where it seems to go beyond this discourse, as in its logical purifications, only the skeleton remains of the same universe—a ghost much more ghostly than those which the analysis combats. If philosophy is more than an occupation, it shows the grounds which made discourse a mutilated and deceptive universe. To leave this task to a colleague in the Sociology or Psychology Department is to make the established division of academic labor into a methodological principle. Nor can the task be brushed aside with the modest insistence that linguistic analysis has only the humble purpose of clarifying "muddled" thinking and speaking. If such clarification goes beyond a mere enumeration and classification of possible meanings in possible contexts, leaving the choice wide open to anyone according to circumstances, then it is anything but a humble task. Such clarification would involve analyzing ordinary language in really controversial areas, recognizing muddled thinking where it *seems* to be the least muddled, uncovering the falsehood in so much normal and clear usage. Then linguistic analysis would attain the level on which the specific societal processes which shape and limit the universe of discourse become visible and understandable.

Here the problem of "metalanguage" arises; the terms which analyze the meaning of certain terms must be other than, or distinguishable from the latter. They must be more and other than mere synonyms which still belong to the same (immediate) universe of discourse. But if this metalanguage is really to break through the totalitarian scope of the established universe of discourse, in which the different dimensions of language are integrated and assimilated, it must be capable of denoting the societal processes which have determined and "closed" the established universe of discourse. Consequently, it cannot be a technical metalanguage, constructed mainly with a view of semantic or logical clarity. The desideratum is rather to make the established language itself speak what it conceals or excludes, for what is to be revealed and denounced is operative *within* the universe of ordinary discourse and action, and the prevailing language *contains* the metalanguage.

This desideratum has been fulfilled in the work of Karl Kraus. He has demonstrated how an "internal" examination of speech and writing, of punctuation, even of typographical errors can reveal a whole moral or political system. This examination still moves within the ordinary universe of discourse; it needs no artificial, "higher-level" language in order to extrapolate and clarify the examined language. The word, the syntactic form, are read in the context in which they appear—for example, in a newspaper which, in a specific city or country, espouses specific opinions through the pen of specific persons. The lexicographic and syntactical context thus opens into another dimension—which is not extraneous but constitutive of the word's meaning and function—that of the Vienna press during and after the First World War; the attitude of its editors toward the slaughter, the monarchy, the republic, etc. In the light of this dimension, the usage of the word, the structure of the sentence assume a meaning and function which do not appear in "unmediated" reading. The crimes against language, which appear in the style of the newspaper, pertain to its political style. Syntax, grammar, and vocabulary become moral and political acts. Or, the context may be an aesthetic and philosophic one: literary criticism, an address before a learned society, or the like. Here, the linguistic analysis of a poem or an essay confronts the given (immediate) material (the language of the respective poem or essay) with that which the writer found in the literary tradition, and which he transformed.

For such an analysis, the meaning of a term or form demands its development in a multi-dimensional universe, where any expressed meaning partakes of several interrelated, overlapping, and antagonistic "systems." For example, it belongs:

(a) to an individual project, i.e., the specific communication (a newspaper article, a speech) made at a specific occasion for a specific purpose;

(b) to an established supra-individual system of ideas, values, and objectives of which the individual project partakes;

(c) to a particular society which itself integrates different and even conflicting individual and supra-individual projects.

To illustrate: a certain speech, newspaper article, or even private communication is made by a certain individual who is the (authorized or unauthorized) spokesman of a particular group (occupational, residential, political, intellectual) in a specific society. This group has its own values, objectives, codes of thought and behavior which enter—affirmed or opposed—with various degrees of awareness and explicitness, into the individual communication. The latter thus "individualizes" a supra-individual system of meaning, which constitutes a dimension of discourse different from, yet merged with, that of the individual communication. And this supra-individual system is in turn part of a comprehensive, omnipresent realm of meaning which has been developed, and ordinarily "closed," by the social system within which and from which the communication takes place.

The range and extent of the social system of meaning varies considerably in different historical periods and in accordance with the attained level of culture, but its boundaries are clearly enough defined if the communication refers to more than the non-controversial implements and relations of daily life. Today, the social systems of meaning unite different nation states and linguistic areas, and these large systems of meaning tend to coincide with the orbit of the more or less advanced capitalist societies on the one hand, and that of the advancing communist societies on the other. While the determining function of the social system of meaning asserts itself most rigidly in the controversial, political universe of discourse, it also operates, in a much more covert, unconscious, emotional manner, in the ordinary universe of discourse. A genuinely philosophic analysis of meaning has to take all these dimensions of meaning into account because the linguistic expressions partake of all of them. Consequently, linguistic analysis in philosophy has an extra-linguistic commitment. If it decides on a distinction between legitimate and non-legitimate usage, between authentic and illusory meaning, sense and non-sense, it invokes a political, aesthetic, or moral judgment.

It may be objected that such an "external" analysis (in quotation marks because it is actually *not* external but rather the internal development of meaning) is particularly out of place where the intent is to capture the meaning of terms by analyzing their function and usage in ordinary discourse. But my contention is that this is precisely what linguistic analysis in contemporary philosophy does *not* do. And it does not do so inasmuch as it transfers ordinary discourse into a special academic universe which is purified and synthetic even where (and just where) it is filled with ordinary language. In this analytic treatment of ordinary language, the latter is really sterilized and anesthetized. Multi-dimensional language is made into one-dimensional language, in which different and conflicting meanings no longer interpenetrate but are kept apart; the explosive historical dimension of meaning is silenced.

Wittgenstein's endless language game with building stones, or the conversing Joe Doe and Dick Roe may again serve as examples. In spite of the simple clarity of the example, the speakers and their situation remain unidentified. They are x and y, no matter how chummily they talk. But in the real universe of discourse, x and y are "ghosts." They don't exist; they are the product of the analytic philosopher. To be sure, the talk of x and y is perfectly understandable, and the linguistic analyst appeals righteously to the normal understanding of ordinary people. But in reality, we understand each other only through whole areas of misunderstanding and contradiction. The real universe of ordinary language is that of the struggle for existence. It is indeed an ambiguous, vague, obscure universe, and is certainly in need of clarification. Moreover, such clarification may well fulfill a therapeutic function, and if philosophy would become therapeutic, it would really come into its own.

Philosophy approaches this goal to the degree to which it frees thought from its enslavement by the established universe of discourse and behavior, elucidates the negativity of the Establishment (its positive aspects are abundantly publicized anyway) and projects its alternatives. To be sure, philosophy contradicts and projects in thought only. It is ideology, and this ideological character is the very fate of philosophy which no scientism and positivism can overcome. Still, its ideological effort may be truly therapeutic—to show reality as that which it really is, and to show that which this reality prevents from being.

In the totalitarian era, the therapeutic task of philosophy would be a political task, since the established universe of ordinary language tends to coagulate into a totally manipulated and indoctrinated universe. Then politics would appear in philosophy, not as a special discipline or object of analysis, nor as a special political philosophy, but as the intent of its concepts to comprehend the unmutilated reality. If linguistic analysis does not contribute to such understanding; if, instead, it contributes to enclosing thought in the circle of the mutilated universe of ordinary discourse, it is at best entirely inconsequential. And, at worst, it is an escape into the non-controversial, the unreal, into that which is only academically controversial.

The Chance of the Alternatives

8: The Historical Commitment
of Philosophy

The commitment of analytic philosophy to the mutilated reality of thought and speech shows forth strikingly in its treatment of *universals*. The problem was mentioned before, as part of the inherent historical and at the same time transcendent, general character of philosophic concepts. It now requires a more detailed discussion. Far from being only an abstract question of epistemology, or a pseudo-concrete question of language and its use, the question of the status of universals is at the very center of philosophic thought. For the treatment of universals reveals the position of a philosophy in the intellectual culture—its historical function.

Contemporary analytic philosophy is out to exorcize such "myths" or metaphysical "ghosts" as Mind, Consciousness, Will, Soul, Self, by dissolving the intent of these concepts into statements on particular identifiable operations, performances, powers, dispositions, propensities, skills, etc. The result shows, in a strange way, the impotence of the destruction—the ghost continues to haunt. While every interpretation or translation may describe adequately a particular mental process, an act of imagining what I mean when I say "I," or what the priest means when he says that Mary is a "good girl," not a single one of these reformulations, nor their sum-total, seems to capture or even circumscribe the full meaning of such terms as Mind, Will, Self, Good. These universals continue to persist in common as well as "poetic" usage, and either usage distinguishes them from the various modes of behavior or disposition that, according to the analytic philosopher, fulfill their meaning.

To be sure, such universals cannot be validated by the

assertion that they denote a whole which is more and other than its parts. They apparently do, but this "whole" requires an analysis of the unmutilated experiential context. If this supra-linguistic analysis is rejected, if the ordinary language is taken at face value—that is, if a deceptive universe of general understanding among people is substituted for the prevailing universe of misunderstanding and administered communication—then the incriminated universals are indeed translatable, and their "mythological" substance can be dissolved into modes of behavior and dispositions.

However, this dissolution itself must be questioned—not only on behalf of the philosopher, but on behalf of the ordinary people in whose life and discourse such dissolution takes place. It is not their own doing and their own saying; it happens to them and it violates them as they are compelled, by the "circumstances," to identify their mind with the mental processes, their self with the roles and functions which they have to perform in their society. If philosophy does not comprehend these processes of translation and identification as societal processes—i.e., as a mutilation of the mind (and the body) inflicted upon the individuals by their society—philosophy struggles only with the ghost of the substance which it wishes to de-mystify. The mystifying character adheres, not to the concepts of "mind," "self," "consciousness," etc. but rather to their behavioral translation. The translation is deceptive precisely because it translates the concept faithfully into modes of actual behavior, propensities, and dispositions and, in so doing, it takes the mutilated and organized appearances (themselves real enough!) for the reality.

However, even in this battle of the ghosts, forces are called up which might bring the phony war to an end. One of the disturbing problems in analytic philosophy is that of statements on universals such as "nation," "state," "the Brit-

ish Constitution," "the University of Oxford," "England." [1]
No particular entities whatsoever correspond to these universals, and still it makes perfect sense, it is even unavoidable, to say that "the nation" is mobilized, that "England"
declared war, that I studied at the "University of Oxford."
Any reductive translation of such statements seems to change
their meaning. We can say that the University is no particular entity over and above its various colleges, libraries, etc.,
but is just the way in which the latter are organized, and
we can apply the same explanation, modified, to the other
statements. However, the way in which such things and people are organized, integrated, and administered operates *as*
an entity different from its component parts—to such an
extent that it can dispose of life and death, as in the case of
the nation and the constitution. The persons who execute
the verdict, if they are identifiable at all, do so not as these
individuals but as "representatives" of the Nation, the Corporation, the University. The U.S. Congress, assembled in
session, the Central Committee, the Party, the Board of
Directors and Managers, the President, the Trustees, and the
Faculty, meeting and deciding on policy are tangible and
effective entities over and above the component individuals.
They are tangible in the records, in the results of their laws,
in the nuclear weapons they order and produce, in the ap-
pointments, salaries, and requirements they establish. Meeting in assembly, the individuals are the spokesmen (often
unaware) of institutions, influences, interests embodied in
organizations. In their decision (vote, pressure, propaganda)
—itself the outcome of competing institutions and interests—

1. See Gilbert Ryle, *The Concept of Mind* loc. cit., p. 17 f. and
passim; J. Wisdom, "Metaphysics and Verification," in: *Philosophy and
Psycho-Analysis*, Oxford 1953; A. G. N. Flew, Introduction to *Logic and
Language* (First Series), Oxford 1955; D. F. Pears, "Universals," in ibid.,
Second Series, Oxford 1959; J. O. Urmson, *Philosophical Analysis*, Oxford
1956; B. Russell, *My Philosophical Development*, New York 1959, p. 223 f;
Peter Laslett (ed.) *Philosophy, Politics and Society*, Oxford 1956, p. 22 ff.

the Nation, the Party, the Corporation, the University is set in motion, preserved, and reproduced—as a (relatively) ultimate, universal reality, overriding the particular institutions or peoples subjected to it.

This reality has assumed a superimposed, independent existence; therefore statements concerning it mean a real universal and cannot be adequately translated into statements concerning particular entities. And yet, the urge to try such translation, the protest against its impossibility indicates that there is something wrong here. To make good sense, "the nation," or "the Party," *ought* to be translatable into its constituents and components. The fact that it is *not*, is a *historical* fact which gets in the way of linguistic and logical analysis.

The disharmony between the individual and the social needs, and the lack of representative institutions in which the individuals work for themselves and speak for themselves, lead to the reality of such universals as the Nation, the Party, the Constitution, the Corporation, the Church—a reality which is not identical with any particular identifiable entity (individual, group, or institution). Such universals express various degrees and modes of reification. Their independence, although real, is a spurious one inasmuch as it is that of particular powers which have organized the *whole* of society. A retranslation which would dissolve the spurious substance of the universal is still a desideratum—but it is a political desideratum.

On croit mourir pour la Classe, on meurt pour les gens du Parti. On croit mourir pour la Patrie, on meurt pour les Industriels. On croit mourir pour la Liberté des Personnes, on meurt pour la Liberté des dividendes. On croit mourir pour le Prolétariat, on meurt pour sa Bureaucratie. On croit mourir sur l'ordre d'un Etat, on meurt pour l'Argent qui le tient. On croit mourir pour une nation, on meurt pour les bandits qui la baillonnent. On croit—

mais pourquoi croirait-on dans une ombre si épaisse? Croire, mourir? . . . quand il s'agit d'apprendre à vivre? [2]

This is a genuine "translation" of hypostatized universals into concreteness, and yet it acknowledges the reality of the universal while calling it by its true name. The hypostatized whole resists analytic dissolution, not because it is a mythical entity behind the particular entities and performances but because it is the concrete, objective ground of their functioning in the given social and historical context. As such, it is a real force, felt and exercised by the individuals in their actions, circumstances, and relationships. They share in it (in a very unequal way); it decides on their existence and their possibilities. The real ghost is of a very forcible reality —that of the separate and independent power of the whole over the individuals. And this whole is not merely a perceived *Gestalt* (as in psychology), nor a metaphysical absolute (as in Hegel), nor a totalitarian state (as in poor political science)—it is the established state of affairs which determines the life of the individuals.

However, even if we grant such a reality to these political universals, do not all the other universals have a very different status? They do, but their analysis is all too easily kept within the limits of academic philosophy. The following discussion does not claim to enter into the "problem of universals," it only tries to elucidate the (artificially) limited scope of philosophic analysis and to indicate the need for going beyond these limits. The discussion will again be

2. "They believe they are dying for the Class, they die for the Party boys. They believe they are dying for the Fatherland, they die for the Industrialists. They believe they are dying for the freedom of the Person, they die for the Freedom of the dividends. They believe they are dying for the Proletariat, they die for its Bureaucracy. They believe they are dying by orders of a State, they die for the money which holds the State. They believe they are dying for a nation, they die for the bandits that gag it. They believe—but why would one believe in such darkness? Believe— die?—when it is a matter of learning to live?" François Perroux, *La Coexistence pacifique*, loc. cit. vol. III, p. 631.

focused on substantive as distinguished from logico-mathematical universals (set, number, class, etc.), and, among the former, on the more abstract and controversial concepts which present the real challenge to philosophic thought.

The substantive universal not only abstracts from concrete entity, it also denotes a different entity. The mind is more and other than conscious acts and behavior. Its reality might tentatively be described as the manner or mode in which these particular acts are synthetized, integrated by an individual. One might be tempted to say *a priori* synthetized by a "transcendental apperception," in the sense that the integrating synthesis which renders the particular processes and acts possible *precedes* them, shapes them, distinguishes them from "other minds." Still, this formulation would do violence to Kant's concept, for the priority of such consciousness is an empirical one, which includes the supra-individual experience, ideas, aspirations, of particular social groups.

In view of these characteristics, consciousness may well be called a disposition, propensity, or faculty. It is not one individual disposition or faculty among others, however, but in a strict sense a general disposition which is common, in various degrees, to the individual members of one group, class, society. On these grounds, the distinction between true and false consciousness becomes meaningful. The former would synthetize the data of experience in concepts which reflect, as fully and adequately as possible, the given society in the given facts. This "sociological" definition is suggested, not because of any prejudice in favor of sociology, but because of the factual ingression of society into the data of experience. Consequently, the repression of society in the formation of concepts is tantamount to an academic confinement of experience, a restriction of meaning.

Moreover, the normal restriction of experience produces a pervasive tension, even conflict, between "the mind" and the mental processes, between "consciousness" and conscious acts. If I speak of the mind of a person, I do not merely refer to his mental processes as they are revealed in his expression, speech, behavior, etc., nor merely of his dispositions or faculties as experienced or inferred from experience. I also mean that which he does *not* express, for which he shows *no* disposition, but which is present nevertheless, and which determines, to a considerable extent, his behavior, his understanding, the formation and range of his concepts.

Thus "negatively present" are the specific "environmental" forces which precondition his mind for the spontaneous repulsion of certain data, conditions, relations. They are present as repelled material. Their *absence* is a reality—a positive factor that explains his actual mental processes, the meaning of his words and behavior. Meaning for whom? Not only for the professional philosopher, whose task it is to rectify the wrong that pervades the universe of ordinary discourse, but also for those who suffer this wrong although they may not be aware of it—for Joe Doe and Richard Roe. Contemporary linguistic analysis shirks this task by interpreting concepts in terms of an impoverished and preconditioned mind. What is at stake is the unabridged and unexpurgated intent of certain key concepts, their function in the unrepressed understanding of reality—in non-conformist, critical thought.

Are the remarks just submitted on the reality content of such universals as "mind" and "consciousness" applicable to other concepts, such as the abstract yet substantive universals, Beauty, Justice, Happiness, with their contraries? It seems that the persistence of these untranslatable universals as nodal points of thought reflects the unhappy consciousness of a divided world in which "that which is" falls short of, and even denies, "that which can be." The irreducible difference between the universal and its particulars seems to be rooted in the primary experience of the inconquerable difference between potentiality and actuality—between two dimensions of the one experienced world. The universal comprehends in one idea the possibilities which are realized, and at the same time arrested, in reality.

Talking of a beautiful girl, a beautiful landscape, a beautiful picture, I certainly have very different things in mind. What is common to all of them—"beauty"—is neither a mysterious entity, nor a mysterious word. On the contrary, nothing is perhaps more directly and clearly experienced than the appearance of "beauty" in various beautiful objects. The boy friend and the philosopher, the artist and the mortician may "define" it in very different ways, but they all define the same specific state or condition—some quality or qualities which, make the beautiful *contrast* with other objects. In this vagueness and directness, beauty is experienced *in* the beautiful—that is, it is seen, heard, smelled, touched, felt, comprehended. It is experienced almost as a shock, perhaps due to the contrast-character of beauty, which breaks the circle of everyday experience and opens (for a short moment) another reality (of which fright may be an integral element).[3]

This description is of precisely that metaphysical character which positivistic analysis wishes to eliminate by translation, but the translation eliminates that which was to be defined. There are many more or less satisfactory "technical" definitions of beauty in aesthetics, but there seems to be only one which preserves the experiential content of beauty and which is therefore the least exact definition—beauty as a "promesse de bonheur." [4] It captures the reference to a condition of men and things, and to a relation between men and things which occur momentarily while vanishing, which

3. Rilke, *Duineser Elegien*, Erste Elegie.
4. Stendhal.

appear in as many different forms as there are individuals and which, in *vanishing*, manifest what can be.

The protest against the vague, obscure, metaphysical character of such universals, the insistence on familiar concreteness and protective security of common and scientific sense still reveal something of that primordial anxiety which guided the recorded origins of philosophic thought in its evolution from religion to mythology, and from mythology to logic; defense and security still are large items in the intellectual as well as national budget. The unpurged experience seems to be more familiar with the abstract and universal than is the analytic philosophy; it seems to be embedded in a metaphysical world.

Universals are primary elements of experience—universals not as philosophic concepts but as the very qualities of the world with which one is daily confronted. What is experienced is, for example, snow or rain or heat; a street; an office or a boss; love or hatred. Particular things (entities) and events only appear in (and even *as*) a cluster and continuum of relationships, as incidents and parts in a general configuration from which they are inseparable; they cannot appear in any other way without losing their identity. They are particular things and events only against a general background which is more than background—it is the concrete ground on which they arise, exist, and pass. This ground is structured in such universals as color, shape, density, hardness or softness, light or darkness, motion or rest. In this sense, universals seem to designate the "stuff" of the world:

"We may perhaps define the 'stuff' of the world as what is designated by words which, when correctly used, occur as subjects of predicates or terms of relations. In that sense, I should say that the stuff of the world consists of things like whiteness, rather

than of objects having the property of being white." "Tradition-
ally, qualities, such as white or hard or sweet, counted as universals, but if the above theory is valid, they are syntactically
more akin to substances." [5]

The substantive character of "qualities" points to the
experiential origin of substantive universals, to the manner
in which concepts originate in immediate experience. Humboldt's philosophy of language emphasizes the experiential
character of the concept in its relation to the word; it leads
him to assume an original kinship not only between concepts
and words, but also between concepts and sounds (*Laute*).
However, if the word, as the vehicle of concepts, is the real
"element" of language, it does not communicate the concept
ready-made, nor does it contain the concept already fixed and
"closed." The word merely suggests a concept, relates itself
to a universal.[6]

But precisely the relation of the word to a substantive
universal (concept) makes it impossible, according to Humboldt, to imagine the origin of language as starting from the
signification of objects by words and then proceeding to
their combination (*Zusammenfügung*):

> In reality, speech is not put together from preceding words,
> but quite the reverse: words emerge from the whole of speech
> (*aus dem Ganzen der Rede*).[7]

The "whole" that here comes to view must be cleared
from all misunderstanding in terms of an independent entity,
of a "Gestalt," and the like. The concept somehow expresses
the difference and tension between potentiality and actuality
—identity in this difference. It appears in the relation
between the qualities (white, hard; but also beautiful, free,

5. Bertrand Russell, *My Philosophical Development* (New York, Simon
and Schuster, 1959), p. 170-171.
6. Wilhelm v. Humboldt, *Ueber die Verschiedenheit des menschlichen
Sprachbaues* . . . loc cit., p. 197.
7. *Ibid.*, p. 74-75.

just) and the corresponding concepts (whiteness, hardness, beauty, freedom, justice). The abstract character of the latter seems to designate the more concrete qualities as part-realizations, aspects, manifestations of a more universal *and* more "excellent" quality, which is experienced *in* the concrete.[8]

And by virtue of this relation, the concrete quality seems to represent a negation as well as realization of the universal. Snow is white but not "whiteness"; a girl may be beautiful, even *a* beauty, but not "beauty"; a country may be free (in comparison with others) because its people have certain liberties, but it is not the very embodiment of freedom. Moreover, the concepts are meaningful only in experienced contrast with their opposites: white with not white, beautiful with not beautiful. Negative statements can sometimes be translated into positive ones: "black" or "grey" for "not white," "ugly" for "not beautiful."

These formulations do not alter the relation between the abstract concept and its concrete realizations: the universal concept denotes that which the particular entity is, and is *not*. The translation can eliminate the hidden negation by reformulating the meaning in a non-contradictory proposition, but the untranslated statement suggests a real want. There is *more* in the abstract noun (beauty, freedom) than in the qualities ("beautiful," "free") attributed to the particular person, thing or condition. The substantive universal intends qualities which surpass all particular experience, but persist in the mind, not as a figment of imagination nor as more logical possibilities but as the "stuff" of which our world consists. No snow is pure white, nor is any cruel beast or man all the cruelty man knows—knows as an almost inexhaustible force in history and imagination.

Now there is a large class of concepts—we dare say, the philosophically relevant concepts—where the quantita-

8. See p. 214.

tive relation between the universal and the particular assumes a qualitative aspect, where the abstract universal seems to designate potentialities in a concrete, historical sense. However "man," "nature," "justice," "beauty" or "freedom" may be defined, they synthetize experiential contents into ideas which transcend their particular realizations as something that is to be surpassed, overcome. Thus the concept of beauty comprehends all the beauty not *yet* realized; the concept of freedom all the liberty not *yet* attained.

Or, to take another example, the philosophic concept "man" aims at the fully developed human faculties which are his distinguishing faculties, and which appear as possibilities of the conditions in which men actually live. The concept articulates the qualities which are considered "typically human." The vague phrase may serve to elucidate the ambiguity in such philosophic definitions—namely, they assemble the qualities which pertain to *all* men as contrasted with other living beings, and, at the same time, are claimed as the most adequate or highest realization of man.[9]

9. This interpretation, which stresses the *normative* character of universals, may be related to the conception of the universal in Greek philosophy —namely, the notion of the most general as the highest, the first in "excellence" and therefore the real reality: ". . . generality is not a subject but a predicate, a predicate precisely of the firstness implicit in superlative excellence of performance. Generality, that is to say, is general precisely because and only to the extent that it is 'like' firstness. It is general, then, not in the manner of a logical universal or class-concept but in the manner of a norm which, only because universally binding, manages to unify a multiplicity of parts into a single whole. It is all-important to realize that the relation of this whole to its parts is *not* mechanical (whole = sum of its parts) but immanently teleological (whole = distinct from the sum of its parts). Moreover, this immanently teleological view of wholeness as functional without being purposive, for all its relevance to the life-phenomenon, is not exclusively or even primarily an 'organismic' category. It is rooted, instead, in the immanent, intrinsic functionality of excellence as such, which *unifies* a manifold precisely in the process of 'aristocratizing' it, excellence and unity being the very conditions of the manifold's full reality even as manifold." Harold A. T. Reiche, *"General Because First": A Presocratic Motive in Aristotle's Theology* (Massachusetts Institute of Technology, Cambridge, 1961, Publications in Humanities no. 52), p. 105 f.

Such universals thus appear as conceptual instruments for understanding the particular conditions of things in the light of their potentialities. They are historical and supra-historical; they conceptualize the stuff of which the experi enced world consists, and they conceptualize it with a view of its possibilities, in the light of their actual limitation, suppression, and denial. Neither the experience nor the judgment is private. The philosophic concepts are formed and developed in the consciousness of a general condition in a historical continuum; they are elaborated from an individual position within a specific society. The stuff of thought is historical stuff—no matter how abstract, general, or pure it may become in philosophic or scientific theory. The abstract-universal and at the same time historical character of these "eternal objects" of thought is recognized and clearly stated in Whitehead's *Science and the Modern World:*[10]

"Eternal objects are . . . in their nature, abstract. By 'abstract' I mean that what an eternal object is in itself—that is to say, its essence—is comprehensible without reference to some one particular experience. To be abstract is to transcend the particular occasion of actual happening. But to transcend an actual occasion does not mean being disconnected from it. On the contrary, I hold that each eternal object has its own proper connection with each such occasion, which I term its mode of ingression into that occasion." "Thus the metaphysical status of an eternal object is that of a possibility for an actuality. Every actual occasion is defined as to its character by how these possibilities are actualized for that occasion."

Elements of experience, projection and anticipation of real possibilities enter into the conceptual syntheses—in respectable form as hypotheses, in disreputable form as "metaphysics." In various degrees, they are unrealistic because they transgress beyond the established universe of behavior, and

10. (New York, Macmillan, 1926), p. 228 f.

they may even be undesirable in the interest of neatness and exactness. Certainly, in philosophic analysis,

"Little real advance . . . is to be hoped for in expanding our universe to include so-called possible entities," [11]

but it all depends on how Ockham's Razor is applied, that is to say, which possibilities are to be cut off. The possibility of an entirely different societal organization of life has nothing in common with the "possibility" of a man with a green hat appearing in all doorways tomorrow, but treating them with the same logic may serve the defamation of undesirable possibilities. Criticizing the introduction of possible entities, Quine writes that such an

"overpopulated universe is in many ways unlovely. It offends the aesthetic sense of us who have a taste for desert landscapes, but this is not the worst of it. [Such a] slum of possibles is a breeding ground for disorderly elements." [12]

Contemporary philosophy has rarely attained a more authentic formulation of the conflict between its intent and its function. The linguistic syndrome of "loveliness," "aesthetic sense," and "desert landscape" evokes the liberating air of Nietzsche's thought, cutting into Law and Order, while the "breeding ground for disorderly elements" belongs to the language spoken by the authorities of Investigation and Information. What appears unlovely and disorderly from the logical point of view, may well comprise the lovely elements of a different order, and may thus be an essential part of the material from which philosophic concepts are built. Neither the most refined aesthetic sense nor the most exact philosophic concept is immune against history. Disorderly elements enter into the purest objects of thought. They too are

11. W. V. O. Quine, *From a Logical Point of View,* loc. cit., p. 4.
12. *Ibid.*

detached from a societal ground, and the contents from which they abstract guide the abstraction.

Thus the spectre of *"historicism"* is raised. If thought proceeds from historical conditions which continue to operate in the abstraction, is there any objective basis on which distinction can be made between the various possibilities projected by thought—distinction between different and conflicting ways of conceptual transcendence? Moreover, the question cannot be discussed with reference to different *philosophic* projects only.[13] To the degree to which the philosophical project is *ideological*, it is part of a *historical* project—that is, it pertains to a specific stage and level of the societal development, and the critical philosophic concepts refer (no matter how indirectly!) to alternative possibilities of this development.

The quest for criteria for judging between different philosophic projects thus leads to the quest for criteria for judging between different historical projects and alternatives, between different actual and possible ways of understanding and changing man and nature. I shall submit only a few propositions which suggest that the internal historical character of the philosophic concepts, far from precluding objective validity, defines the ground for their objective validity.

In speaking and thinking for himself, the philosopher speaks and thinks from a particular position in his society, and he does so with the material transmitted and utilized by this society. But in doing this, he speaks and thinks into a common universe of facts and possibilities. Through the various individual agents and layers of experience, through the different "projects" which guide the modes of thought from the business of everyday life to science and philosophy, the interaction between a collective subject and a common world persists and constitutes the objective validity of the universals. It is objective:

13. For this use of the term "project" see Introduction, p. xvi.

(1) by virtue of the matter (stuff) opposed to the apprehending and comprehending subject. The formation of concepts remains determined by the structure of matter not dissoluble into subjectivity (even if the structure is entirely mathematical-logical). No concept can be valid which defines its object by properties and functions that do not belong to the object (for example, the individual cannot be defined as capable of becoming identical with another individual; man as capable of remaining eternally young). However, matter confronts the subject in a historical universe, and objectivity appears under an open historical horizon; it is changeable.

(2) by virtue of the structure of the specific society in which the development of concepts takes place. This structure is common to all subjects in the respective universe. They exist under the same natural conditions, the same regime of production, the same mode of exploiting the social wealth, the same heritage of the past, the same range of possibilities. All the differences and conflicts between classes, groups, individuals unfold within this common framework.

The objects of thought and perception as they appear to the individuals prior to all "subjective" interpretation have in common certain primary qualities, pertaining to these two layers of reality: (1) to the physical (natural) structure of matter, and (2) to the form which matter has acquired in the collective historical practice that has made it (matter) into objects *for a subject*. The two layers or aspects of objectivity (physical and historical) are interrelated in such a way that they cannot be insulated from each other; the historical aspect can never be eliminated so radically that only the "absolute" physical layer remains.

For example, I have tried to show that, in the technological reality, the object world (including the subjects) is experienced as a world of *instrumentalities*. The technological context predefines the form in which the objects appear. They appear to the scientist *a priori* as value-free elements or complexes of relations, susceptible to organization in an effective mathematico-logical system; and they appear to common sense as the stuff of work or leisure, production or consumption. The object-world is thus the world of a specific historical project, and is never accessible outside the historical project which organizes matter, and the organization of matter is at one and the same time a theoretical and a practical enterprise.

I have used the term "project" so repeatedly because it seems to me to accentuate most clearly the specific character of historical practice. It results from a determinate choice, seizure of one among other ways of comprehending, organizing, and transforming reality. The initial choice defines the range of possibilities open on this way, and precludes alternative possibilities incompatible with it.

I shall now propose some criteria for the truth value of different historical projects. These criteria must refer to the manner in which a historical project realizes given possibilities—not formal possibilities but those involving the modes of human existence. Such realization is actually under way in any historical situation. Every established society *is* such a realization; moreover, it tends to prejudge the rationality of *possible* projects, to keep them within its framework. At the same time, every established society is confronted with the actuality or possibility of a qualitatively different historical practice which might destroy the existing institutional framework. The established society has already demonstrated its truth value as historical project. It has succeeded in organizing man's struggle with man and with nature; it reproduces and protects (more or less adequately) the human existence (always with the exception of the existence of those who are the declared outcasts, enemy-aliens, and other victims of the system). But against this project in full realization emerge other projects, and among them those which would change the established one in its totality. It is with reference to such a transcendent project that the criteria for objective historical truth can best be formulated as the criteria of its rationality:

(1) The transcendent project must be in accordance with the real possibilities open at the attained level of the material and intellectual culture.

(2) The transcendent project, in order to falsify the established totality, must demonstrate its own *higher* rationality in the threefold sense that

(a) it offers the prospect of preserving and improving the productive achievements of civilization;

(b) it defines the established totality in its very structure, basic tendencies, and relations;

(c) its realization offers a greater chance for the pacification of existence, within the framework of institutions which offer a greater chance for the free development of human needs and faculties.

Obviously, this notion of rationality contains, especially in the last statement, a value judgment, and I reiterate what I stated before: I believe that the very concept of Reason originates in this value judgment, and that the concept of truth cannot be divorced from the value of Reason.

"Pacification," "free development of human needs and faculties"—these concepts can be empirically defined in terms of the available intellectual and material resources and capabilities and their systematic use for attenuating the struggle for existence. This is the objective ground of historical rationality.

If the historical continuum itself provides the objective ground for determining the truth of different historical projects, does it also determine their sequence and their limits? Historical truth is comparative; the rationality of the possible depends on that of the actual, the truth of the transcending project on that of the project in realization. Aristotelian science was falsified on the basis of its achievements; if capitalism were falsified by communism, it would be by virtue of its own achievements. Continuity is preserved through rupture: quantitative development becomes qualitative change if it attains the very structure of an established system; the established rationality becomes irrational when, in the course of its *internal* development, the potentialities of the system have outgrown its institutions. Such internal refutation pertains to the historical character of reality, and the same character confers upon the concepts which comprehend this reality their critical intent. They recognize and anticipate the irrational in the established reality—they project the historical negation.

Is this negation a "determinate" one—that is, is the internal succession of a historical project, once it has become a totality, necessarily pre-determined by the structure of this totality? If so, then the term "project" would be deceptive. That which is historical possibility would sooner or later be real; and the definition of liberty as comprehended necessity would have a repressive connotation which it does not have. All this may not matter much. What does matter is that such historical determination would (in spite of all subtle ethics and psychology) absolve the crimes against humanity which civilization continues to commit and thus facilitate this continuation.

I suggest the phrase "determinate choice" in order to emphasize the ingression of liberty into historical necessity; the phrase does no more than condense the proposition that men make their own history but make it under given conditions. Determined are (1) the specific contradictions which develop within a historical system as manifestations of the conflict between the potential and the actual; (2) the material and intellectual resources available to the respective system; (3) the extent of theoretical and practical freedom compatible with the system. These conditions leave open alternative possibilities of developing and utilizing the available resources, alternative possibilities of "making a living," of organizing man's struggle with nature.

Thus, within the framework of a given situation, industrialization can proceed in different ways, under collective or private control, and, even under private control, in different directions of progress and with different aims. The choice is primarily (but only primarily!) the privilege of those groups which have attained control over the productive process. Their control projects the way of life for the whole, and the ensuing and enslaving necessity is the result of their freedom. And the possible abolition of this necessity depends on a new ingression of freedom—not any freedom, but that of men who comprehend the given necessity as insufferable pain, and as unnecessary.

As historical process, the dialectical process involves consciousness: recognition and seizure of the liberating potentialities. Thus it involves freedom. To the degree to which consciousness is determined by the exigencies and interests of the established society, it is "unfree"; to the degree to which the established society is irrational, the consciousness becomes free for the higher historical rationality only in the struggle *against* the established society. The truth and the freedom of negative thinking have their ground and reason in this struggle. Thus, according to Marx, the proletariat is the liberating historical force only as revolutionary force; the determinate negation of capitalism occurs *if* and *when* the proletariat has become conscious of itself and of the conditions and processes which make up its society. This consciousness is prerequisite as well as an element of the negating practice. This "if" is essential to historical progress —it is the element of freedom (and chance!) which opens the possibilities of conquering the necessity of the given facts. Without it, history relapses into the darkness of unconquered nature.

We have encountered the "vicious circle" of freedom and liberation before;[14] here it reappears as the dialectic of the determinate negation. Transcendence beyond the established conditions (of thought and action) presupposes transcendence *within* these conditions. This negative freedom— i.e., freedom from the oppressive and ideological power of given facts—is the *a priori* of the historical dialectic; it is the element of choice and decision in and against historical determination. None of the given alternatives is *by itself* determinate negation unless and until it is consciously seized in order to break the power of intolerable conditions and attain the more rational, more logical conditions rendered possible by the prevailing ones. In any case, the rationality and logic invoked in the movement of thought and action is that *of* the given conditions to be transcended. The negation proceeds on empirical grounds; it is a historical project within and beyond an already going project, and its truth is a chance to be determined on these grounds.

However, the truth of a historical project is not validated *ex post* through success, that is to say, by the fact that it is accepted and realized by the society. Galilean science was true while it was still condemned; Marxian theory was already true at the time of the Communist Manifesto; fascism remains false even if it is in ascent on an international scale ("true" and "false" always in the sense of historical rationality as defined above). In the contemporary period, all historical projects tend to be polarized on the two conflicting totalities—capitalism and communism, and the outcome seems to depend on two antagonistic series of factors: (1)

14. See p. 41.

the greater force of destruction; (2) the greater productivity without destruction. In other words, the higher historical truth would pertain to the system which offers the greater chance of pacification.

9: The Catastrophe of Liberation

Positive thinking and its neo-positivist philosophy counteract the historical content of rationality. This content is never an extraneous factor or meaning which can or cannot be included in the analysis; it enters into conceptual thought as constitutive factor and determines the validity of its concepts. To the degree to which the established society is irrational, the analysis in terms of historical rationality introduces into the concept the negative element—critique, contradiction, and transcendence.

This element cannot be assimilated with the positive. It changes the concept in its entirety, in its intent and validity. Thus, in the analysis of an economy, capitalist or not, which operates as an "independent" power over and above the individuals, the negative features (overproduction, unemployment, insecurity, waste, repression) are not comprehended as long as they appear merely as more or less inevitable by-products, as "the other side" of the story of growth and progress.

True, a totalitarian administration may promote the efficient exploitation of resources; the nuclear-military establishment may provide millions of jobs through enormous purchasing power; toil and ulcers may be the by-product of the acquisition of wealth and responsibility; deadly blunders and crimes on the part of the leaders may be merely the way of life. One is willing to admit economic and political madness—and one buys it. But this sort of knowledge of "the other side" is part and parcel of the solidification of the state of affairs, of the grand unification of opposites which counteracts qualitative change, because it pertains to a thoroughly hopeless or thoroughly preconditioned existence that has made its home in a world where even the irrational is Reason.

225

The tolerance of positive thinking is enforced tolerance —enforced not by any terroristic agency but by the overwhelming, anonymous power and efficiency of the technological society. As such it permeates the general consciousness—and the consciousness of the critic. The absorption of the negative by the positive is validated in the daily experience, which obfuscates the distinction between rational appearance and irrational reality. Here are some banal examples of this harmonization:

(1) I ride in a new automobile. I experience its beauty, shininess, power, convenience—but then I become aware of the fact that in a relatively short time it will deteriorate and need repair; that its beauty and surface are cheap, its power unnecessary, its size idiotic; and that I will not find a parking place. I come to think of *my* car as a product of one of the Big Three automobile corporations. The latter determine the appearance of my car and make its beauty as well as its cheapness, its power as well as its shakiness, its working as well as its obsolescence. In a way, I feel cheated. I believe that the car is not what it could be, that better cars could be made for less money. But the other guy has to live, too. Wages and taxes are too high; turnover is necessary; we have it much better than before. The tension between appearance and reality melts away and both merge in one rather pleasant feeling.

(2) I take a walk in the country. Everything is as it should be: Nature at its best. Birds, sun, soft grass, a view through the trees of the mountains, nobody around, no radio, no smell of gasoline. Then the path turns and ends on the highway. I am back among the billboards, service stations, motels, and roadhouses. I was in a National Park, and I now know that this was not reality. It was a "reservation," something that is being preserved like a species dying out. If it were not for the government, the billboards, hot dog stands, and motels would long since have invaded that piece of Nature. I am grateful to the government; we have it much better than before . . .

(3) The subway during evening rush hour. What I see of the people are tired faces and limbs, hatred and anger. I feel someone might at any moment draw a knife—just so. They read, or rather they are soaked in their newspaper or magazine or paperback. And yet, a couple of hours later, the same people, deodorized, washed, dressed-up or down, may be happy and tender, really smile, and forget (or remember). But most of them will probably have some awful togetherness or aloneness at home.

These examples may illustrate the happy marriage of the positive and the negative—the *objective* ambiguity which adheres to the data of experience. It is objective ambiguity because the shift in my sensations and reflections responds to the manner in which the experienced facts are actually interrelated. But this interrelation, if comprehended, shatters the harmonizing consciousness and its false realism. Critical thought strives to define the irrational character of the established rationality (which becomes increasingly obvious) and to define the tendencies which cause this rationality to generate its own transformation. "Its own" because, as historical totality, it has developed forces and capabilities which themselves become projects beyond the established totality. They are possibilities of the advancing technological rationality and, as such, they involve the whole of society. The technological transformation is at the same time political transformation, but the political change would turn into qualitative social change only to the degree to which it would alter the direction of technical progress—that is, develop a new technology. For the established technology has become an instrument of destructive politics.

Such qualitative change would be transition to a higher stage of civilization if technics were designed and utilized for the pacification of the struggle for existence. In order to indicate the disturbing implications of this statement, I submit that such a new direction of technical progress would be the catastrophe of the established direction, not merely the quantitative evolution of the prevailing (scientific and technological) rationality but rather its catastrophic transformation, the emergence of a new idea of Reason, theoretical and practical.

The new idea of Reason is expressed in Whitehead's proposition: "The function of Reason is to promote the art of life." [1] In view of this end, Reason is the "direction of the attack on the environment" which derives from the "threefold urge: (1) to live, (2) to live well, (3) to live better." [2]

Whitehead's propositions seem to describe the actual development of Reason as well as its failure. Or rather they seem to suggest that Reason is still to be discovered, recognized, and realized, for hitherto the historical function of Reason has also been to repress and even destroy the urge to live, to live well, and to live better—or to postpone and put an exorbitantly high price on the fulfillment of this urge.

In Whitehead's definition of the function of Reason, the term "art" connotes the element of determinate negation. Reason, in its application to society, has thus far been opposed to art, while art was granted the privilege of being rather irrational—not subject to scientific, technological, and operational Reason. The rationality of domination has separated the Reason of science and the Reason of art, or, it has falsified the Reason of art by integrating art into the universe of domination. It was a separation because, from the beginning, science contained the aesthetic Reason, the free play and even the folly of imagination, the fantasy of transformation; science indulged in the rationalization of possibilities. However, this free play retained the commitment to the prevailing unfreedom in which it was born and from which it abstracted; the possibilities with which science played were also those of liberation—of a higher truth.

1. A. N. Whitehead, *The Function of Reason* (Boston: Beacon Press, 1959), p. 5.
2. *Ibid.*, p. 8.

Here is the original link (within the universe of domination and scarcity) between science, art, and philosophy. It is the consciousness of the discrepancy between the real and the possible, between the apparent and the authentic truth, and the effort to comprehend and to master this discrepancy. One of the primary forms in which this discrepancy found expression was the distinction between gods and men, finiteness and infinity, change and permanence.[3] Something of this mythological interrelation between the real and the possible survived in scientific thought, and it continued to be directed toward a more rational and true reality. Mathematics was held to be real and "good" in the same sense as Plato's metaphysical Ideas. How then did the development of the former become *science*, while that of the latter remained metaphysics?

The most obvious answer is that, to a great extent, the *scientific* abstractions entered and proved their truth in the actual conquest and transformation of nature, while the *philosophic* abstractions did not—and could not. For the conquest and transformation of nature occurred within a law and order of life which philosophy transcended, subordinating it to the "good life" of a different law and order. And this other order, which presupposed a high degree of freedom from toil, ignorance, and poverty, was *unreal*, at the origins of philosophic thought and throughout its development, while scientific thought continued to be applicable to an increasingly powerful and universal *reality*. The final philosophic concepts remained indeed metaphysical; they were not and could not be verified in terms of the established universe of discourse and action.

But if this is the situation, then the case of metaphysics, and especially of the meaningfulness and truth of metaphysical propositions, is a historical case. That is, historical rather than purely epistemological conditions determine the truth,

3. See chapter V.

the cognitive value of such propositions. Like all propositions that claim truth, they must be verifiable; they must stay within the universe of possible experience. This universe is never co-extensive with the established one but extends to the limits of the world which can be created by transforming the established one, with the means which the latter has provided or withheld. The range of verifiability in this sense grows in the course of history. Thus, the speculations about the Good Life, the Good Society, Permanent Peace obtain an increasingly realistic content; on technological grounds, the metaphysical tends to become physical.

Moreover, if the truth of metaphysical propositions is determined by their historical content (i.e., by the degree to which they define historical possibilities), then the relation between metaphysics and science is strictly historical. In our own culture, at least, that part of Saint-Simon's Law of the Three Stages is still taken for granted which stipulates that the metaphysical *precedes* the scientific stage of civilization. But is this sequence a final one? Or does the scientific transformation of the world contain its own metaphysical transcendence?

At the advanced stage of industrial civilization, scientific rationality, translated into political power, appears to be the decisive factor in the development of historical alternatives. The question then arises: does this power tend toward its own negation—that is, toward the promotion of the "art of life"? Within the established societies, the continued application of scientific rationality would have reached a terminal point with the mechanization of all socially necessary but individually repressive labor ("socially necessary" here includes all performances which can be exercised more effectively by machines, even if these performances produce luxuries and waste rather than necessities). But this stage would also be the end and limit of the scientific rationality in its established structure and direction. Further progress would mean the *break*, the turn of quantity into quality. It would open the possibility of an essentially new human reality—namely, existence in free time on the basis of fulfilled vital needs. Under such conditions, the scientific project itself would be free for trans-utilitarian ends, and free for the "art of living" beyond the necessities and luxuries of domination. In other words, the completion of the technological reality would be not only the prerequisite, but also the rationale for *transcending* the technological reality.

This would mean reversal of the traditional relationship between science and metaphysics. The ideas defining reality in terms other than those of the exact or behavioral sciences would lose their metaphysical or emotive character as a result of the scientific transformation of the world; the scientific concepts could project and define the possible realities of a free and pacified existence. The elaboration of such concepts would mean more than the evolution of the prevailing sciences. It would involve the scientific rationality as a whole, which has thus far been committed to an unfree existence and would mean a new idea of science, of Reason.

If the completion of the technological project involves a break with the prevailing technological rationality, the break in turn depends on the continued existence of the technical base itself. For it is this base which has rendered possible the satisfaction of needs and the reduction of toil—it remains the very base of all forms of human freedom. The qualitative change rather lies in the reconstruction of this base—that is, in its development with a view of different ends.

I have stressed that this does not mean the revival of "values," spiritual or other, which are to supplement the scientific and technological transformation of man and nature.[4] On the contrary, the historical achievement of

4. See chapter I, esp. p. 18.

science and technology has rendered possible the *translation of values into technical tasks*—the materialization of values. Consequently, what is at stake is the redefinition of values in *technical terms*, as elements in the technological process. The new ends, as technical ends, would then operate in the project and in the construction of the machinery, and not only in its utilization. Moreover, the new ends might assert themselves even in the construction of scientific hypotheses —in pure scientific theory. From the quantification of secondary qualities, science would proceed to the quantification of values.

For example, what is calculable is the minimum of labor with which, and the extent to which, the vital needs of all members of a society could be satisfied—provided the available resources were used for this end, without being restricted by other interests, and without impeding the accumulation of capital necessary for the development of the respective society. In other words; quantifiable is the available range of freedom from want. Or, calculable is the degree to which, under the same conditions, care could be provided for the ill, the infirm, and the aged—that is, quantifiable is the possible reduction of anxiety, the possible freedom from fear.

The obstacles that stand in the way of materialization are definable political obstacles. Industrial civilization has reached the point where, with respect to the aspirations of man for a human existence, the scientific abstraction from final causes becomes obsolete in science's own terms. Science itself has rendered it possible to make final causes the proper domain of science. Society,

"par une élévation et un élargissement du domaine technique, doit remettre à leur place, *comme techniques*, les problèmes de finalité, considérés à tort comme éthiques et parfois comme religieux. L'*inachèvement* des techniques sacralise les problèmes de finalité et asservit l'homme au respect de fins qu'il se représente comme des absolus." [5]

Under this aspect, "neutral" scientific method and technology become the science and technology of a historical phase which is being surpassed by its own achievements— which has reached its determinate negation. Instead of being separated from science and scientific method, and left to subjective preference and irrational, transcendental sanction, formerly metaphysical ideas of liberation may become the proper object of science. But this development confronts science with the unpleasant task of becoming *political*—of recognizing scientific consciousness as political consciousness, and the scientific enterprise as political enterprise. For the transformation of values into needs, of final causes into technical possibilities is a new stage in the conquest of oppressive, unmastered forces in society as well as in nature. It is an act of *liberation:*

"L'homme se libère de sa situation d'être asservi par la finalité du tout en apprenant à faire de la finalité, à organiser un tout finalisé qu'il juge et apprécie, pour n'avoir pas à subir passivement une intégration de fait." . . . "L'homme dépasse l'asservissement en organisant consciemment la finalité . . ." [6]

However, in constituting themselves *methodically* as political enterprise, science and technology would *pass beyond* the stage at which they were, because of their neutrality, *subjected* to politics and against their intent func-

5. "through a raising and enlarging of the technical sphere, must treat *as technical* problems, questions of finality considered wrongly as ethical and sometimes religious. The *incompleteness* of technics makes a fetish of problems of finality and enslaves man to ends which he thinks of as absolutes." Gilbert Simondon, *loc. cit.* p. 151; my italics.

6. "Man liberates himself from his situation of being subjected to the finality of everything by learning to create finality, to organise a "finalised" whole, which he judges and evaluates. Man overcomes enslavement by organising consciously finality." *Ibid.*, p. 103.

tioning as political instrumentalities. For the technological redefinition and the technical mastery of final causes *is* the construction, development, and utilization of resources (material and intellectual) *freed* from all *particular* interests which impede the satisfaction of human needs and the evolution of human faculties. In other words, it is the rational enterprise of man as man, of mankind. Technology thus may provide the historical correction of the premature identification of Reason and Freedom, according to which man can become and remain free in the progress of self-perpetuating productivity on the basis of oppression. To the extent to which technology has developed on this basis, the correction can never be the result of technical progress per se. It involves a political reversal.

Industrial society possesses the instrumentalities for transforming the metaphysical into the physical, the inner into the outer, the adventures of the mind into adventures of technology. The terrible phrases (and realities of) "engineers of the soul," "head shrinkers," "scientific management," "science of consumption," epitomize (in a miserable form) the progressing rationalization of the irrational, of the "spiritual"—the denial of the idealistic culture. But the consummation of technological rationality, while translating ideology into reality, would also transcend the materialistic antithesis to this culture. For the translation of values into needs is the twofold process of (1) material satisfaction (materialization of freedom) and (2) the free development of needs on the basis of satisfaction (non-repressive sublimation). In this process, the relation between the material and intellectual faculties and needs undergoes a fundamental change. The free play of thought and imagination assumes a rational and directing function in the realization of a pacified existence of man and nature. And the ideas of justice, freedom, and humanity then obtain their truth and good conscience on the sole ground on which they could ever have truth and good conscience—the satisfaction of man's material needs, the rational organization of the realm of necessity.

"Pacified existence." The phrase conveys poorly enough the intent to sum up, in one guiding idea, the tabooed and ridiculed *end* of technology, the repressed final cause behind the scientific enterprise. If this final cause were to materialize and become effective, the Logos of technics would open a universe of qualitatively different relations between man and man, and man and nature.

But at this point, a strong caveat must be stated—a warning against all technological fetishism. Such festishism has recently been exhibited mainly among Marxist critics of contemporary industrial society—ideas of the future omnipotence of technological man, of a "technological Eros," etc. The hard kernel of truth in these ideas demands an emphatic denunciation of the mystification which they express. Technics, as a universe of instrumentalities, may increase the weakness as well as the power of man. At the present stage, he is perhaps more powerless over his own apparatus than he ever was before.

The mystification is not removed by transferring technological omnipotence from particular groups to the new state and the central plan. Technology retains throughout its dependence on other than technological ends. The more technological rationality, freed from its exploitative features, determines social production, the more will it become dependent on political direction—on the collective effort to attain a pacified existence, with the goals which the free individuals may set for themselves.

"Pacification of existence" does not suggest an accumulation of power but rather the opposite. Peace and power, freedom and power, Eros and power may well be contraries! I shall presently try to show that the reconstruction of the material base of society with a view to pacification may involve a qualitative as well as quantitative *reduction* of power, in order to create the space and time for the development of productivity under self-determined incentives. The notion of such a reversal of power is a strong motive in dialectical theory.

To the degree to which the goal of pacification determines the Logos of technics, it alters the relation between technology and its primary object, Nature. Pacification presupposes mastery of Nature, which is and remains the object opposed to the developing subject. But there are two kinds of mastery: a repressive and a liberating one. The latter involves the reduction of misery, violence, and cruelty. In Nature as well as in History, the struggle for existence is the token of scarcity, suffering, and want. They are the qualities of blind matter, of the realm of immediacy in which life passively suffers its existence. This realm is gradually mediated in the course of the historical transformation of Nature; it becomes part of the human world, and to this extent, the qualities of Nature are historical qualities. In the process of civilization, Nature ceases to be mere Nature to the degree to which the struggle of blind forces is comprehended and mastered in the light of freedom.[7]

History is the negation of Nature. What is only natural is overcome and recreated by the power of Reason. The metaphysical notion that Nature comes to itself in history points to the unconquered limits of Reason. It claims them as historical limits—as a task yet to be accomplished, or rather yet to be undertaken. If Nature is in itself a rational, legiti-

7. Hegel's concept of freedom presupposes consciousness throughout (in Hegel's terminology: self-consciousness). Consequently, the "realization" of Nature is not, and never can be Nature's own work. But inasmuch as Nature is in itself negative (i.e., wanting in its own existence), the historical transformation of Nature by Man is, as the overcoming of this negativity, the liberation of Nature. Or, in Hegel's words, Nature is in its essence non-natural—"Geist."

mate object of science, then it is the legitimate object not only of Reason as power but also of Reason as freedom; not only of domination but also of liberation. With the emergence of man as the *animal rationale*—capable of transforming Nature in accordance with the faculties of the mind and the capacities of matter—the merely natural, as the sub-rational, assumes negative status. It becomes a realm to be comprehended and organized by Reason.

And to the degree to which Reason succeeds in subjecting matter to rational standards and aims, all sub-rational existence appears to be want and privation, and their reduction becomes the historical task. Suffering, violence, and destruction are categories of the natural as well as human reality, of a helpless and heartless universe. The terrible notion that the sub-rational life of nature is destined to remain forever such a universe, is neither a philosophic nor a scientific one; it was pronounced by a different authority:

"When the Society for the Prevention of Cruelty to Animals asked the Pope for his support, he refused it, on the ground that human beings owe no duty to lower animals, and that ill-treating animals is not sinful. This is because animals have no souls." [8]

Materialism, which is not tainted by such ideological abuse of the soul, has a more universal and realistic concept of salvation. It admits the reality of Hell only at one definite place, here on earth, and asserts that this Hell was created by Man (and by Nature). Part of this Hell is the ill-treatment of animals—the work of a human society whose rationality is still the irrational.

All joy and all happiness derive from the ability to transcend Nature—a transcendence in which the mastery of Nature is itself subordinated to liberation and pacification of existence. All tranquillity, all delight is the result

8. Quoted in: Bertrand Russell, *Unpopular Essays* (New York: Simon and Schuster, 1950) p. 76.

of conscious *mediation,* of autonomy and contradiction. Glorification of the natural is part of the ideology which protects an unnatural society in its struggle against liberation. The defamation of birth control is a striking example. In some backward areas of the world, it is also "natural" that black races are inferior to white, and that the dogs get the hindmost, and that business must be. It is also natural that big fish eat little fish—though it may not seem natural to the little fish. Civilization produces the means for freeing Nature from its own brutality, its own insufficiency, its own blindness, by virtue of the cognitive and transforming power of Reason. And Reason can fulfill this function only as post-technological rationality, in which technics is itself the instrumentality of pacification, organon of the "art of life." The function of Reason then converges with the function of *Art.*

The Greek notion of the affinity between art and technics may serve as a preliminary illustration. The artist possesses the ideas which, as final causes, guide the construction of certain things—just as the engineer possesses the ideas which guide, as final causes, the construction of a machine. For example, the idea of an abode for human beings determines the architect's construction of a house; the idea of wholesale nuclear explosion determines the construction of the apparatus which is to serve this purpose. Emphasis on the essential relation between art and technics points up the specific *rationality* of art.

Like technology, art creates another universe of thought and practice against and within the existing one. But in contrast to the technical universe, the artistic universe is one of illusion, semblance, *Schein.* However, this semblance is resemblance to a reality which exists as the threat and promise of the established one.[9] In various forms of mask and silence, the artistic universe is organized by the images of a

9. See chapter III.

life without fear—in mask and silence because art is without power to bring about this life, and even without power to represent it adequately. Still, the powerless, illusory truth of art (which has never been more powerless and more illusory than today, when it has become an omnipresent ingredient of the administered society) testifies to the validity of its images. The more blatantly irrational the society becomes, the greater the rationality of the artistic universe.

Technological civilization establishes a specific relation between art and technics. I mentioned above the notion of a reversal of the Law of the Three Stages and of a "revalidation" of metaphysics *on the basis* of the scientific and technological transformation of the world. The same notion may now be extended to the relation between science-technology and art. The rationality of art, its ability to "project" existence, to define yet unrealized possibilities could then be envisaged as *validated by and functioning in the scientific-technological transformation of the world.* Rather than being the handmaiden of the established apparatus, beautifying its business and its misery, art would become a technique for destroying this business and this misery.

The technological rationality of art seems to be characterized by an aesthetic "reduction":

"Art is able to reduce the apparatus which the external appearance requires in order to preserve itself—reduction to the limits in which the external may become the manifestation of spirit and freedom.[10]

According to Hegel, art reduces the immediate contingency in which an object (or a totality of objects) exists, to a state in which the object takes on the form and quality of freedom.

10. Hegel, *Vorlesungen über die Aesthetik*, in: *Sämtliche Werke*, ed. H. Glockner (Stuttgart, Frommann, 1929), vol. XII, p. 217 f. See also Osmaston's translation, in Hegel, *The Philosophy of Fine Art* (London, Bell and Sons, 1920), vol. I, p. 214.

Such transformation is reduction because the contingent situation suffers requirements which are external, and which stand in the way of its free realization. These requirements constitute an "apparatus" inasmuch as they are not merely natural but rather subject to free, rational change and development. Thus, the artistic transformation violates the natural object, but the violated is itself oppressive; thus the aesthetic transformation is liberation.

The aesthetic reduction appears in the technological transformation of Nature where and if it succeeds in linking mastery and liberation, directing mastery toward liberation. In this case, the conquest of Nature reduces the blindness, ferocity, and fertility of Nature—which implies reducing the ferocity of man against Nature. Cultivation of the soil is qualitatively different from destruction of the soil, extraction of natural resources from wasteful exploitation, clearing of forests from wholesale deforestation. Poverty, disease, and cancerous growth are natural as well as human ills—their reduction and removal is liberation of life. Civilization has achieved this "other," liberating transformation in its gardens and parks and reservations. But outside these small, protected areas, it has treated Nature as it has treated man—as an instrument of destructive productivity.

In the technology of pacification, aesthetic categories would enter to the degree to which the productive machinery is constructed with a view of the free play of faculties. But against all "technological Eros" and similar misconceptions, "labor cannot become play . . ." Marx's statement precludes rigidly all romantic interpretation of the "abolition of labor." The idea of such a millenium is as ideological in advanced industrial civilization as it was in the Middle Ages, and perhaps even more so. For man's struggle with Nature is increasingly a struggle with his society, whose powers over the individual become more "rational" and therefore more necessary than ever before. However, while the realm of necessity continues, its organization with a view of qualitatively different ends would change not only the mode, but also the extent of socially necessary production. And this change in turn would affect the human agents of production and their needs:

"free time transforms its possessor into a different Subject, and as different Subject he enters the process of immediate production." [11]

I have recurrently emphasized the historical character of human needs. Above the animal level even the necessities of life in a free and rational society will be other than those produced in and for an irrational and unfree society. Again, it is the concept of "reduction" which may illustrate the difference.

In the contemporary era, the conquest of scarcity is still confined to small areas of advanced industrial society. Their prosperity covers up the Inferno inside and outside their borders; it also spreads a repressive productivity and "false needs." It is repressive precisely to the degree to which it promotes the satisfaction of needs which require continuing the rat race of catching up with one's peers and with planned obsolescence, enjoying freedom from using the brain, working with and for the means of destruction. The obvious comforts generated by this sort of productivity, and even more, the support which it gives to a system of profitable domination, facilitate its importation in less advanced areas of the world where the introduction of such a system still means tremendous progress in technical and human terms.

However, the close interrelation between technical and

11. Marx, *Grundrisse der Kritik der politischen Oekonomie* loc. cit., p. 559. (My translation).

political-manipulative know-how, between profitable productivity and domination, lends to the conquest of scarcity the weapons for containing liberation. To a great extent, it is the sheer *quantity* of goods, services, work, and recreation in the overdeveloped countries which effectuates this containment. Consequently, qualitative change seems to presuppose a *quantitative* change in the advanced standard of living, namely, *reduction of overdevelopment.*

The standard of living attained in the most advanced industrial areas is not a suitable model of development if the aim is pacification. In view of what this standard has made of Man and Nature, the question must again be asked whether it is worth the sacrifices and the victims made in its defense. The question has ceased to be irresponsible since the "affluent society" has become a society of permanent mobilization against the risk of annihilation, and since the sale of its goods has been accompanied by moronization, the perpetuation of toil, and the promotion of frustration.

Under these circumstances, liberation from the affluent society does not mean return to healthy and robust poverty, moral cleanliness, and simplicity. On the contrary, the elimination of profitable waste would increase the social wealth available for distribution, and the end of permanent mobilization would reduce the social need for the denial of satisfactions that are the individual's own—denials which now find their compensation in the cult of fitness, strength, and regularity.

Today, in the prosperous warfare and welfare state, the human qualities of a pacified existence seem asocial and unpatriotic—qualities such as the refusal of all toughness, togetherness, and brutality; disobedience to the tyranny of the majority; profession of fear and weakness (the most rational reaction to this society!); a sensitive intelligence sickened by that which is being perpetrated; the commitment to the feeble and ridiculed actions of protest and refusal. These expressions of humanity, too, will be marred by necessary compromise—by the need to cover oneself, to be capable of cheating the cheaters, and to live and think in spite of them. In the totalitarian society, the human attitudes tend to become escapist attitudes, to follow Samuel Beckett's advice: "Don't wait to be hunted to hide. . . ."

Even such personal withdrawal of mental and physical energy from socially required activities and attitudes is today possible only for a few; it is only an inconsequential aspect of the redirection of energy which must precede pacification. Beyond the personal realm, self-determination presupposes free available energy which is not expended in superimposed material and intellectual labor. It must be free energy also in the sense that it is not channeled into the handling of goods and services which satisfy the individual, while rendering him incapable of achieving an existence of his own, unable to grasp the possibilities which are repelled by his satisfaction. Comfort, business, and job security in a society which prepares itself for and against nuclear destruction may serve as a universal example of enslaving contentment. Liberation of energy from the performances required to sustain destructive prosperity means decreasing the high standard of servitude in order to enable the individuals to develop that rationality which may render possible a pacified existence.

A new standard of living, adapted to the pacification of existence, also presupposes reduction in the future population. It is understandable, even reasonable, that industrial civilization considers legitimate the slaughter of millions of people in war, and the daily sacrifices of all those who have no adequate care and protection, but discovers its moral and religious scruples if it is the question of avoiding the production of more life in a society which is still geared to the planned annihilation of life in the National Interest, and to the unplanned deprivation of life on behalf of private interests. These moral scruples are understandable and reasonable because such a society needs an ever-increasing number of customers and supporters; the constantly regenerated excess capacity must be managed.

However, the requirements of profitable mass production are not necessarily identical with those of mankind. The problem is not only (and perhaps not even primarily) that of adequately feeding and caring for the growing population—it is first a problem of number, of mere quantity. There is more than poetic license in the indictment which Stefan George pronounced half a century ago: "Schon eure Zahl ist Frevel!"

The crime is that of a society in which the growing population aggravates the struggle for existence in the face of its possible alleviation. The drive for more "living space" operates not only in international aggressiveness but also *within* the nation. Here, expansion has, in all forms of teamwork, community life, and fun, invaded the inner space of privacy and practically eliminated the possibility of that isolation in which the individual, thrown back on himself alone, can think and question and find. This sort of privacy— the sole condition that, on the basis of satisfied vital needs, can give meaning to freedom and independence of thought —has long since become the most expensive commodity, available only to the very rich (who don't use it). In this respect, too, "culture" reveals its feudal origins and limitations. It can become democratic only through the abolition of mass democracy, i.e., if society has succeeded in restoring the prerogatives of privacy by granting them to all and protecting them for each.

To the denial of freedom, even of the possibility of freedom, corresponds the granting of liberties where they strengthen the repression. The degree to which the population is allowed to break the peace wherever there still is peace and silence, to be ugly and to uglify things, to ooze familiarity, to offend against good form is frightening. It is frightening because it expresses the lawful and even organized effort to reject the Other in his own right, to prevent autonomy even in a small, reserved sphere of existence. In the overdeveloped countries, an ever-larger part of the population becomes one huge captive audience—captured not by a totalitarian regime but by the liberties of the citizens whose media of amusement and elevation compel the Other to partake of their sounds, sights, and smells.

Can a society which is incapable of protecting individual privacy even within one's four walls rightfully claim that it respects the individual and that it is a free society? To be sure, a free society is defined by more, and by more fundamental achievements, than private autonomy. And yet, the absence of the latter vitiates even the most conspicuous institutions of economic and political freedom—by denying freedom at its hidden roots. Massive socialization begins at home and arrests the development of consciousness and conscience. The attainment of autonomy demands conditions in which the repressed dimensions of experience can come to life again; their liberation demands repression of the heteronomous needs and satisfactions which organize life in this society. The more they have become the individual's own needs and satisfactions, the more would their repression appear to be an all but fatal deprivation. But precisely by virtue of this fatal character, it may create the primary subjective prerequisite for qualitative change —namely, the *redefinition of needs.*

To take an (unfortunately fantastic) example: the mere absence of all advertising and of all indoctrinating media of information and entertainment would plunge the individual into a traumatic void where he would have the chance to wonder and to think, to know himself (or rather the negative of himself) and his society. Deprived of his false fathers, leaders, friends, and representatives, he would have to learn his ABC's again. But the words and sentences which he would form might come out very differently, and so might his aspirations and fears.

To be sure, such a situation would be an unbearable nightmare. While the people can support the continuous creation of nuclear weapons, radioactive fallout, and questionable foodstuffs, they cannot (for this very reason!) tolerate being deprived of the entertainment and education which make them capable of reproducing the arrangements for their defense and/or destruction. The non-functioning of television and the allied media might thus begin to achieve what the inherent contradictions of capitalism did not achieve—the disintegration of the system. The creation of repressive needs has long since become part of socially necessary labor—necessary in the sense that without it, the established mode of production could not be sustained. Neither problems of psychology nor of aesthetics are at stake, but the material base of domination.

10: Conclusion

The advancing one-dimensional society alters the relation between the rational and the irrational. Contrasted with the fantastic and insane aspects of its rationality, the realm of the irrational becomes the home of the really rational—of the ideas which may "promote the art of life." If the established society manages all normal communication, validating or invalidating it in accordance with social requirements, then the values alien to these requirements may perhaps have no other medium of communication than the abnormal one of fiction. The aesthetic dimension still retains a freedom of expression which enables the writer and artist to call men and things by their name—to name the otherwise unnameable.

The real face of our time shows in Samuel Beckett's novels; its real history is written in Rolf Hochhut's play *Der Stellvertreter*. It is no longer imagination which speaks here, but Reason, in a reality which justifies everything and absolves everything—except the sin against its spirit. Imagination is abdicating to this reality, which is catching up with and overtaking imagination. Auschwitz continues to haunt, not the memory but the accomplishments of man—the space flights; the rockets and missiles; the "labyrinthine basement under the Snack Bar"; the pretty electronic plants, clean, hygienic and with flower beds; the poison gas which is not really harmful to people; the secrecy in which we all participate. This is the setting in which the great human achievements of science, medicine, technology take place; the efforts to save and ameliorate life are the sole promise in the disaster. The willful play with fantastic possibilities, the ability to act with good conscience, *contra naturam*, to experiment with men and things, to convert illusion into reality and fiction into truth, testify to the extent to which Imagination has become an instrument of progress. And it is one which, like others in the established societies, is methodically abused. Setting the pace and style of politics, the power of imagination far exceeds Alice in Wonderland in the manipulation of words, turning sense into nonsense and nonsense into sense.

The formerly antagonistic realms merge on technical and political grounds—magic and science, life and death, joy and misery. Beauty reveals its terror as highly classified nuclear plants and laboratories become "Industrial Parks" in pleasing surroundings; Civil Defense Headquarters display a "deluxe fallout-shelter" with wall-to-wall carpeting ("soft"), lounge chairs, television, and Scrabble, "designed as a combination family room during peacetime (sic!) and family fallout shelter should war break out." [1] If the horror of such realizations does not penetrate into consciousness, if it is readily taken for granted, it is because these achievements are (a) perfectly rational in terms of the existing order, (b) tokens of human ingenuity and power beyond the traditional limits of imagination.

The obscene merger of aesthetics and reality refutes the philosophies which oppose "poetic" imagination to scientific and empirical Reason. Technological progress is accompanied by a progressive rationalization and even realization of the imaginary. The archetypes of horror as well as of joy, of war as well as of peace lose their catastrophic character. Their appearance in the daily life of the individuals is no longer that of irrational forces—their modern avatars are elements of technological domination, and subject to it.

In reducing and even canceling the romantic space of imagination, society has forced the imagination to prove

1. According to *The New York Times,* November 11, 1960, displayed at the New York City Civil Defense Headquarters, Lexington Ave. and Fifty-fifth Street.

itself on new grounds, on which the images are translated into historical capabilities and projects. The translation will be as bad and distorted as the society which undertakes it. Separated from the realm of material production and material needs, imagination was mere play, invalid in the realm of necessity, and committed only to a fantastic logic and a fantastic truth. When technical progress cancels this separation, it invests the images with its own logic and its own truth; it reduces the free faculty of the mind. But it also reduces the gap between imagination and Reason. The two antagonistic faculties become interdependent on common ground. In the light of the capabilities of advanced industrial civilization, is not all play of the imagination playing with technical possibilities, which can be tested as to their chances of realization? The romantic idea of a "science of the Imagination" seems to assume an ever-more-empirical aspect.

The scientific, rational character of Imagination has long since been recognized in mathematics, in the hypotheses and experiments of the physical sciences. It is likewise recognized in psychoanalysis, which is in theory based on the acceptance of the specific rationality of the irrational; the comprehended imagination becomes, redirected, a therapeutic force. But this therapeutic force may go much further than in the cure of neuroses. It was not a poet but a scientist who has outlined this prospect:

Toute une psychanalyse matérielle peut . . . nous aider à guérir de nos images, ou du moins nous aider à limiter l'emprise de nos images. On peut alors espérer . . . *pouvoir rendre l'imagination heureuse,* autrement dit, pouvoir donner bonne conscience à l'imagination, en lui accordant pleinement tous ses moyens d'expression, toutes les images matérielles qui se produisent dans les *rêves naturels,* dans l'activité onirique normale. Rendre heureuse l'imagination, lui accorder toute son exubérance, c'est précisément donner à l'imagination sa véritable fonction d'entraîne-ment psychique.[2]

Imagination has not remained immune to the process of reification. We are possessed by our images, suffer our own images. Psychoanalysis knew it well, and knew the consequences. However, "to give to the imagination all the means of expression" would be regression. The mutilated individuals (mutilated also in their faculty of imagination) would organize and destroy even more than they are now permitted to do. Such release would be the unmitigated horror—not the catastrophe of culture, but the free sweep of its most repressive tendencies. Rational is the imagination which can become the *a priori* of the reconstruction and redirection of the productive apparatus toward a pacified existence, a life without fear. And this can never be the imagination of those who are possessed by the images of domination and death.

To liberate the imagination so that it can be given all its means of expression presupposes the repression of much that is now free and that perpetuates a repressive society. And such reversal is not a matter of psychology or ethics but of politics, in the sense in which this term has here been used throughout: the practice in which the basic societal institutions are developed, defined, sustained, and changed. It is the practice of individuals, no matter how organized they may be. Thus the question once again must be faced: how can the administered individuals—who have made their mutilation into their own liberties and satisfactions, and thus

2. "An entire psychoanalysis of matter can help us to cure us of our images or at least help us to limit the hold of our images on us. One may then hope *to be able to render imagination happy,* to give it good conscience in allowing it fully all its means of expression, all material images which emerge in *natural dreams,* in normal dream activity. To render imagination happy, to allow it all its exuberance, means precisely to grant imagination its true function as psychological impulse and force." Gaston Bachelard, *Le Matérialisme rationnel* (Paris. Presses Universitaires, 1953), p. 18 (Bachelard's emphasis).

reproduce it on an enlarged scale—liberate themselves from themselves as well as from their masters? How is it even thinkable that the vicious circle be broken?

Paradoxically, it seems that it is not the notion of the new societal *institutions* which presents the greatest difficulty in the attempt to answer this question. The established societies themselves are changing, or have already changed the basic institutions in the direction of increased planning. Since the development and utilization of all available resources for the universal satisfaction of vital needs is the prerequisite of pacification, it is incompatible with the prevalence of particular interests which stand in the way of attaining this goal. Qualitative change is conditional upon planning for the whole against these interests, and a free and rational society can emerge only on this basis.

The institutions within which pacification can be envisaged thus defy the traditional classification into authoritarian and democratic, centralized and liberal administration. Today, the opposition to central planning in the name of a liberal democracy which is denied in reality serves as an ideological prop for repressive interests. The goal of authentic self-determination by the individuals depends on effective social control over the production and distribution of the necessities (in terms of the achieved level of culture, material and intellectual).

Here, technological rationality, stripped of its exploitative features, is the sole standard and guide in planning and developing the available resources for all. Self-determination in the production and distribution of vital goods and services would be wasteful. The job is a technical one, and as a truly technical job, it makes for the reduction of physical and mental toil. In this realm, centralized control is rational if it establishes the preconditions for meaningful self-determination. The latter can then become effective in its own realm—in the decisions which involve the production and distribution of the economic surplus, and in the individual existence.

In any case, the combination of centralized authority and direct democracy is subject to infinite variations, according to the degree of development. Self-determination will be real to the extent to which the masses have been dissolved into individuals liberated from all propaganda, indoctrination, and manipulation, capable of knowing and comprehending the facts and of evaluating the alternatives. In other words, society would be rational and free to the extent to which it is organized, sustained, and reproduced by an essentially new historical Subject.

At the present stage of development of the advanced industrial societies, the material as well as the cultural system denies this exigency. The power and efficiency of this system, the thorough assimilation of mind with fact, of thought with required behavior, of aspirations with reality, militate against the emergence of a new Subject. They also militate against the notion that the replacement of the prevailing control over the productive process by "control from below" would mean the advent of qualitative change. This notion was valid, and still is valid, where the laborers were, and still are, the living denial and indictment of the established society. However, where these classes have become a prop of the established way of life, their ascent to control would prolong this way in a different setting.

And yet, the facts are all there which validate the critical theory of this society and of its fatal development: the increasing irrationality of the whole; waste and restriction of productivity; the need for aggressive expansion; the constant threat of war; intensified exploitation; dehumanization. And they all point to the historical alternative: the planned utilization of resources for the satisfaction of vital needs with a minimum of toil, the transformation of leisure into free time, the pacification of the struggle for existence.

But the facts and the alternatives are there like fragments which do not connect, or like a world of mute objects without a subject, without the practice which would move these objects in the new direction. Dialectical theory is not refuted, but it cannot offer the remedy. It cannot be positive. To be sure, the dialectical concept, in comprehending the given facts, transcends the given facts. This is the very token of its truth. It defines the historical possibilities, even necessities; but their realization can only be in the practice which responds to the theory, and, at present, the practice gives no such response.

On theoretical as well as empirical grounds, the dialectical concept pronounces its own hopelessness. The human reality is its history and, in it, contradictions do not explode by themselves. The conflict between streamlined, rewarding domination on the one hand, and its achievements that make for self-determination and pacification on the other, may become blatant beyond any possible denial, but it may well continue to be a manageable and even productive conflict, for with the growth in the technological conquest of nature grows the conquest of man by man. And this conquest reduces the freedom which is a necessary *a priori* of liberation. This is freedom of thought in the only sense in which thought can be free in the administered world—as the consciousness of its repressive productivity, and as the absolute need for breaking out of this whole. But precisely this absolute need does not prevail where it could become the driving force of a historical practice, the effective cause of qualitative change. Without this material force, even the most acute consciousness remains powerless.

No matter how obvious the irrational character of the whole may manifest itself and, with it, the necessity of change, insight into necessity has never sufficed for seizing the possible alternatives. Confronted with the omnipresent efficiency of the given system of life, its alternatives have always appeared utopian. And insight into necessity, the consciousness of the evil state, will not suffice even at the stage where the accomplishments of science and the level of productivity have eliminated the utopian features of the alternatives—where the established reality rather than its opposite is utopian.

Does this mean that the critical theory of society abdicates and leaves the field to an empirical sociology which, freed from all theoretical guidance except a methodological one, succumbs to the fallacies of misplaced concreteness, thus performing an ideological service while proclaiming the elimination of value judgments? Or do the dialectical concepts once again testify to their truth—by comprehending their own situation as that of the society which they analyze? A response might suggest itself if one considers the critical theory precisely at the point of its greatest weakness—its inability to demonstrate the liberating tendencies *within* the established society.

The critical theory of society, was, at the time of its origin, confronted with the presence of real forces (objective and subjective) *in* the established society which moved (or could be guided to move) toward more rational and freer institutions by abolishing the existing ones which had become obstacles to progress. These were the empirical grounds on which the theory was erected, and from these empirical grounds derived the idea of the liberation of *inherent* possibilities—the development, otherwise blocked and distorted, of material and intellectual productivity, faculties, and needs. Without the demonstration of such forces, the critique of society would still be valid and rational, but it would be incapable of translating its rationality into terms of historical practice. The conclusion? "Liberation of inherent possibilities" no longer adequately expresses the historical alternative.

The enchained possibilities of advanced industrial societies are: development of the productive forces on an enlarged scale, extension of the conquest of nature, growing satisfaction of needs for a growing number of people, creation of new needs and faculties. But these possibilities are gradually being realized through means and institutions which cancel their liberating potential, and this process affects not only the means but also the ends. The instruments of productivity and progress, organized into a totalitarian system, determine not only the actual but also the possible utilizations.

At its most advanced stage, domination functions as administration, and in the overdeveloped areas of mass consumption, the administered life becomes the good life of the whole, in the defense of which the opposites are united. This is the pure form of domination. Conversely, its negation appears to be the pure form of negation. All content seems reduced to the one abstract demand for the end of domination—the only truly revolutionary exigency, and the event that would validate the achievements of industrial civilization. In the face of its efficient denial by the established system, this negation appears in the politically impotent form of the "absolute refusal"—a refusal which seems the more unreasonable the more the established system develops its productivity and alleviates the burden of life. In the words of Maurice Blanchot:

"Ce que nous refusons n'est pas sans valeur ni sans importance. C'est bien à cause de cela que le refus est nécessaire. Il y a une raison que nous n'accepterons plus, il y a une apparence de sagesse qui nous fait horreur, il y a une offre d'accord et de

conciliation que nous n'entendrons pas. Une rupture s'est pro-
duite. Nous avons été ramenés à cette franchise qui ne tolère
plus la complicité." [8]

But if the abstract character of the refusal is the result
of total reification, then the concrete ground for refusal
must still exist, for reification is an illusion. By the same
token, the unification of opposites in the medium of technological rationality must be, *in all its reality*, an illusory unification, which eliminates neither the contradiction between
the growing productivity and its repressive use, nor the vital
need for solving the contradiction.

But the struggle for the solution has outgrown the
traditional forms. The totalitarian tendencies of the one-
dimensional society render the traditional ways and means of
protest ineffective—perhaps even dangerous because they
preserve the illusion of popular sovereignty. This illusion
contains some truth: "the people," previously the ferment of
social change, have "moved up" to become the ferment of
social cohesion. Here rather than in the redistribution of
wealth and equalization of classes is the new stratification
characteristic of advanced industrial society.

However, underneath the conservative popular base is
the substratum of the outcasts and outsiders, the exploited
and persecuted of other races and other colors, the unemployed and the unemployable. They exist outside the democratic process; their life is the most immediate and the most
real need for ending intolerable conditions and institutions.
Thus their opposition is revolutionary even if their consciousness is not. Their opposition hits the system from without

3. "What we refuse is not without value or importance. Precisely because of that, the refusal is necessary. There is a reason which we no longer
accept, there is an appearance of wisdom which horrifies us, there is a
plea for agreement and conciliation which we will no longer heed. A break
has occurred. We have been reduced to that frankness which no longer
tolerates complicity." "Le Refus," in *Le 14 Juillet*, no. 2, Paris, Octobre
1958.

and is therefore not deflected by the system; it is an elementary force which violates the rules of the game and, in doing so, reveals it as a rigged game. When they get together and go out into the streets, without arms, without protection, in order to ask for the most primitive civil rights, they know that they face dogs, stones, and bombs, jail, concentration camps, even death. Their force is behind every political demonstration for the victims of law and order. The fact that they start refusing to play the game may be the fact which marks the beginning of the end of a period.

Nothing indicates that it will be a good end. The economic and technical capabilities of the established societies are sufficiently vast to allow for adjustments and concessions to the underdog, and their armed forces sufficiently trained and equipped to take care of emergency situations. However, the spectre is there again, inside and outside the frontiers of the advanced societies. The facile historical parallel with the barbarians threatening the empire of civilization prejudges the issue; the second period of barbarism may well be the continued empire of civilization itself. But the chance is that, in this period, the historical extremes may meet again: the most advanced consciousness of humanity, and its most exploited force. It is nothing but a chance. The critical theory of society possesses no concepts which could bridge the gap between the present and its future; holding no promise and showing no success, it remains negative. Thus it wants to remain loyal to those who, without hope, have given and give their life to the Great Refusal.

At the beginning of the fascist era, Walter Benjamin wrote:

> *Nur um der Hoffnungslosen willen ist uns die Hoffnung gegeben.*
> It is only for the sake of those without hope that hope is given to us.

Index

Abstractness of theory, xiv, 134
Adorno, Theodor W., 11, 69, 99, 120, 139
Alienation, 8, 9, 11, 23; artistic, 60, 62, 72
Aristotle, 127, 130, 136 f., 147
Art: and reason, 228 f., 238; and technology, 238, 247 f.
Austin, J. L., 173, 175 f.
Automation, 25 f., 35 f.

Bachelard, Gaston, 153, 250
Backward countries, 45 f.
Barthes, Roland, 68 f., 84, 91, 100 f.
Beckett, Samuel, 243
Bell, Daniel, 28 f.
Benjamin, Walter, 257
Blanchot, Maurice, 255
Bloch, Ernst, 120
Born, Max, 149
Brecht, Bertolt, 66, 70
Bridgman, P. W., 12 f.

Capitalism-socialism: relation, transition, 22, 37, 41 f.
Choice in history, xvi, 219 f.
Communist Parties: France, Italy, 20
Concept, general, 105, 137, 203 f.
Concreteness, false, 174, Ch. 8 passim
Conscience, 79
Consciousness: happy, 76 f., 79 f., 84; unhappy, 61, 76, 209; false, 208
Cook, Fred J., xviii

Descartes, René, 15, 152 f.
Desublimation, institutionalized, 74
Dewey, John, 167
Dialectic, 97, 100, 124 f., 133, 140 f., 222 f., 253
Dingler, Herbert, 149
Dumont, René, 47

Flaubert, Gustave, 62
Fourier, Charles, 172

Frank, Philipp G., 150
Freedom: changing content, 1 f., 7; inner, 10
Freud, Sigmund, 78, 82, 183

George, Stefan, 65, 244
Gerr, Stanley, 87
Grünbaum, Adolf, 149

Hegel, Georg, 96, 140, 152, 185, 236, 239
Heidegger, Martin, 153
Heisenberg, Werner, 149, 153
Historical rationality, 220 f
Historicism, 217 f.
History: as negation of nature, 236 f.; suppression of, 97 f.
Hobbes, Thomas, 15
Horkheimer, Max, 137, 157
Humboldt, Wilhelm v., 96, 212
Hume, David, 173
Husserl, Edmund, 130, 153, 162 f.

Ideology, 11, 119 f., 188, 199
Imagination, 248 f.
Introjection, 10
Ionesco, E., 80

Janowitz, Morris, 114

Kahn, Herman, 80
Kant, Immanuel, 15
Kraus, Karl, 177, 196

Laboring classes: transformation, 24
Locke, John, 15
Logic: dialectical, see Dialectic; formal, 131, 137 f., 167
Lowenthal, Leo, 92

Mallarmé, Stéphane, 68
Mallet, Serge, 28 f., 30
Marvick, Dwaine, 114
Marx, Karl, 16, 21, 23 f., 26, 28, 35, 41, 154, 222, 241
Meacham, Stewart, 33

Index   *260*

Metalanguage, 179, 195 f.
Metaphysics, post-technological 229 f., 234, 239
Mills, C. Wright, xvii, 38
Mystification, 188 f., 204

Needs: historical character, 4, 241; true and false, 4 f., 245

Operationalism, behaviorism, 12, 85 f., 156; therapeutic method, 107, 170, 183, 199
Orwellian language, 88, 100

Pacification of existence, 16, 167, 220, 235, 249
Packard, Vance, xvii
Perroux, François, 33, 54, 206
Piaget, Jean, 160 f.
Plato, 127 f., 131 f., 147
Pluralism, 3, 50 f.
Poetic language, 67 f., 184, 192
Pollock, Frederick, 102
Popper, Karl, 151
Positivism, 172
Progress, 16, 166, 227

Quine, W. V. O., 149, 216

Reason, as power of the negative, 123, 171, 225
Reichenbach, Hans, 149
Reification, 168, 181, 206, 256
Rimbaud, Arthur, 68

Roper, Elmo, 118 f.
Rousseau, Jean Jacques, 40
Russell, Bertrand, 211
Ryle, Gilbert, 174

Saint-Simon, Claude-Henri de, 172
Sartre, Jean-Paul, 26, 177
Simondon, Gilbert, 24, 27, 159 232 f.
Soviet society, 39 f.
Stalin, 43, 101
Sublimation, non-repressive, 73, 75 f.
Surrealism, 68

Technological rationality: as art, 231 f.; as political xvi, 11 f., 18, 154, 158, 168, 227, 233; as totalitarian, xv
Technological veil, 32
Totalitarian, 3
Transcendence of social theory, xi, 15, 106, 118; historical 37, 220 f.

Valéry, Paul, 67, 179
Value judgments, x, 147, 156, 220
Values, quantification of, 232, 234

Walker, Charles R., 25 f., 30
Weizsäcker, G. F. v., 151, 155
Western Electric Company, Hawthorne plant study, 108 f.
Whitehead, Alfred N., 215, 228
Whyte, William H., xvii
Wittgenstein, Ludwig, 173 f.
Woodward, Julian L., 118 f.